A CULTURAL HISTORY OF THE HOME

VOLUME 1

A Cultural History of the Home
General Editor: Amanda Flather

Volume 1
A Cultural History of the Home in Antiquity
Edited by Andrew Wallace-Hadrill and Joanne Berry

Volume 2
A Cultural History of the Home in the Medieval Age
Edited by Katherine L. French

Volume 3
A Cultural History of the Home in the Renaissance
Edited by Amanda Flather

Volume 4
A Cultural History of the Home in the Age of Enlightenment
Edited by Clive Edwards

Volume 5
A Cultural History of the Home in the Age of Empire
Edited by Jane Hamlett

Volume 6
A Cultural History of the Home in the Modern Age
Edited by Despina Stratigakos

A CULTURAL HISTORY OF THE HOME

IN ANTIQUITY

Edited by Andrew Wallace-Hadrill
and Joanne Berry

BLOOMSBURY ACADEMIC
LONDON • NEW YORK • OXFORD • NEW DELHI • SYDNEY

BLOOMSBURY ACADEMIC
Bloomsbury Publishing Plc
50 Bedford Square, London, WC1B 3DP, UK
1385 Broadway, New York, NY 10018, USA

BLOOMSBURY, BLOOMSBURY ACADEMIC and the Diana logo are
trademarks of Bloomsbury Publishing Plc

First published in Great Britain 2021

Copyright © Bloomsbury Publishing, 2021

Andrew Wallace-Hadrill and Joanne Berry have asserted their right under the Copyright,
Designs and Patents Act, 1988, to be identified as Editors of this work.

Cover image © DEA / M. SEEMULLER / Getty Images

All rights reserved. No part of this publication may be reproduced or transmitted in any form or
by any means, electronic or mechanical, including photocopying, recording, or any information
storage or retrieval system, without prior permission in writing from the publishers.

Bloomsbury Publishing Plc does not have any control over, or responsibility for, any third-party
websites referred to or in this book. All internet addresses given in this book were correct at
the time of going to press. The author and publisher regret any inconvenience caused if
addresses have changed or sites have ceased to exist, but can accept no responsibility
for any such changes.

A catalogue record for this book is available from the British Library.

Library of Congress Cataloging-in-Publication Data
Names: Stratigakos, Despina, editor.
Title: A cultural history of the home.
Description: New York, NY : Bloomsbury Academic, 2020. |
Series: The cultural histories series | Includes bibliographical references and index.
Contents: volume 1. A cultural history of the home in antiquity /
edited by Andrew Wallace-Hadrill and Joanne Berry –
volume 2. A cultural history of the home in the medieval age /
edited by Katherine L. French – volume 3. A cultural history of the home in the renaissance /
edited by Amanda Flather – volume 4. A cultural history of the home in the age of
enlightenment / edited by Clive Edwards – volume 5. A cultural history of the home
in the age of empire / edited by Jane Hamlett – volume 6. A cultural history of the
home in the modern age / edited by Despina Stratigakos.
Identifiers: LCCN 2020030967| ISBN 9781472584229 (v. 1 ; hardback) |
ISBN 9781472584236 (v. 2 ; hardback) | ISBN 9781472584243 (v. 3 ; hardback) |
ISBN 9781472584250 (v. 4 ; hardback) | ISBN 9781472584298 (v. 5 ; hardback) |
ISBN 9781472584304 (v. 6 ; hardback) | ISBN 9781472584410 (Set)
Subjects: LCSH: Home–History. | Families–History.
Classification: LCC HQ503 .C856 2020 | DDC 306.8509—dc23
LC record available at https://lccn.loc.gov/2020030967

ISBN: HB: 978-1-4725-8422-9
       Set: 978-1-4725-8441-0

Series: The Cultural Histories Series

Typeset by RefineCatch Limited, Bungay, Suffolk
Printed and bound in Great Britain

To find out more about our authors and books visit www.bloomsbury.com
and sign up for our newsletters.

CONTENTS

LIST OF ILLUSTRATIONS   vii

SERIES PREFACE   ix
Amanda Flather

Introduction   1
Andrew Wallace-Hadrill

1   The Meaning of Home   15
    Andrew Wallace-Hadrill

2   Family and Household   35
    Michele George

3   The House   59
    Lisa Nevett

4   Furniture and Furnishings   81
    Joanne Berry

5   Home and Work   103
    Nicolas Tran

6   Gender and Home   119
    Kate Wilkinson

7   Hospitality and Home   141
    Marie-Adeline Le Guennec

8 Religion and Home *Carlos Machado*	161
BIBLIOGRAPHY	181
NOTES ON CONTRIBUTORS	197
INDEX OF ARCHAEOLOGICAL SITES	199
INDEX OF ANCIENT SOURCES CITED	201
GENERAL INDEX	203

ILLUSTRATIONS

INTRODUCTION

0.1	Olynthos, House A vii 4.	8
0.2	Herculaneum, House of the Bicentenary.	11
0.3	Carthage, House of the Hill of Juno, Mosaic of Dominus Julius.	13

CHAPTER TWO

2.1	Wedding scene, red-figure *lebes gamikos*, 430–420 BCE.	39
2.2	Women working at a loom, *lekythos*, 550–530 BCE.	41
2.3	Women folding cloth and spinning wool, *lekythos*, 550–530 BCE.	42
2.4	Women at fountain house, black-figure *hydria*, 510–500 BCE.	43
2.5	Family scene, red-figure *hydria*, 440–430 BCE.	44
2.6	Roman funerary altar with wedding scene, 40–50 CE.	52
2.7	Sarcophagus for a child, 120–130 CE.	57
2.8	Funerary relief of the Vettii, 20 BCE.	58

CHAPTER THREE

3.1	Sketch plan showing the topography of ancient Athens in relation to the Classical city wall.	62
3.2	Plan of three Classical Houses from the Areopagus.	64
3.3	Photograph of the House of the Parakeet Mosaic, showing the walls of the *andron*.	66
3.4	Plan of House 1 at Thorikos.	69
3.5	Plans of House of Dionysus, Delos and the early Roman house from the northwest shoulder of the Areopagus.	73

3.6 Plans of later Roman houses from the Areopagus.   76

CHAPTER FOUR

4.1 House of the Chaste Lovers (IX.12.6), Pompeii.   82
4.2 Stele of Hegeso, National Archaeological Museum of Athens.   85
4.3 The Poet Menander, from the House of Menander, Pompeii.   89
4.4 Bisellium depicted on the Tomb of Navoleia Tyche at Pompeii.   89
4.5 Carbonized wooden table from Herculaneum.   93
4.6 Plan of Region I, *insulae* 7, 8 and 9 at Pompeii.   94
4.7 Garden *triclinium* in the House of the Ephebe (I.7.10–12).   98
4.8 Plan of the House of Ceres (I.9.13).   100

CHAPTER FIVE

5.1 Plan of the Coroplast's House, Halos.   107
5.2 Plan of the fullery of Mustius, Pompeii.   109
5.3 Painted pillar in the fullery of L. Veranius Hypsaeus, Pompeii.   115

CHAPTER SIX

6.1 Projecta casket.   123
6.2 Statuette of a nurse with child.   132
6.3 Mosaic of lucky hunchback (a *kai su* mosaic).   138

CHAPTER SEVEN

7.1 *Tessera hospitalis* in the form of a hand from Contrebia Belaisca.   149
7.2 Proxeny Decree (Attic, fourth century BCE).   149
7.3 Representation of a Greek *symposion*.   153
7.4 Organization of the Roman *triclinium*.   155
7.5 Plan of the House of the Deer.   157

CHAPTER EIGHT

8.1 Domus della Fortuna Annonaria, Ostia.   163
8.2 Athenian *pyxis*, showing Hestia holding a sceptre and fruit in a wedding procession.   166
8.3 Painted *lararium* from the *domus* of Julius Polybius, Pompeii.   170
8.4 Mosaic with scene of Venus, House of Amphitrite, Bulla Regia.   172
8.5 *Lararium* and *Mithraeum* of *domus* on Via Giovanni Lanza, Rome.   179

GENERAL EDITOR'S PREFACE

AMANDA FLATHER

A Cultural History of the Home is an authoritative, interdisciplinary, six-volume series investigating the changing meaning of home, both as an idea and as a place to live, from ancient times until the present. Each volume follows the same basic structure and begins with an overview of the cultural, social, political and economic factors that shaped ideas and requirements of home in the period under consideration. Experts examine important aspects of the cultural history of home under eight main headings: the meaning of home; house and home; family and home; gender and home; work and home; furniture and furnishings; religion and home; hospitality and home. A single volume can be read to obtain a thorough knowledge of the period or one of the eight themes can be followed through history by reading the relevant chapter in each of the six volumes, providing an understanding of developments over the longer term.

Individual volumes in the series will cover six historical periods:

Volume 1: *A Cultural History of the Home in Antiquity* (800 BCE–800 CE)
Volume 2: *A Cultural History of the Home in the Medieval Age* (800–1450)
Volume 3. *A Cultural History of the Home in the Renaissance* (1450–1650)
Volume 4. *A Cultural History of the Home in the Age of Enlightenment* (1650–1800)
Volume 5. *A Cultural History of the Home in the Age of Empire* (1800–1920)
Volume 6. *A Cultural History of the Home in the Modern Age* (1920–2000+)

Introduction

ANDREW WALLACE-HADRILL

Home is an essentially modern concept, with its own culturally specific parameters, and one that does not map onto the past without making allowance for large differences (see e.g. Harvey 2012: 12). Terms like the Greek *oikos* and the Latin *domus* have a wide semantic range that covers the physical structure of the house and the social structure of its inhabitants, and each at some points carries some, but not all, of the sense of 'home'. Nevertheless, it is a rewarding challenge to look at the past though a new lens, and in the way of the dialogue between past and present, to cast new light on both sides. Many aspects of the modern (and to some extent specifically Anglo-Saxon) concept of home find abundant echoes in antiquity. If European literature goes back at one level to Homer, so the idea of 'home' goes back to the *Odyssey*, and the epic battle of Odysseus to return to his home and – having done so – to establish his home as his own through both contest (against the suitors of Penelope) and recognition by his own family.

But if there are some aspects of the ancient home that are instantly recognizable, there are others that may seem alien. The modern home may seem to be defined by contrasts with what it is not. Home is frequently in contrast to work, in a relationship of tension ('work/life balance'). That is a separation that only seems to have been established with the industrial revolution, with the creation of factories and offices physically removed from places of residence (Wall 1994). Separated from the place of work, the home becomes the place of family, of privacy, of relaxation. There is something of this in the ancient home too. There is always a contrast between the spheres of inside and outside, which overlap with the spheres of private and public, and critically of female and male. But the oppositions are not those of modernity, because the home is indeed a place of work, whether in town or country, the essential place of production as well as consumption. That affects the shopkeeper living in a garret above his shop or the rich and powerful, for whom the expectations of hospitality must compromise the privacy of home. The same is true of early modern Europe (Sarti 2002).

But it is above all the institution of slavery that must make the ancient home unrecognizable to modern eyes. To some extent the post-industrial, nineteenth-century practice of domestic service may seem to make slavery recognizable: the juxtaposition of two worlds, upstairs and downstairs, of the wealthy living in comfort and careless leisure versus their support system, characterized by poverty and hard work. Such a contrast seems to excite the endless curiosity of television audiences, whose modern domesticities separate them from both worlds. Yet ancient slavery (which the modern audience seems to recognize only from images of the plantations of the American antebellum South) is a wholly different matter. An Athenian lady, like the wife of Ischomachus as portrayed by Xenophon, busy managing the slaves in her house, fretting over the neatest way to store things, or the Roman *domina* surrounded by her *ancillae*, struggling to pile her coiffure into the right number of curls, may seem to be the ancestors of Mrs Beeton's housewife, as rather remotely they are. But slaves are the entire labour force of a home that is a place of work: not just 'domestics', in the sense of cooks, butlers, chambermaids and tweenies, but the workforce of production, in weaving, manufacture, commerce, book-keeping and management, and even in reproduction of the next generation of slaves. These patterns affect all levels of ancient society, and at the top end on a stupefying scale. When the prefect of the city of Rome, Pedanius Secundus, was found murdered at home by a slave, the senate insisted on carrying out the legal sentence, that *all* slaves in the home should be executed (because all had equally the duty to protect their master), despite the fact that they numbered 400 (Tacitus, *Annals* 14.42). These were not all the slaves Pedanius owned, but all who lived under the same roof (a precise legal expression, which covered the multiple sets of roofs of a grand home). He will certainly have owned houses elsewhere in the city, and villas staffed by slaves across Italy, but the law only covered slaves who lived in the same home as the murdered master. Only the largest modern hotel would have a staff of 400, and most of them, being free not slaves, and separating residence from place of work, would not live under the same roof as their clients.

This volume, then, sets out to explore an ancient home that is simultaneously familiar and unfamiliar. It cannot be said that the 'home' has been a conscious focus of attention in classical studies. It represents, rather, a point of potential convergence between several other streams of study. Thanks in particular to the growth of gender studies, there has been extensive discussion of women in antiquity, and more specifically of the family. Both these themes have been covered by previous volumes in the Cultural History series; but though there is clear overlap, the theme of this volume is quite distinct. Critically, 'home' involves location: it is a place, though like all aspects of space, this is not simply defined topographically, but rather as a form of social production (Lefebvre 1991). In the case of antiquity, the evidence for domestic space is above all archaeological, though literary descriptions also abound, and attempts to relate the two have become a good deal more sophisticated and less mechanical. Over the course of recent decades there has been an upsurge of interest in domestic space, which runs in parallel with, and at some points intersects with, the upsurge of interest in gender and family. Ever since the eighteenth-century beginnings of excavation at Herculaneum and Pompeii, the physical evidence of the ancient house has become more familiar, though it is only the introduction of anthropological and sociological approaches that has made it possible to read the physical evidence as a text for social life and relations. A volume on 'home' has the advantage of bringing together these streams of interest, the one (on family and gender) based principally on study of literary evidence, the other (on housing) on physical evidence, enabling one to look at familiar material from a different angle.

An important feature of this series is that in setting the same thematic titles for the chapters, irrespective of period, it provides a framework that will encourage cross-period and cross-cultural comparisons. The exploration of the theme requires a combination of sources of information, the written word, in the form of literature and documents, and material culture. 'Meaning' emerges most readily from the written form in the literature, often imaginative, that explores the ideals and sentiment within the concept (chapter 1), though such meaning is also implicit in the material remains of houses and burials, the tomb being the home of the dead, and its imagery replicating the scenes of the home of the living, with its companionship and feasting, its furnishings reflecting the furniture of the houses of the living. The family is best grasped through the literary record, and here legal frameworks are especially significant (chapter 2). The essential feature here is the intimate relationship between household and state: the *oikos/domus* is simultaneously the essential building block of the state, the *polis/res publica*, and its image. The family operates within a legal framework designed by and for the state, and it is when the Classical, city-based form of state is challenged in late antiquity that the continuity of ancient conceptions of the home is hardest to trace. The house, by contrast, explored here primarily through the Greek world, gives material expression to the home, and in doing so raises questions about the representation of the home in literature, which suggests a simpler division between male and female spheres than is borne out by the physical evidence (chapter 3). Furnishings are again principally understood through material evidence, thanks in particular to the unusually detailed evidence offered by the Vesuvian sites, which enable us to enrich the finds record of other less well-preserved sites, though here too preservation has notable limits, with wooden furniture little understood outside Herculaneum, while it is literature that allows us to see the importance of fabrics, extremely rare in the archaeological record (chapter 4).

When it comes to the theme of the home as place of work, literary and archaeological evidence converge. The modernizing assumption that the home should be a place of residence and not of work led to persistent misreadings of the archaeological record: evidence of commercial activities within the houses of Pompeii was seen as a social crisis precipitated by natural catastrophe. That reading can now be refuted, and it is only if we recognize the home as a place of work throughout antiquity that we can read the evidence aright (chapter 5). One corollary is that slaves, as we have seen, play a fundamental role in the conception of home, as they do indeed in the conception of 'family': it is no coincidence that the Latin *familia* refers more often to the slave household than to a nuclear grouping. Just as in the early modern period 'family' was used to include the servants living in a household, so *familia* combines owners and dependants (Tadmor 2001). It is the presence of slaves within the home that most complicates the gendered divisions we might expect (chapter 6). Here it is the literary evidence that suggests an ideal of the home as the sphere of female production: the traditional virtue of the housewife is closely associated with weaving. But the idea that the men worked the fields outside while the women spun inside is far too simplistic, for slavery means that the home is the place of work of male slaves. It also complicates sexual relations: the ideal of the chaste wife sits alongside an acceptance of sexual relations by the husband with slaves both female and male. This in turn links to the perception of the home as the place of hospitality (chapter 7). From the *Odyssey* onwards, Greek and Roman writers assume that a fundamental function of the home is the obligation to entertain friends and even strangers. That creates a constant tension between ideals of privacy that might in some sense separate the women of the house from the eyes of male strangers, in a *gynaeceum*, or rather contain the presence of the stranger within the defined hospitality area of the *andrôn*. Such separations work at best only partially for the Greek world (chapter 3), while in the Roman world they almost entirely dissolve. Hospitality depends heavily on the presence of slaves, male and female, preparing and serving food and drink, and entertaining, by song and sex. In the Christianized world of late antiquity, preachers struggled, often in vain, to control such social patterns.

It might be imagined that it was precisely religion that most changed the sense of home in antiquity. But the contrast that suggests paganism was essentially communal and located outside the house, while Christianity was inherently domestic, will not stand (chapter 8). If the pagan home was a microcosm of the state, or rather of the citizen community expressed in the city, so the gods of the community were the gods of the home. Hestia/Vesta, the goddess of the hearth, might claim to be above all the religious expression of the home: but she was also the goddess of the community, and the fires of Vesta tended in Rome by her Virgins were a visceral symbol of the state as a shared home. Alongside Vesta, any of the deities worshipped in temples and in public ceremony might be found worshipped in domestic *lararia*: tens of thousands of bronze statuettes of deities are the domestic correlate of state religion. By the same token, Christianity may be thought of as in origin a domestic cult, the *ekklesia* in the *oikos*; but that is only so long as persecution makes public expressions of faith unthinkable. The moment that Constantine makes Christianity a state cult, the parallel trajectory becomes visible: even as new basilicas make the public face of the religion visible, the now dominant religion insists on the domestic sphere, demanding adherence to its morality by a new emphasis on sexual conduct, one which however continues to overlook the abuse of slaves provided that the marital vows are respected by the wife.

The eight themes are convergent in piecing together an account of the home in antiquity, and one that depends on a combination of written voices and material culture, albeit in different proportions for different themes. A more complex challenge is presented by the timescale covered in this volume (800 BCE–800 CE). Any periodization requires reflection: it may be at once arbitrary and determined by questionable ideological assumptions. The definition of 'antiquity' is certainly open to question. It is the expression conventionally used in Western scholarship to describe a specific period of Mediterranean history embodied in Greek and Latin literature. The period begins with the approximate introduction of the alphabet to Greece, despite the fact that Bronze Age and Iron Age Greece used the same language, and the Bronze Age was far from illiterate. We can also account for this period in terms of the emergence of the *polis*, a form of society based on citizenship, and typically including an urban centre at the heart of an agricultural hinterland. But the break is not total – Mycenaean settlements also had urban centres, albeit based on palaces. What makes the difference is the emergence of Greek literature and the traditions of Classical education in Europe that made this literature 'classical'. There are other definitions of antiquity that would include Egypt and the Near East, and start considerably earlier.

At the far end of the period is a perceived break between antiquity and the Middle Ages. This border too is fluid and disputed. Some would end antiquity with the collapse of Roman imperial control in the western Mediterranean at the end of the fifth century. Some would start the early medieval with the conversion of Constantine in the early fourth century, for the creation of a Christian state is the start of a story rather different from that of the *polis*. The coronation of Charlemagne in 800 CE as Holy Roman Emperor (thirty-two years into his reign in Francia) might be taken as the beginning of the nation states of Europe after the relative confusion of the 'Dark Age' period of barbarian invasions, though in truth the story of Charlemagne's Francia makes little sense without going back to the arrival of the Franks in Roman Gaul in the fifth century. Above all, the date 800 encompasses the spectacular Arab conquest of half the territory of the Roman Empire in the course of the seventh and eighth centuries: by that date, a swathe of land from Syria through Egypt and North Africa to the south of Spain is under the control of Islamic caliphates. The survival of the East Roman Empire as what we rather dismissively label 'Byzantine' represents another point at which the story of antiquity has no clean breaks. Garth Fowden has urged a new periodization of the 'First Millennium' that would embrace Islamic culture with its deep debt to Greek philosophy alongside the 'western European' story (Fowden 2014). That would represent a stimulating shift of perspective, though this is not the place to embark on it.

For many reasons it is impracticable to pursue the history of the home throughout the full potential sweep of the period as defined by this series: not only is the chronological scope too vast for any one historian, but the sheer diversity of human experience across space as well as time means that any attempt at coherence would be defeated. Above all, we are limited by the state of the current scholarship. It is only relatively recently that the 'domestic', in the sense both of family and of the physical environment, has attracted serious attention. There has been intensive work in the traditional heartlands of Classical Greece and Rome. Ever since Sarah Pomeroy's *Goddesses, Whores and Slaves* of 1975, the study of women, or better gender, in the Greco-Roman worlds has been highly active (e.g. Foxhall 2013). Understanding of the family in Greece has moved on significantly (compare Lacey 1980 [1968] with Patterson 1998). The family in the Roman world has been a major focus of attention since Beryl Rawson's series of conferences on this theme, which successfully pulled together work on the literary and especially legal sources with study of the tens of thousands of funerary inscriptions, and work on the built environment of the house (Rawson 2011). A new wave of interest in the physical environment of the Roman house (Clarke 1991; Wallace-Hadrill 1994; Ellis 2000) has led to extensive work in this field (recently, Tuori and Nissin 2015), while the work of Lisa Nevett and others on the Greek house has led to a far more nuanced understanding (Nevett 1999, 2010; Ault and Nevett 2005). Work on the Classical Greco-Roman world has been paralleled by, and has interacted with, interest by scholars of early Christianity, both in the family (Moxnes 1997; Osiek and Balch 1997), and specifically in the house as location for both family and worship (Balch and Osiek 2003; Cooper 2011; Adams 2016). Work on the pagan and Christian worlds converge in a new wave of studies of the family in late antiquity (Nathan 2000; Cooper 2007; Bowes 2008) and of housing in the same period (Lavan et al. 2007).

It is up to this point, stretching into the fifth century and a little beyond, that there is a certain coherence, both in terms of the sources deployed and the traditions of investigation (Harlow and Loven 2012; Southon, Harlow and Callow 2013). But at this point scholarship breaks up into specialist areas with limited contact with antiquity. Germanic law codes have been used to give some insight into the early Germanic family, but both the idea that they had much in common and that the idea of kin or *Sippe* was a defining feature is now discounted (Wood 2003; Mitchell 2007: 25–46). The Islamic family, with its traditions of polygamy, is a large and complex subject with limited contact with the Classical world (Mitchell 2007: 63–78). As Julia Bray observes, 'Family is an under-researched topic in Islamic history' (Bray 2013), and it deserves more space than this volume can afford, and different chronological parameters. Similarly, there is much still to say about the family in the Byzantine world, which would exceed our scope (Brubaker and Tougher 2013). As in previous volumes in this series, the focus of most contributors is on the Classical Greek and Roman worlds, extending as appropriate into late antiquity (cf. Harlow and Laurence 2010: 6).

To what extent can a coherent story be told within these tighter limits, stretching from early Greece to the later Roman empire? The themes that make up this volume constantly intersect, and one point that emerges from the different themes is the extent to which, despite all changes over time, it is actually possible to speak about 'the home in antiquity'. One way to illustrate this is to start from the physical environment of the home. In what follows I will take three examples of homes from across the millennium at the core of this book, from the fifth century BCE to the fifth century CE. I start from the site which has long served as the 'type' of the Classical Greek house, Olynthos in northern Greece (Chalkidike). In fact, the site is less typical than appears, since it experienced within a century first a major expansion, as Perdikkas of Macedon built it up as a centre to resist Athenian control (432), and then complete destruction by Philip II of Macedon (348). As excavated by Robinson in the 1930s, what we see is a large area clearly laid out and built at the same time, occupied so briefly as to have relatively few of the constant modifications that housing stock normally experiences over time, and then abandoned in one moment of destruction (though there are signs of very partial reoccupation) that meant finds belong to a single period, albeit the pale relics of a city sacking rather than a full occupational record (Cahill 2002).

The most obvious feature of the plan of Olynthos, or rather the northern 'new city' of the fifth century, is the extreme mathematical regularity of the house plots. Each block of houses (or in Roman terms, *insula*) is of a standard size, and subdivided into ten equal plots (though even here there have been some modifications over the course of a century). Each plot is square in plan. One way to interpret this is as an expression of Greek democracy (Hoepfner and Schwandner 1994): each citizen is mathematically equal. Behind this equality, we may guess at the influence of Hippodamus of Miletus, famous for his

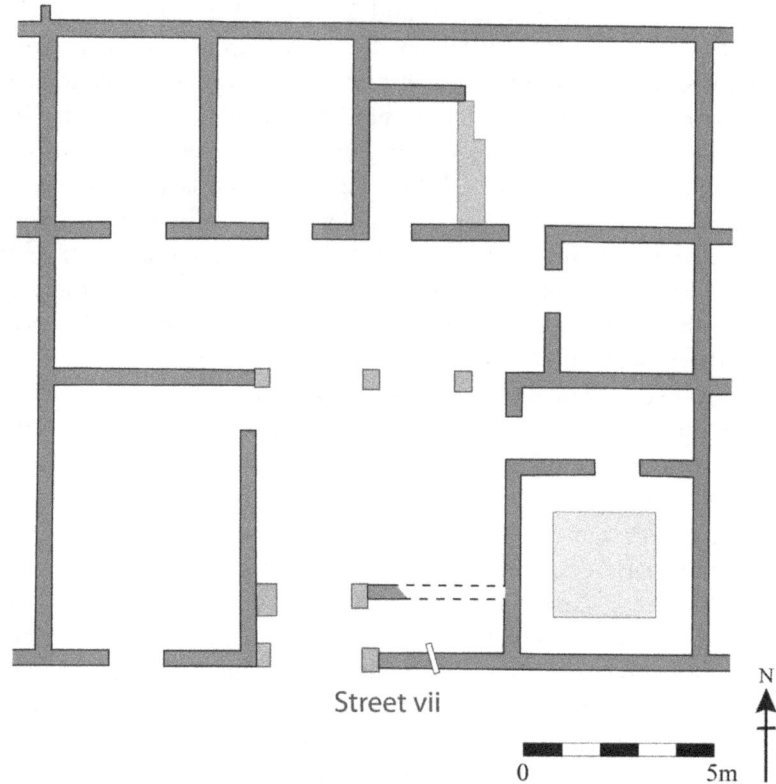

FIGURE 0.1: Olynthos, House A vii 4 (Cahill 2002). Credit: Sophie Hay.

orthogonal planning and ideas of the ideal community expressed in city layout. But if ever that was the intention, it is clear that the citizens were in practice far from equal: sharp variations in the lavishness of decoration, archaeologically visible thanks to the use of pebble-based mosaics, point to inequalities of wealth, and also sharp variations in recorded house sale prices (Cahill 2002: 276–9). City planners often have ideals, but the truth is that regularity of layout makes life easy for them, in simplification of layout and construction. Perhaps the most important point is not equality, but a conception of the relationship between house and city: the *polis* is an assemblage of *oikoi*; the home complete to itself (a square) is a component part of a city complete to itself (but in this case the regularity is limited to the new layout, not all of Olynthos).

Within the square of the *oikos*, there is not so much a separation as an integration of components. This is where the world of women relates to that of men; where the family relates to the community; where masters relate to slaves; where work relates to leisure; where the sacred relates to the profane. We are on controversial ground here. In recent decades, since Susan Walker suggested that the Greek house could be understood with the aid of the Islamic house, as a division between men and women (Walker 1983), there has been debate as to how, or indeed whether, Greek houses as excavated illustrate a separation of male and female spheres (Jameson 1990; Nevett 1999: 174–5; Cahill 2002: 148–53; Trümper 2011: 37–9; Foxhall 2013: 116–21 and Nevett, below, chapter 3). Taking an example from Olynthos, and bearing in mind that there was endless variation in house layouts (Cahill 2002: 204–6), we can see how the square is divided into two parts, one nearer the entrance to the street and the other more secluded from access. In this example (House A vii 4, Figure 0.1), the nearer part consists of a courtyard immediately beyond the doors; a rectangular space to its left which has a separate entrance to the street and is probably a shop or workshop; and a special square room to its right marked by a mosaic floor, and conventionally labelled an *andrôn* (see below Fig. 3.3).

Because several writers, both Greek and Roman, refer to a typical distinction in the Greek house between the women's quarters (*gynaeconitis*) and the men's quarters (*andronitis*), it has been suggested that we should look for a strict gender separation in houses like this at Olynthos. And yet, while it is clear that the room labelled *andrôn*, marked by a slightly raised platform round the sides for dining couches, was designed around the ritual of evening drinking in the symposium (*symposion*), and consequently by widespread Greek custom excluded the wife and daughters of the house, this is not quite the same as making it a men-only area, as female entertainers were allowed. The courtyard through which you had to pass to reach it was evidently a 'common' area to the genders, and indeed in this instance the find of a cluster of loom weights suggests female activity. There are no watertight divisions to be detected, and at best one may suggest that the 'women's quarters' meant no more than that male outsiders were not allowed within – the husband, male children and male slaves having full access. What the house shows is not so much separation as integration, a solution in terms of physical spaces that allowed for the entertainment of male visitors (which added to the house's esteem) without compromising the perceived honour of the women by unsupervised exposure.

The house permits simultaneously the integration of male and female spheres and the integration of the world outside with that inside. The world outside is represented in this example in two different forms. One is the entertainment of guests. It is striking just how many of the houses of Olynthos have recognizable rooms for symposia. The importance attributed to hospitality is underlined both by the careful layout of these rooms (typically square) and by their superior decoration: it is here that mosaics cluster. Ironically, the finds record fails to deliver the sort of furnishings that helped to mark the importance of these spaces: the wooden beds and fabric coverlets have not survived the destruction, and the higher-quality drinking vessels, especially wine-mixing bowls (*krateres*) which are found in these houses are almost never found in the *andrôn*, and very rarely in houses with an *andrôn*. The most plausible explanation is that higher-status houses used metal drinking vessels, of bronze and silver, which were obvious targets for the looting of the city (Cahill 2002: 186–90).

The second presence of the world outside is represented by the shop space to the left of the front door. Direct access from the street is enabled by a separate door, though there is also a door that links it to the interior of the house. What craft or commercial activities took place in this house is unclear from the record, but the finds clustered in the courtyard and back portico (*pastas*) as well as room (b) point to weaving, and a balance with bronze weights suggests sales (Cahill 2002: 107). Again, it is evident that the world of work is both separable from and integrated with that of private domesticity. By the same token, it is impossible to distinguish the world of slaves from that of 'family'. It is impossible to tell whether the looms were worked by the housewife, the ideal Penelope, or by her slaves; or whether the food preparation in the kitchen (e) involved free or slaves. As ever in antiquity, they lived and worked alongside each other.

A final blind spot here is the place of religion in the home. A few Olynthian houses had masonry altars in their courtyards; rather more had small portable altars, sometimes in pairs (Cahill 2002: 87, Morgan 2011: 450). If, as is likely, they had images of the gods in bronze, these will have been pillaged. By a curious parallelism, it is very hard to see the public face of religion in Olynthos, where (unlike so many other cities) no temples have been excavated. What seems safe to say is that such religion as there was in the home was intimately linked to that of the *polis*: we cannot envisage private and personal cults at variance with that of the community at large (Morgan 2011). And whether visible as a religious space or not, the hearth, Hestia, was by definition a sacred space, the ritual embodiment of home, one to which even an adulterer caught in the act could flee for asylum (Lysias 1.27).

The remains of a brutally sacked and looted city cannot be expected to reveal everything. Life upstairs is invisible, though stairs show that upper floors were common: was the upper floor for women rather than men, or for slaves rather than family? There can be no answer, since domestic usage is constantly fluid, changing not merely over time, but even in the course of a day. Had Olynthos survived longer, property boundaries would surely have changed, and with the increased prosperity of the Hellenistic world might have become more elaborately articulated, and richer in mosaics, like those of Delos (Trümper 2011). But one snapshot is enough to hint at a theme that will become apparent in the chapters of this volume, that the idea of the *oikos* integrated the household with the city, the male sphere with the female, the world of work with that of leisure, the sacred with the profane.

We might look in the Roman world for contrasts, and differences there certainly are, but the theme of integration remains the same. Take for instance the House of the Bicentenary in Herculaneum (V.15–16) (Figure 0.2), belonging

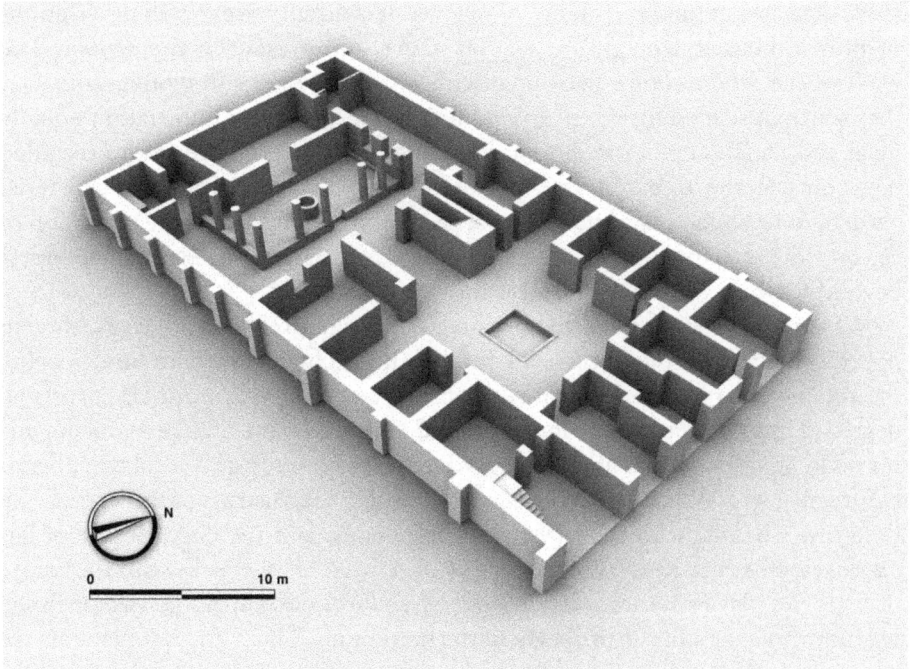

FIGURE 0.2: Herculaneum, House of the Bicentenary. Credit: Brian Donovan.

in its visible structures to the first century CE, though with origins going back to the second or third BCE (Wallace-Hadrill 2011: 223–6). The four shops in the facade of this large house, opening onto the main street of the town (the 'Decumanus Maximus'), belong to the physical fabric and layout of the house, though one operates as an independent unit with its own residential quarters upstairs, while two others interconnect with the inside. The world of work and commerce can be separated and integrated with the household at will. The most conspicuous feature architecturally, familiar from many other examples in Roman cities of this period, is the central hall or *atrium*, notable from its generous dimensions including its height, and also its marked axial symmetry. It is traditional to explain such *atria* and their associated spaces, especially the large open *tablinum* at the opposite side from the door, in terms of Roman social practices of patronage and reception of clients at the *salutatio*, but much more is at stake (Wallace-Hadrill 1994: 12). This is the space which above all others integrates the worlds that meet in the home. Its size and symmetry are an invitation to the world outside to come in, and with its position on the main street, the invitation is a generous one, enhanced, we imagine, by the custom of leaving the front doors open during the day. But it also integrates the worlds of men and women, and given the self-conscious Roman distance from the Greek sense of shame at public visibility of women, it is no surprise that in descriptions of Roman houses, women are seen as active and present in the *atrium*. The walls of the *tablinum* are decorated with images of men and women together, the principal scene hinting at marital unity. Bedrooms, by implication equally male and female, open off this space, though there were other more secluded bedrooms in the upper floors. Beyond the *atrium* opens a small cloistered garden, onto which open the principal reception rooms: again, the invitation of the outsider into the furthest recesses of the house suggests a degree of openness beyond what we have encountered in Olynthos.

What is not visible from the architecture is the presence of slaves, though doubtless they were busy preparing food in the kitchen at the back, and keeping the mosaic floors well swept. But the presence of slaves, and their surprising degree of integration into the family, is made explicit by the bundle of documents found in an upper room above the garden. They come from a legal case, heard before magistrates in Rome, between the *domina*, the mistress of the household, Calatoria Themis, widow of Petronius Stephanus, and the child of one of her ex-slaves, Petronia Justa. The dispute is over whether the girl was born before or after her slave mother was given her freedom; on that hinges whether she was born free, or still the property of the household. The witness statements are surprisingly indecisive, as other ex-slaves or neighbours swear to have been there at the time, or to have witnessed discussions, including the reproach from Themis to the mother of the child, that they have always treated the girl like a daughter. Whether Petronius Stephanus and his wife ever owned this entire and magnificent house is far from clear; but they certainly had a slave household, and the fuzzy boundaries between child and slave are explicit in Themis' reproach.

Religion too served to integrate slave and free. The gods of the hearth, the *lares*, are met here as in numerous other houses, most frequently in the depiction of two dancing figures flanking an alar, which is approached from below by crested snakes, but also through bronze figurines, keeping company with the gods of the pagan pantheon, Jupiter, Minerva, Fortune and – much favoured in Herculaneum – Hercules. The cult of the *lares* at the *lararium*, and with them the spirit of the master of the household, the *genius domini*, symbolizes the loyalty of the slaves to the *familia*, just as the parallel cult of the emperor in the street shrines symbolizes the loyalty of the citizen.

For a final image of the home, we may turn to Roman Africa at the end of the fourth or beginning of the fifth century CE, shortly before the Vandal invasion was to shatter the peace of one of Rome's richest provinces. The great mosaic of 'Julius Dominus' was found in a large town house in the city of Carthage on the 'Hill of Juno': displayed in the Bardo Museum, it has rather lost its context (Figure 0.3; Dunbabin 1978: 119–21, catalogue Carthage 32, plate 109). But it reminds us of the intimate connection of town and country

FIGURE 0.3: Carthage, House of the Hill of Juno, Mosaic of Dominus Julius.
Credit: DEA/Archivio J. Lange via Getty Images.

typical of the ancient city: the settlers of new Olynthos were in all probability simultaneously given allotments in the country (they frequently have storage facilities that exceed urban needs), and the owners of the House of the Bicentenary could perfectly well have had country estates as well as shops. Here in Carthage, the owners displayed the country estate that was one source of their prosperity. The villa at the centre of the composition is rather different from a town house: the strongly built facade flanked by turrets offers not only a vision of security but also the idea of the villa as a city in miniature. Above the ashlar masonry of the walls is a long arcade of columns, suggesting a world of elegant pleasures, of shady walks and vistas over the countryside. Behind is the cluster of domes which in a later world would have pointed to a mosque, but here surely represent a luxurious bath building.

The villa is surrounded by images of the owners, the *dominus* and the *domina*, their slave workers and their rich prosperity. To the left of the villa the *dominus* approaches on horseback, followed by a slave carrying the bags. To the right (and one surely reads first left to right), having arrived safely at his country estate, he sets off on a hunt, with spear and net and hound. From Odysseus onwards, hunting has been a sport for the antique noble. The upper and lower registers introduce us to the *domina*. Above, she is seen seated outside on a bench on a summer's day, fanning herself. To the left, a peasant brings her ducks, while peasant children shake down olives from a tree; to the right a girl brings a lamb, and a shepherd tends sheep in front of a peasant's hut of reeds and a field of ripe corn. In the language of these mosaics, she is flanked by winter and summer. In the lower register, she appears again to the left, this time leaning like a seductive Venus on a column, while a slave girl offers her a necklace from her jewellery box; behind the roses bloom. On the right, she is balanced by the *dominus*, to whom a slave offers a scroll addressed to IV DOM (hence the name of the mosaic, if we can trust the extrapolation); behind him peasants tread the grapes of the vintage (Ghedini and Bullo 2007, Rossiter 2007).

This image of aristocratic wealth, and the emphasis on the country estate as source of wealth, would be familiar to the families of Rome whom Jerome courted (he would doubtless have persuaded the *domina* to take an oath of virginity, and to leave the estate to the church after her husband's death). For once, the mosaic allows the importance of the slave household, and maybe peasant tenants, to be visible. Of the children of the house there is no trace, which of course does not mean they had none, much as a Jerome would have liked it. The home is a twin concern, of town and country. The villa is a place of abundant agricultural productivity, but also of leisure and pleasure, of elegant dinners (why else the necklace?) and of bathing. Whether the owners were Christian, as so many in the Carthage of around 400 CE, they do not here reveal, but the Venus pose of the mistress was no obstacle. There is no image here of hospitality; but we remind ourselves, this mosaic belonged to a town house, and was surely intended for the admiration of the guests at a dinner party: the game and sheep and olives and wine on which they feasted are advertised as produce of this villa, where *dominus* and *domina* together held sway among their staff.

The Olynthos and Herculaneum houses were offered as examples of the integration of spheres the antique home aspired to. Here too we find integration: of town and country, and master and mistress, of owner and slaves or tenants, of work and play. There is a continuity here, or rather a contrast to modernity. The privacy, the intimacy, the nuclearity of the modern home seem very distant. For all that, home, *oikos* or *domus*, was a powerful integrative concept that was seen as an essential building block of ancient societies.

CHAPTER ONE

The Meaning of Home

ANDREW WALLACE-HADRILL

THE LANGUAGE OF HOME

A figure sits on a beach, staring disconsolately over the barren waves. Tears pour from his eyes, tears he does not trouble to wipe away: his pain is eating him away, consuming him. Behind him stands a fair-haired nymph, ever young, ever lovely, for she is an immortal god. She cannot understand the man. She has saved his life, and offered to make him immortal like herself; given him an enchanted place to dwell: a great cave scented with the cedar from the hearth, by which she weaves with a golden shuttle, singing the while with her lovely voice. But he wants none of it. Though they make love, he desires her no more. He yearns for another woman, who is weaving far away by another hearth: his Penelope, his home (*Odyssey* 5, esp. 148–213). The homesickness of Odysseus is the model for all nostalgia: the pain of longing for the *nostos*, the return home. The *Odyssey* poetically is a *nostos*, a poem about homesickness and homecoming, about the meaning of home.

The idea of the home spans cultures: if Homer is the foundation of Western literature, the *Odyssey* places the importance of 'home' at its heart. The word clusters by which we articulate this shared idea are more varied. The sharp distinction of 'house' and 'home' is specific to English and other Germanic languages. I can have a house that is not a home, and a home that is not a house: I may own several houses that I rent out, yet make my home in a penthouse suite in an apartment block. It is harder to make the same distinction in the Romance languages: in Italian my home is *casa mia*, yet every house is a *casa*; in French a house is a *maison*, but for my home I must turn to an adverbial expression, *chez moi*, at the root of which is the Latin *casa*, or to the hearth as symbol of household, *feu* (Italian *fuoco*). To express homesickness, the Romance languages hark back to Homeric roots, in 'nostalgia', the pain of yearning for return.

Greek and Latin each have two separate word clusters: Greek *domos/dôma* versus *oikos/oikia*; Latin *domus* versus *aedes*, and differently, *familia*. Yet in neither case does the contrast map onto our house/home distinction. Odysseus heads back indifferently to his *domos*, *dôma*, even just *dô*, and to his *oikos*. His going home is both *domonde* and *oikonde* – the difference is metric, not semantic. But *oikos* is also his family, and so it remains through Classical Greek (Foxhall 2013: 24–6, Patterson 1998: 1–4). Modern Greek, by contrast, uses a Latin derivative, *spiti* from *hospitium*, a guesthouse: *spiti mou* is *casa mia*, *chez moi*. Family is *oikogeneia*, the people of the *oikos*. But in ancient Greek, *domos* can equally mean 'family'. *Oikos* is not home *as opposed to* house: it is house, home and family altogether, a singularly powerful amalgam (MacDowell 1989). The management of house, home, family and property is *oikonomia*: economics.

In Latin, *domus* has the same power – house, home and family – while *familia* embraces all those, wife, children and slaves, who were under the authority of the *paterfamilias* (Saller 1984). The owner of the house is the *dominus*: lord and master to house, family and slaves. *Aedes* is pale by comparison, a building, though including a building for the gods, a temple (the grammarians ruled: singular, a temple; plural, a house). To build not only a house but any building is *aedificare*, the building an *aedificium*, an edifice, while ancient Greek uses both the *oikos* and *domos* root for building in *oikodomeo*. *Casa*, from which the Romance languages name house and home, is indeed a Latin word; but restricted in the Classical period to the peasant's hut, like the thatched hut of Rome's founder, the *casa Romuli*. Only in medieval Latin does *domus* move up scale to the church, the *domus ecclesiae*, morphed in Italian to the *duomo* with its 'dome'; and *casa* correspondingly moves upwards, from hut to house, to take its place. Linguistic usage matters, but is not in itself a sufficient guide to the complex topographies of culture.

OIKOS IN GREEK THOUGHT

Because of its status as a literary charter, it is worth exploring the *Odyssey* in greater detail. To Victorian eyes, noting its domestic focus, the *Odyssey* was differently gendered from the *Iliad*, authored even by a woman. Unnecessary though this explanation is, the contrast is real: the *Iliad* deals with the world of manly war, while the *Odyssey* is about the home. Having opened with a glimpse of Calypso, the homewrecker, set on making a husband of the man who only yearns for home and wife (1.11–62), the action, anything but linear, at once focuses not on Odysseus but his home. There the suitors are consuming the substance of the hero's household as they pay court to his wife (1.103–229).

There are homewreckers at both ends of the action. And through them we learn the meaning of home (Patterson 1998: 46–50).

It falls to the son, Telemachus, to take action in defence of his mother and home; but by an extended exercise in distraction, the goddess Athene sends him off on a journey around Greece, to see if he can get word of his missing father (books 1–4). A distraction this may be in plotline; but if the *Odyssey* is about home, it is essential. By leaving his own home and visiting the homes of his father's friends, Telemachus both echoes his father's wanderings, and learns the value of home by absence from it. Essentially, he also learns about hospitality. His father's friends are under moral obligation, the laws of Zeus Xenios, the guardian of hospitality, to welcome him into their homes as long as he wants, and send him on his way laden with precious gifts, each one of which comes with a long tale of the chain of hospitality it represents. Just as Telemachus and Penelope are obligated to entertain the suitors, to the damage of their own household, so Telemachus relies on the hospitable obligations of others. But good hospitality has its code of honour, as he is reminded more than once: you should keep a visitor as long as he wants, but not detain him for longer than he wants. Telemachus is a man with a mission; he returns home without news of his father, but the wiser about hospitality. The Homeric home is thus not a private space to the exclusion of others, but a place where others should be welcomed and entertained. Unless indeed, like the suitors, they behave grossly and outstay their welcome.

Odysseus in the meantime is multiply tempted, like Athanasius' St Anthony in the desert. He is offered chance after chance to forget his home and make a new one. As if Calypso was not enough, there is Circe. As Odysseus recounts to the hospitable Phaeacians, it was not only the divine Calypso who longed to make him her husband; so did the tricksy Circe. But she could not persuade his heart, 'for there is nothing sweeter than your homeland or your parents, even if you live away from your rich home in a foreign land, far from your parents' (*Odyssey* 9.34ff.). For him, then, home has multiple components that hang together: homeland (*patria* or fatherland), parents, house, wife, wealth. He begs the Phaeacians to take him home, and they oblige, though the meeting on the beach between the naked, shipwrecked hero and Nausicaa, the king's daughter with her laughing maids, seems to be a set-up for him to make a new home in a country that proves idyllic. As we listen to the description of the city of Phaeacia with its twin harbours (6.262–9), we are transported to the sort of location favoured by Greek colonists who from the eighth century onwards left their homes to make new home cities overseas (*apoikiai*).

Odysseus returns to Ithaca, laden with the gifts of the hospitable Phaeacians, and returns with a vengeance. After twenty years of absence, it would be no wonder if he were unrecognizable; and to fool the suitors he renders himself the more so by dressing as a beggar. But the test of home is not only that you recognize it, but that it recognizes you. The old dog, symbol of fidelity, is the first to know its master (17.300–10). Then it is the aged nursemaid, Eurycleia, who knows her master by the scar he bears from an old boar hunt (19.357–502). But the final test of recognition is Penelope herself. This happens only after he has revealed his strength, rid his house of its unwelcome guests and punished the faithless household servants, the maids who had slept with the suitors (22.419–73). Despite all this, Penelope is not content with appearances: she wants to know her husband from the secrets that only they know and which bind them together. The location of the secret is the very symbol of their union, the marriage bed; and the secret is that Odysseus himself had carved the bed from the great olive tree at the core of the house (23.173–208). Home, then, is not just a place, and not just a place shared by people, but a place of shared memories. Odysseus, who has spent his wanderings sharing memories with strangers, memories of monsters he has outwitted, and seductresses with whom he has slept and yet escaped, now shares with his wife the most ancient and intimate of their memories. At last he is home.

The world of Odysseus may be located in the never-never land of myth: it is neither Mycenaean Greece nor the Archaic present, but all times. Moses Finley recognized in it the sort of primitive society with Marcel Mauss had studied in *The Gift*: one of gift-exchange (Finley [1956] 1977). But the image of home, home values and home-yearning which it offered retained its validity and power throughout antiquity. Calypso weaves and offers a false home; Penelope weaves and unravels by night to defeat the impatient suitors, and represents the true home. The image of the wife, weaving by the hearth, is equally evocative in the Roman world: the virtuous wife as the *lanifica*, the wool-maker, like Lucretia who is found in her atrium, the location of the *lectus genialis*, the marriage bed, by the rapist Tarquin, quietly weaving (Livy 1.58–9), or Augustus' wife Livia who claimed to weave him his toga (Suetonius, *Augustus* 73).

Greek tragedy, even if fifth-century Athens represents a different society and culture from the world of Odysseus, plays constantly on Homeric themes. The home is pervasive as a theme: whether in an Oedipus cast out of his home as a baby to return and subvert it, even as he saves the city, by parricide and incest, and blind himself on the bed on which he was conceived and on which he conceived children by his mother, or a Medea who, having betrayed father and country to save Jason, is driven by his infidelity to destroy the home by murdering her own children. Perhaps the most powerful extended examination of the home in its disruption is Aeschylus' *Oresteia* trilogy (Goldhill 1992: 24–41; Patterson 1998: 140–8).

For Agamemnon too it is a *nostos*, a long-delayed return to his home. The action opens at his home in Argos: the night watchman tells us that it is an *oikos* which, if it had a tongue, would have many stories to tell (*Agamemnon* 37–9). Gradually they are revealed. Agamemnon's wife, Clytemnestra, pretending to rejoice at the news of his imminent return, sends word to him that he will find a faithful wife in his home, as he left her, a fine watchdog for the house, a deliberate echo of Odysseus and his faithful hound (606–8). But even in leaving home ten years before, he had struck a blow to the heart of home by allowing his virgin daughter to be sacrificed in the hopes of a following wind. The resentment of Clytemnestra has never gone. She too has betrayed the home by her infidelity with Aegisthus. There is betrayal on both sides. She greets his homecoming with a scene designed to symbolize the destruction of home. She spreads a purple carpet to welcome him, a gesture redolent of Oriental tyranny and luxury. Agamemnon recognizes it as a destruction of the substance of the house; as Clytemnestra laughs it off ('there is the sea, and who will exhaust it?'), the theme of the home is drummed in insistently: his *oikos* has wealth aplenty to spare, this is no poor *domos*, and she would have sacrificed far more to have him home to his *domos* before; his return to hearth and home, *domatitin hestian*, is like the warmth of spring after winter (958–74). Beside Agamemnon in his chariot is his war-captive, Cassandra, raped and wretched. Clytemnestra recognizes in her the serial infidelity of her husband, while she, Cassandra, recognizes the doom that awaits them both, and the blood curse that hangs over the house. Agamemnon advances down the purple carpet to the bath that will be stained purple with his blood.

The dysfunctional home of the *Oresteia* stretches into past and future. After the murder of Agamemnon and Cassandra, Clytemnestra lays claim to justice for her daughter's sacrifice (1431–47), and finally her own concealed lover is revealed, Aegisthus, the son of Thyestes, whom Agamemnon's father Atreus had subjected to the ghastly feast of the flesh of his own children (1577–1611). The meal and hospitality, which is fundamental for the home, have been revoltingly perverted, and Aegisthus claims the moral high ground, though the chorus recognizes in him only the sneaky adulterer (1625–7). Agamemnon's children, Orestes and Electra, are obligated to avenge their father by killing their mother; for that the Furies, the Erinyes, cannot forgive them until they are persuaded to hand them over to Athenian justice. Here the unHomeric touch is that the state, or rather the people, the *demos*, intervenes to resolve the problems of the family (*Eumenides* 681ff.). In Homer, the power is with the kings and the *demos* follows, however much a Thersites may grumble. The Athenian home is no longer in isolation, or one of a series of homes tied together by hospitality and gift-exchange, but a component of a collaborative citizen community, ruled by law and the administration of justice.

This representation of the *oikos* as an integral part of the state is no Aeschylean whimsy, a way of celebrating the contemporary reform of the homicide court. Throughout the Archaic and Classical periods, the *oikos* is bound up with the community. When a Greek community sent out settlers to form a colony overseas, it was an *apoikia*, a home from home, led by an *oikistes*, a homemaker. Those who moved into your city from outside were *metoikoi*, home-changers. The *oikos*, as Plato and Aristotle recognized, was the building block of the *polis*. The just city is there to defend and limit the rights of the *oikos*: justice cannot be delivered by feud, as in the house of Atreus, but by the judgment of fellow citizens.

We can see this operation of *polis* justice at work most vividly in the speech delivered in the late fifth century before an Athenian court by Lysias, *On the Murder of Eratosthenes* (Patterson 1998: 163–74). The defendant, Euphiletos, has killed his wife's adulterer, caught *in flagrante* in his home. This brief speech offers not only one of the fullest descriptions we have of an Athenian house, for which it is frequently cited, but also a discussion of the values, imagined and subverted, of the home, and of the ties of *oikos* to *polis*. Euphiletos needs to demonstrate to the court that the killing is unpremeditated, in a *raptus* of passion, not a carefully planned trap, though his own narrative scarcely bears out his version. No matter. He depicts the ideal home: a young wife whom he looked after solicitously, and on the birth of their child came to trust implicitly on the basis of the intimacy of their relationship (*oikeiotes*). She seemed the perfect housewife, *oikonomos*, sparing and precise in her household management (Lacey 1980: 169–70). Their little house (*oikidion*) was on two floors, the upper reached by a ladder; and though normally upstairs was the women's quarters (*gynaikônitis*) and the lower the men's quarters (*andrônitis*), he let his wife have the downstairs to save her climbing down the ladder to breastfeed the baby. She abused his trust. Having caught the eye of Eratosthenes while at his mother's funeral, she started an affair, with the assistance of her maid. He recalls an occasion when she had to leave his room upstairs and go down because the baby was crying, and jokingly locked him in to stop him getting up to anything with the maid. Bangs in the night indicated that the doors were opened. The house probably had a courtyard, with an outer and an inner door. Just what has been happening is revealed by a nosy neighbour who tips him off – as an act of revenge, because she had previously had a fling with the same Eratosthenes. At her suggestion, he follows the maid out to the market, and gives her a choice, to be flogged and put to mill work, or to tell all. She tells, and arranges to tip Euphiletos off on Eratoshenes' next visit. When the moment comes, he slips out and summons a posse of neighbours, who burst in, and find the lovers in the act. Eratosthenes' pleas for mercy fall on deaf ears.

It is at this point that Euphiletos' story most creaks. He had the confessed and naked adulterer bound, and begging for his life, offering to make it up: did he really need to kill him? Here the defendant deploys the relationship of *oikos* and *polis*: it is not he who killed him, but the *polis* itself, which enjoined on the husband the killing of an adulterer caught in the act in his own home. The laws of the city are read out in detail, and the citizen jurors implored to defend their own interests: he has acted in the interests of all, in the defence of marriage as an institution. To punish him would be to wipe out the laws of the *polis* and give the green light to every adulterer.

Euphiletos pushes his argument too far. While the homicide laws doubtless allowed legitimate defence to the man killing an adulterer, though limiting this to the adulterer of his own wife in his own home, and caught in the act, they surely did not enjoin that the offended husband *must* kill him. It was in the interest of the *polis* to limit family feud within the *oikos*, as in the case of Orestes. The default position was that the state monopolized the right to take life, and made that harder by due process of a jury trial before fellow citizens. The old right of Odysseus to return home and slay the adulterers in his home (not that Penelope had let them get their way) was preserved, but in a strictly limited way. It is unlikely, whatever the jury found, that Euphiletos' knowing entrapment was permitted (Lacey 1980: 114–15).

The case provides us with a snapshot of so many features of the ideal home: not just its physical structures, and the formal separation of men's from women's sphere which was widely regarded as typical of the Greek house, but also the ideals of happy family and domesticity (Nevett 1999), the wife's role in household management (the husband is often away on business, but as a farmer working the land), the intersection between the inside and outside worlds and its gendering (the lady of the house goes out for funerals and festivals, maids go to market), relations with neighbours (the jealous neighbour who tips Euphiletos off, the posse of men he is able to gather in a hurry), and the integration of home and state, which strictly limits the power of action, even for a *crime passionelle*.

The role of Euphiletos' wife within the home was of the *oikonomos*, household management. How to manage an Athenian household is best spelt out in Xenophon's treatise, the *Oeconomicus*: though in some ways this is the first work of economics, it is often closer to Mrs Beeton. The treatise, which opens with the usual interrogation by Socrates, moves on to an account of how ideally to manage your *oikos* by the perfect gentleman, *kalos kai agathos*, Ischomachus (Pomeroy 1994). A definition of *oikos* is established: it is not merely your dwelling place or house, *oikia*, but covers all your property, including your slaves: the scope is expanded to estate as well as household, and the second half of the treatise is about estate management. The first half, by contrast, is defined as the sphere of control of the wife: inside rather than outside; storage and consumption of produce rather than production; spending rather than earning. Ischomachus married his wife as a teenage girl, and could hardly expect her to arrive with the art of household management already mastered; consequently he teaches, or gently guides, her (and the reader) in this demanding art.

Interestingly, Ischomachus sees the roles of husband and wife as separate but reciprocal: each depends on the other. It is a *koinônia*, a joint enterprise or partnership. The wife, to whom nature has given the role of bearing and raising children, operates indoors, the husband outdoors in farming. Within her sphere, the wife reigns supreme, a queen bee commanding the worker bees, that is, the domestic household. She rules by knowledge and an understanding of order, *taxis*, which is parallel to the general's tactical order: every household item in its right place, known to her. Work is to be delegated, and the wife will act like a commander, conducting inspections and spot checks. By her management of resources, the wife increases the resources of the household, as does the husband by management of the estate. She is responsible for storage, for feeding and for weaving. The image of Penelope is not far away, but this wife will supervise weaving performed by slaves. Nor will she try to render herself more attractive by the use of cosmetics: better healthy exercise, even in household tasks like kneading dough. (Given the use of white lead in cosmetics, Ischomachus is probably right that this is a healthier option.) As the housekeeping wife grows in wisdom and skill at good management, so does her value to her husband, and it is this, rather than her fading beauty, which will ensure that the bond between them grows.

Politically incorrect though his advice may be by modern standards, it fits surprisingly well with a tradition that stretches from Penelope to Mrs Beeton. The wife bears the heavy responsibility of the homemaker: care for children and household staff, responsibility for food and clothes sit in a tradition of differentiated female and male spheres. What is refreshing and perhaps surprising about the gentlemanly, if undeniably patronizing, Ischomachus is his willingness to allow an equality of standing to his wife, a balance of power that cedes her control in her sphere. That Xenophon idealizes is obvious, though it is an amusing footnote to discover that Ischomachus' wife had been accused in court not merely of infidelity, but of seducing her own son-in-law (Harvey 1984).

Xenophon's take seems to be different from that of Aristotle, at least in nuance. Aristotle opens his *Politics* (1.1–4) with the human relationships he sees as natural. In a series of lopsided relationships, the male naturally commands the female, the master the slave, the father the child, though he emphasizes that women and slaves are not treated the same by Greeks, only by barbarians. Man is a 'political animal' in his instinct to form communities: the first *koinônia* or association is the household, *oikia* (note that here unlike in Xenophon the word means family rather than the physical house), and he cites Hesiod in the *Works and Days* recommending, 'first get a house and a wife and a ploughing ox' (1252b10–12, though oddly enough for his argument, in the text we have of Hesiod, the following line defines the woman as a slave girl). The village is made up of *oikiai*, and the *polis* is an association of villages. He then goes on to examine the *oikia*, as Xenophon the *oikos*, as comprehending all property, animate and inanimate: hence slaves are animate property and part of the house.

Aristotle goes on to draw a distinction familiar from Xenophon between generation of wealth (*chrêmatistikê*) and household management (*oikonomikê*). But his interest is at the levels of the *polis*, in politics, not in the house and its management, and he does not follow Xenophon's model in dilating on the theme. Indeed, his cold analytics and his hierarchical model of human relations seem far from the more humane vision in Xenophon of an ideal home. But though Aristotle gives little space to the emotive aspect of the 'home', it is striking that he sees the *oikia* as the fundamental building block of the *polis*. His analysis also underlines the vital role of slaves in the *oikos*, and the fact that the power relationship between owner and slave was parallel to that between husband and wife, or parent and child.

DOMUS IN ROMAN LIFE AND LAW

It would be wrong to draw too sharp a contrast between Greek and Roman ideas of the home. At all points Hellenophone and Latinophone populations were in close contact with each other, and particularly if we are to judge the Roman idea of home from literary texts, we are looking at a literature strongly influenced by close knowledge of Greek. It is true that Latin texts themselves point to some basic contrasts between Greek and Roman practice. The biographer Cornelius Nepos, writing at the end of the first century BCE, alerts his readers at the start of his lives of Greek figures to the different treatment of women: Greek women were segregated, he suggests, while the Roman *matrona* was at the heart of things, circulating freely among men (*Preface* 4–7). The architect Vitruvius, writing a few years later, elaborates that contrast in physical terms: the Roman home knows no separation of *gynaeconitis* and *andronitis*, a separation he sees as basic to the Greek home. In this there must be some truth, though different Greeks at different periods in different areas will have played such separation differently, and the pursuit of a clear male/female separation proves a phantasm (Nevett 2001 and chapter 3 below). Even Lysias, in one of the few close descriptions we have of such practices, is describing an inversion of the normal relationship, in which the part of the house least accessible from the door is given to men instead of women, and for that we have only Euphiletos' rather unreliable word (above).

If there is a real contrast, and if we can generalize across time and space without caveats, it seems to be not so much that the Greek home segregates women in a way the Roman does not, but that the boundaries between inside and out, between *domi* (at home) and *foris* (abroad), and between private (*privatus*) and public (*publicus*) are significantly more permeable in the Roman home. The modern concept of home, forged in its essentials in the early nineteenth century, relies on the alignment of three polarities: home:work, female:male and private:public. It is because home is normalized as *not* a place of work, and at the same time the woman is normalized as *not* a worker (a norm that the twentieth century was to jettison) that the privacy of the home acquires its sense of a refuge from the outside world of men and work: the more recent idea of a work/life balance also privileges the home as the place of personal and private life. The *oikia* of Ischomachus in Xenophon maps broadly onto these distinctions; the Roman *domus* in some significant ways does not. The separation of the 'home' from work and its essentially private nature is constantly breached in the Roman *domus*, and far more so than in the Greek equivalent.

The Roman comedy of the second century BCE offers many pictures of domesticity. The different genres of drama offered different stage sets, reflected, as Vitruvius observed (7.5.2), in the domestic decoration of his own day, the late first century BCE. Tragedy was set in palaces; satyr plays in the countryside; and comedy in houses and streets populated by ordinary people. The plays of Plautus and Terence, translated (more or less) from Attic New Comedies, paint a world that hovers between fourth-century Athens and second-century Rome. A good example is Plautus' *Mostellaria, The Haunted House*. The scene is set in the street onto which two neighbouring houses open. The owner of one, Theopropides, has been away on business, and in his absence his son has been partying extensively, and has set up with an unsuitable girl, Philemation (Kiss-Kiss), a slave girl whose freedom he has purchased on borrowed money. The unexpected return of the father leads to the cunning slave cooking up a complex story about his son's debt, suggesting that Theopropides' house is haunted, so the son has borrowed to buy the neighbour's house. The neighbour is duped into letting Theopropides look round his house, supposedly to get some ideas for improving his own. The setting in Athens comes out clearly from the details of the house he is to imitate: the *gynaeceum* and the portico (754–65). And despite the fact that the neighbour's wife is resting in bed, hoping to be joined by her husband, the party is urged to make themselves at home, and visit every room, even the women's quarters.

We must presume, assuming Vitruvius does not mislead in suggesting Roman houses did not have women's quarters, that the audience would recognize this as a partially alien Greek world. Even so, it was an alien world the Romans were busy imitating, in architecture as well as literature, and the second century is precisely the period at which porticos, such as the one here so admired, became a common domestic feature in Italy (Gowers 1993: 60–6). It is also significant that the world of husbands and wives, fathers and sons, masters and slaves (mostly deceitful), let alone the world of parties and prostitutes, was one the Romans recognized in their own society. Underlying the play is a set of assumptions about the home which the Romans would cheerfully sign up to: the importance for the master in not wasting the resources of the house on high living, and the constant danger of status barriers being broken (son falls in love with a tart). In the opening scene, Theopropides' wastrel son nicely compares himself to a house (*aedes*), once well built, that has been allowed to go to rack and ruin by lack of maintenance to roof tiles and gutters. Love and Lust have leaked through his roof and ruined him (84–117). The very word that repeatedly describes his behaviour, *pergraecamini*, 'Greeking it up', enshrines the perceived influence on Rome.

A century later, Cicero's thinking on the home shows the continued influence of Greek models. In his philosophical writings, he does not devote much space to the theme (though he had translated Xenophon's *Oeconomicus*), but what he says is fully in line with Socratic thought:

> Because the urge to reproduce is an instinct common to all animals, the first social bond is between the conjugal pair; the next with children, and then the unified house with all things in common. This is the beginning of the city and the seed-bed of the state.
> —*De Officiis* 1.54, Gardner and Wiedemann 1991, 2–3

Here as in Aristotle the household (*domus*) is the primal building block of the city and state (*urbs* and *res publica*, where Aristotle would have said *polis*). It depends on the bonds of affection between man and woman, parent and child and beyond them the whole household, which might embrace extended family, and surely household slaves. From the point of view of Roman law, it was the power of the father of the family, *patria potestas*, an untrammelled power over wife, children and slaves, that held the household together; yet Cicero is insistent that the root is the bond of affection, *ipsa caritas generis humani* (*De Finibus* 5.65). For him, law and human instinct converge (Treggiari 1991: 208).

It is its emotional charge that for us most clearly distinguishes home from house, and when Cicero most famously speaks about his own home, emotion is charged to the fullest. Indeed, he can talk of a house as a political asset: the statesman is justified in building his house in a prominent position overlooking the forum, in full view of his fellow citizens, and in investing it with a degree of luxury which his reception of numerous visitors makes appropriate, though there is an important balance to be struck so that the owner's standing does as much for the house as the house for his standing (*De Officiis* 1.139, 'nec domo dominus sed domino domus honestanda est'). Cicero's house on the lower slopes of the Palatine fitted his prescription. But it is only when he is sent into exile by Clodius, and his house is ritually demolished and dedicated as a shrine to Libertas, that the full emotive power of his house is put on show. His return from exile is a *nostos* to match that of Odysseus. The ritual demolition of his house sought to place him in line with the figures of the past accused of aiming to make themselves tyrants, from Spurius Maelius to Fulvius Flaccus (*De Domo*

Sua 101–2). Clodius wants to mark Cicero as a tyrant and enemy of Liberty. But Clodius' Liberty is spurious, a statue robbed from the tomb of a prostitute outside Tanagra (111). Clodius in reality was after enlarging his own house on the Palatine, with a portico 300 feet long with fancy flooring and a peristyle (116). A citizen's house is more than a building: it is a sacred space, containing altars, hearths, household gods, rites, religion and ceremonies, the holy refuge of which nobody can be deprived (109). Cicero's return is a restitution of his home, the recovery of his seat, his altars, his hearth and his household gods (143). The emotions Cicero sought to stir were basic to Roman practice: the household gods, the *lares* and *di penates*, gods of the hearth and food-store, defined the home. They were exactly what Aeneas brought with him from Troy.

If the *Odyssey* is the ultimate homecoming, Virgil's *Aeneid* mirrors its themes to become the ultimate homemaking (or remaking). Aeneas too wanders the seas, passing his own Cyclops, and setting up house with his own Calypso, the Carthaginian Dido. As the gods periodically remind him, his mission is to found a new home. But it is the fact that he carries with him his *di penates*, and his father on his shoulder, his son at his hand, that means that his new home will be a reincarnation of his old home. The cruel death of his wife Creusa means that with a new home he must find a new wife; but the memories and household gods he carries with him will endow his new home with deeper meaning. Aeneas is the archetypal refugee, the eventual founder of a city that would pride itself on giving a home to refugees, Romulus' asylum (Dench 2005).

The Latin text most mined for illumination of the Roman house is Vitruvius' *On Architecture*. There is no need here to revisit his prescriptions for the Roman *atrium* house, its room names and its decoration. The issue is home not house, and here too, Vitruvius illuminates. It is precisely his much-discussed chapters on adapting the house suitably to different status groups that proves most relevant. What strikes the modern reader as unexpected in his account is the picture he gives of the privacy, or rather lack of privacy, of the Roman home. Privacy has been a defining characteristic of the modern home since the nineteenth century. The gentleman's home, as prescribed by the Victorian writer Robert Kerr, was based on a separation between the quiet and comfort of the family and the convenience of the domestics (Kerr 1871). The architect must make every effort to ensure privacy for family rooms. In Vitruvius' Roman house, the privacy of the home is interrupted by the existence of 'common spaces', accessible to visitors, even without invitation, who came in as 'of right' (6.5.1). Of course it was convention, not law, that threw open the private space of the house to the passing visitor. It is not a helpful reading of Vitruvius to suggest that there were separate 'public' and 'private' zones in the house. His distinction is rather between rooms where the visitor entered invited and uninvited. The privacy of the dining and sleeping rooms where guests were invited was compromised by Victorian standards (Wallace-Hadrill 1994: 17–37).

It is more illuminating to grasp why the presence of visitors was so important, and what is distinctive about the Roman pattern. After all, from the *Odyssey* to the *Mostellaria*, the house was a place of hospitality, and entertainment of guests a vital function, indeed an obligation. But Vitruvius is not talking about house-guests and dinner parties, but about business. He distinguishes different status groups. The class of office holders needs grand 'public' spaces, lofty vestibules and vast atria and peristyles, because their political life means doing their duties (*officia*) by their fellow citizens: these are not social friends, but fellow citizens seeking their advice and judgment on public and private affairs. Common folk, by contrast, needed to 'go round' (*ambire*) to do their duties to others. Nor is it only the top flight of politically active statesmen who need to receive visitors. Moneylenders, contractors of public works, lawyers and advocates need to entertain their clients. Farmers by contrast need space for the business of the farm and especially storage (6.5.2).

The Vitruvian house achieves no separation from the world of work (Wallace-Hadrill 1994: 46–7, 118–42; see further below, chapter 5). Privacy is not inconceivable; but it is relative within the spaces of the houses. If the Greek house separates the world of women, the secluded interior, from the world of men, close to the door, the Roman house distances sociability from the accessible business life of the house. It was particularly difficult to separate the servile staff of the house from the family. If the houses of the Vesuvian cities show separate service areas, this is in the grandest houses, and the separation is nothing like the Victorian upstairs/downstairs (Wallace-Hadrill 1994: 57–60). Indeed, *familia* is more often used to refer to domestic staff than to close family; all together form the *domus*, the household. Vitruvius' attention to the rank and occupation of the owner shows that it is not mere houses, but homes he is building. But the homeliness of these homes is much compromised according to modern standards by the use of the home as a place of work, indeed, specific types of work outside the home, *foris*: the political, economic and religious life of the community. But the house served not as a castle, an exclusion of the world outside, but as a complex and powerful mechanism for integrating the outside with the inside on the owner's terms.

Numerous Roman texts take us within the home as a place of intimacy: family letters, in a tradition stretching from Cicero to the Younger Pliny, or funerary epitaphs in their thousands and tens of thousands that represent family members, husbands and wives, parents and children, patrons and freedmen, bonded by affection (Gardner and Wiedemann 1991). Let one phrase stand for them all, Lucretius' summary of what we fear to lose in death:

> Now no happy home will welcome you back, neither your best of wives nor your sweet children will rush up to steal your kisses and touch your heart with silent sweetness.
>
> —*de Rerum Natura* 3.894–6

It is precisely because Lucretius offers us this scene as a cliché that it is revealing of Roman expectations. The *nostos* of Odysseus, welcomed home by his dog, his nursemaid and his faithful wife, has become the everyday banality of every Roman coming back home in the evening. The emotional charge of the Roman *domus* should not be underestimated, even if we meet in it features that seem alien: the intrusion of strangers and the world of work, and the legal powers given by the state to the *paterfamilias*, and the centrality of slavery. But while the Roman family was determined by legal structures, and the house by architectural structures, the Roman home, for all its differences from the modern, was defined by emotional bonds, by the religious ties embodied in the *di penates* and the *lares*, and by the affection not only for persons but also for place, which held past and present together in *domus una*.

At the same time, we should be aware that the ideal of the happy home in which the wife manages the household is precisely that, an ideal. It did not always match reality, as Columella, writing in the mid-first century CE, complains in giving advice on how to run a villa:

> Among the Greeks, and later among the Romans up to the time which our own fathers could remember, almost all work in the house was done by the women, with the heads of households (*patresfamiliarum*) leaving all their cares behind them and returning to their homes as though to recuperate from the strains of public life. For there was then total respect, harmony and diligence, and even the most attractive woman burned with the competitive spirit, wishing to make her husband's affairs increase and prosper by her efforts . . . But now most women have given themselves up to luxury and idleness to such an extent that they do not even bother to concern themselves with wool-working and disdain clothes produced within the household . . .
> —Columella, *On Agriculture* 12, pref., cited by Gardner and Wiedemann 1991, 72–3

Columella is surely optimistic in placing this ideal in the memories of the previous generation. It was never more than an ideal. Just as the reality of Ischomachus' wife seems to have fallen far short of the ideal depicted, so the ideal of the Roman happy home, sustaining itself on its own produce, sat alongside the realities of slave labour and slave management, and women caught up in highly competitive social life beyond the home.

HOME IN EARLY CHRISTIAN THOUGHT

Classical Greco-Roman thought, as we have seen, took the family, *oikos/domus*, to be a building block of citizen society, *polis/civitas*. That connection underpinned and was reinforced by the family legislation of Augustus, which was to remain a basic element of Roman law until Constantine (Treggiari 1991: 60–80; see further chapter 2). The citizen was urged and incentivized to marry and have children: fail to do so and he lost his right to inherit outside his own family; do so and he gained precedence, in election to office, national or local, even in seating at the games. These novel measures were far from popular, and Augustus is said to have read out a speech made by a censor, Metellus Macedonicus, over a century before, in which he urged procreation as a citizen's duty, adding that marriage was a burden one would willingly avoid, but that since one could neither live with a wife without difficulties, nor live without one at all, it was best to do one's duty as a citizen (Aulus Gellius, *Attic Nights* 1.6). Nor for Augustus was the death of a spouse an excuse for avoiding reproduction: a widow was required to remarry within a year or two of losing her husband, and this despite the traditional praise for the wife who never married again, the *univira* (Treggiari 1991: 232–6).

At the same time, the legitimacy of the citizen offspring, born of a *iustum matrimonium*, a recognized marriage between citizen man and citizen woman, was reinforced by legislation making adultery a criminal offence, with exile as a penalty, and penalties for any husband who connived with a wife's infidelity. The documentation of legitimate offspring was also regularized, with the requirement to register the birth of any legitimate child. Curiously, since under common law (*ius gentium*) any child of a citizen mother, even without a citizen father, was a full citizen, these *spurii* while enjoying citizen rights were not registered.

It is evident that the Augustan legislation sought to promote the family, and specifically the legitimate family. But when even the legislator took such a bleak view of the pleasures of marriage, how did it impact on the sense of 'home' with its necessary emotional bonds? An interesting commentary is provided by the works of two Stoic philosophers, writing a century after the Augustan reforms, one, Musonius Rufus, a Roman of high social standing, the other, his pupil Epictetus, a slave by origin. Both are firm supporters of family life. Musonius' fourteenth *Discourse* addresses the question of whether marriage is an obstacle to the philosophical life, a suggestion he unhesitatingly refutes. Every philosopher originates in a home, *oikia*, even surrounded by slaves, *oiketai*: how can he reject the family? Men are inherently sociable, like bees: they cannot exist in isolation. The bond between man and woman, their *koinonia*, sharing in marriage, is the deepest of human bonds, deeper than that between parent and child or brothers and sisters. 'The basis of the protection of the home (*oikos*) is marriage. Thus, whoever destroys human marriage destroys the home, the city, and the whole human race' (Musonius, *Discourse* 14.34–6, cited by Barton 1997: 97).

His pupil Epictetus concurred, mocking the position of the Cynic, who rejects human sociability. The Cynic consequently rejects marriage and the home:

> Look at me, who am without a city (*apolis*), without a home (*anoikos*), without possessions; without a slave; I sleep on the ground; I have no wife, no children; no headquarters, only the earth and sky, and one poor cloak.
> —Epictetus 3.22.45

It is a package deal which the Cynic rejects: home, wife, children, slaves, property, the classic contents of Xenophon's *oikos*, and to reject that is to reject the *polis*, or human society. In both Musonius and Epictetus, we see in rather less ironical terms than those of the Metellus Macedonicus quoted by Augustus a philosophical defence of the family as standing at the heart of society and the state.

How far is this traditional picture of the home changed by Christian beliefs and eventually by the adoption of Christianity as the religion of the Roman empire? There are unmistakable traces in the Gospels of the call to follow Jesus as an abandonment of the family and home (Osiek and Balch 1997: 125–8; Osiek 2011). They represent Jesus as demanding greater love than that for father and mother or son or daughter (Matthew 10.37), to the extent of abandoning a family funeral ('Let the dead bury their dead', Matthew 8.22). When in Mark's Gospel Peter says the disciples have abandoned everything to follow him, the reply of Jesus is to spell out the components of the abandoned home:

> I tell you this: there is no one who had given up home (*oikia*), brothers or sisters, mother, father or children, or land, for my sake and for the Gospel, who will not receive in this age a hundred times as much – houses, brothers and sisters, mothers and children, and land.
> —Mark 10.29–30

The reply spells out full awareness of what normally made a home.

But the call to the disciples to abandon what they held dear merely underlines the perceived value of these things; it is far from the proposal of a social revolution that would destroy the home. This becomes quite clear in the narrative of Paul's spreading of the word to the gentiles in the Acts, and in the pastoral letters written by him or in his name. Paul spreads the word within the structure of the *oikos*: he converts not just individuals but households, like Stephanas of Corinth and his *oikia* (1 Corinthians 16.15) or Lydia of Philippi, the dealer in purple cloth, and her *oikos* (Acts 16.14–15); he greets the congregation in households, like that of Priscilla and Aquila (Romans 16.4, *kat'oikon ekklesian*); and the household is where these first-century converts meet to worship, in what have become known to scholarship as 'house-churches', perhaps too simplistically (Adams 2016). Not only is the *oikos* the location of the *ekklesia*: the *ekklesia*, the assembly of the faithful, is itself a household, the *oikos Theou* (1 Timothy 3.15).

There were indeed elements of Paul's preaching that might be seen as disruptive of the family (Martin 1997). His own abstinence from sexual contact, and his view that marriage was a way for the weak-willed to avoid *porneia*, since sex within marriage was acceptable (1 Corinthians 7.9), opened the way for later generations of Christian thinkers to embrace monastic asceticism, and like Jerome to elevate virginity above marriage. This vision of Paul as the enemy of family is captured in the fifth-century *Life of Thecla*, an elaboration on the already apocryphal Acts of Paul. Having heard him preach from a neighbouring house, Thecla breaks with her fiancé, Thamyris, who raises a hue-and-cry against Paul:

> This man has introduced a new teaching, bizarre and disruptive of the human race. He denigrates marriage: yes, marriage, which you might say is the beginning, root and fountainhead of our nature. From it spring fathers, mothers, children and families. Cities, villages and cultivation have appeared because of it.
> —*vita Theclae* 16, cited by Brown 1988: 5

The home is still seen as the basis for the city and civilization itself. But if those on the more ascetic wing of the movement did indeed challenge it, there were plenty of voices to reassert the role of the *oikos* within their faith.

A clear example is the set of 'household codes' spelled out in a number of pastoral epistles (Ephesians 5.22–6.9; Colossians 3.18–4.1; 1 Peter 2.18–3.7; Osiek and Balch 1997: 118–23). The message of patriarchal obedience is one that any Roman *paterfamilias* would recognize: wives must be subject to their husbands, children obey their parents, and slaves obey their masters with fear and trembling. But the message of authority is tempered by one of mutual respect: husbands must love their wives as they love their own bodies; fathers instruct their children without provoking resentment; and masters avoid threatening their slaves. Seneca might not have disagreed, though no pagan source makes the mutuality of the pact so explicit.

It is not in lack of appreciation of the importance of marriage, family and household that early Christian doctrine diverges from pagan Roman society. Paradoxically, the doctrine that from the point of view of Roman law and society would prove most radical was the firmly expressed ruling of Jesus on divorce: though the law of Moses permitted a man to divorce his wife, in leaving his father and mother for marriage a man became one flesh with his wife: 'What God has joined together, man must not separate' (Mark 10.1–9). This may have been in line with contemporary Judaic thought (Nathan 2000: 40), but it ran entirely against the Roman idea and practice of marriage, and specifically against the Augustan family legislation, which not only permitted remarriage, but required it in the case of widowhood (Treggiari 1991: 498–502). This was no mere detail: it goes to the heart of the conception of marriage. The Roman marriage was a contract entered into between citizens, and subject only to the law of the citizen-state; from Augustus onwards the state prioritized the production of children over personal sentiment.

The Christian concept of marriage as an indissoluble bond under God is predicated on a quite different relationship, not that between citizen and state, but that between believer and divinity. The *ekklesia* as the *oikos* of God took precedence over the relationship of citizen and state. One of the earliest edicts of Constantine, in 320, was the revocation of the *lex Julia* on celibacy and childlessness:

> Those persons who were formally considered celibates by the ancient law shall be freed from the threatening terrors of the law, and they shall live as though numbered among married men and supported by the bonds of matrimony, and all men shall have an equal status in that they shall be able to accept anything to which they are entitled. Nor indeed shall any person be considered childless, and the prejudices attached to that name shall not harm him.
>
> —*Codex Theodosianus* 8.16.1

The idea that Constantine's legislative programme was driven by Christianity is questionable (Evans Grubbs 1995: 103–39), but here at very least the effect of his repeal was that he removed legal obstacles to the Christian enthusiasm for celibacy, and indeed to the opposition to remarriage (Nathan 2000: 60).

We can witness the impact that the new ideal of celibacy had on the Roman aristocracy in the late fourth and early fifth centuries in the repeated exhortations by Jerome to rich Roman matrons to embrace celibacy. He makes explicit that their dedication of their lives to Christ is an abandonment of home. As he imagines Eustochium saying, 'I have left the home (*domus*) of my childhood, I have forgotten my father, I am born again in Christ' (*Letters* 22. 1).

He reminds her of the disadvantages of marriage:

> You should recognize from the outset of reading this that I am not now going to sing the praises of virginity, which you have demonstrated excellently in embracing it, nor am I about to enumerate the disagreeable features of marriage, such as when the belly swells, the baby cries, the husband's mistress causes you agony, the household management (*domus cura*) is stressful, and all the supposed advantages of marriage are cut short by death. And yet wives have their position, in an honourable marriage and an untarnished bed.
>
> —ibid.: 2

The married state to which Jerome offers an alternative in celibate widowhood and the dedication of self (and of course considerable property) to the church would have been perfectly recognizable to Xenophon or Lysias – the role of the wife as homemaker, fretting over household chores, producing children who cry in the night, and agonizing over the husband's affairs while keeping her own bedchamber free of taint of suspicion.

Jerome's ascetic position was extreme. His contemporary Augustine would have recognized his portrait of marriage from his own childhood: his devoted and Christian mother, Monnica, quietly putting up with the infidelity of her pagan husband Patricius, and yet astonishing her female friends by getting on with him so well through her tactic of submissive compromise:

> Many married women who had husbands gentler than him bore on their faces the signs of beatings, and criticised their husbands' ways in their chats with friends ... They were amazed, knowing what a fierce husband (Monnica) put up with, that they had never heard a whisper nor seen a trace of Patricius striking his wife, or indeed that they had been split for a single day over a domestic dispute.
> —*Confessions* 9.9, cited by Nathan 2000: 104

Augustine deeply admired his mother's ability to broker domestic peace, and although he personally backed down from marriage, despite having a son by his long-term mistress, unlike Jerome he was able to write a treatise *On the Goodness of the Marital State* (*de bono coniugali*). In this he grappled with the problem that though it was carnal knowledge between Adam and Eve that brought about the fall, nevertheless, the union of man and woman was the fundamental part of the natural order that enabled obedience to the divine instruction to go forth and multiply.

The obsession of Christian thinkers, growing from its partial roots in Paul to Augustine and beyond, with the sinfulness of carnal desire problematized marriage in a way unfamiliar to previous Greek and Roman thought (Brown 1988). But in practice, despite the renunciations of these ascetic over-achievers, the home as the point of convergence between house, family, property including slaves, and sentiment survived unscathed. It can be argued that the Roman household was transformed, even 'fell', in late antiquity, to the extent that the householder, the *paterfamilias*, had to cede his power to that of the church in the person of the bishop (Cooper 2007). Yet we still find the ideal of the mistress of the wealthy household administering her slave staff in a way Xenophon would have recognized: and we still find reality failing to match the ideal. Salvian of Marseilles, lamenting the loss of much of Gaul to the barbarians in the early fifth century, felt that the rich Romans of Aquitaine had brought disaster on their own heads by marital infidelity, and specifically sleeping with the slave girls, an activity he denounced as reducing the wife to the level of her slaves, and fatally undermining the home (*On the Governance of God* 7. 3).

But for all Salvian's lamentations, the Roman *domus* was resilient, and its utility understood by the church. In seventh-century Spain, now ruled by Visigoths, Bishop (and Saint) Isidore in his *Etymologies* could draw on centuries of Classical learning to define the *domus*:

> Citizens, *cives*, are so called because they live coming together in common, to make common life richer and safer. The *domus* is the dwelling of a single family, just as the city is of a single people, and just as the world is of the human race. *Domus* is however descent group, family, or the conjunction of man and wife.
>
> —*Etymologies* 9.4.1–2

For Isidore, as for Aristotle or Cicero, the *domus* is the fundamental building block of civil society, of the city, even of human civilization: in a fractal relationship, not merely a component of the whole, but its image.

CHAPTER TWO

Family and Household

MICHELE GEORGE

If we are to understand the texture of the home in antiquity, we must have some understanding of its framework and of the most important social institutions that formed it. This chapter will look at the social structure of the ancient household and consider key issues such as family structure, family formation and the nature of the emotional bonds that kept it together.

In both the Greek and Roman worlds, the family was at the core of the social order, and the locus for production and reproduction. Yet despite the crucial importance of the family, in neither society was there a single, unambiguous word for the nuclear group of mother, father and children. In ancient Greece, the term *oikos* is the closest word for 'family', but in fact it embraces both the people who belonged to the nuclear group and members of the close kin group or extended family (*anchisteia*) and also the physical house and all property or goods in its ownership. In the Roman era, the nuclear family was simply referred to with the possessive adjective 'mine', 'yours', i.e. 'my people' (*mei*), while the Latin word *familia*, whence comes the modern word 'family', is used most commonly of household slaves, rather than their masters. This apparent semantic gap underlines the need to examine carefully the shape of the ancient family, in order to understand what it meant to them. The sources for contextualizing family and household differ from one period to the other. For the Greek era, there is political theory from the philosopher Aristotle, home economics from the historian Xenophon and fragments of the dynamics of family life from Greek drama. Among the most useful texts are the extant speeches of the Athenian orators, whose social commentary, although anecdotal and rhetorically driven, lay out the mix of legal boundaries, social customs and attitudes that defined family life. In the Roman period, the existence of extensive juridical sources gives us attitudes and customs codified by law, while other accounts, such as the forensic speeches of Cicero or the letters of Pliny the Younger, expose the reality. The Roman penchant for setting words in stone, the so-called 'epigraphic habit', is particularly illuminating, especially in the many thousands of funerary inscriptions that illustrate cultural ideals and emotional bonds within the household.

THE GREEK HOUSEHOLD

Family Structure

The majority of our sources are Athenocentric, and thus in much of what follows, 'Greek' often means 'Athenian' in particular. However, the pattern that emerges at Athens seems to have pertained in many other city-states (*poleis*) with the exception of Sparta, which will be examined separately. Although Aristotle describes all Greek households as partnerships, they are not equal but hierarchical, following nature's design: 'the primary and smallest parts of the household (*oikia*) are master and slave, husband and wife, father and children' (Aristotle, *Politics* 1253b5, Loeb trans.).

The underlying goal of each household was its own perpetuation and the protection of its property and wealth. The term *oikos* in ancient Greece did not only refer to people, but also included the wherewithal – property, cash and any objects of value – that formed its economic basis. The *oikos* was also, however, the basis of the Greek political system as well as its social core, and for men, membership in an *oikos* was the first essential step towards membership in the *polis* itself. In contrast to the modern era, where membership in the state is based on individual identity, in antiquity family identity, with the *oikos* at its core, was the necessary foundation for civic engagement; without it, a man could not be a full participant in the *polis*. At Athens this is demonstrated on a number of levels: each *oikos* belonged to a phratry or brotherhood, a pseudo-kinship group involved in the oversight of citizenship and inheritance matters, and beyond that, each *oikos* was also enrolled in a *deme*, another important political division. The *oikos* was therefore a constituent part of political organization in the Greek city-state; protection of the *oikos* was thus of paramount concern because it also meant protection of the city-state itself.

Given its central role, it is not surprising that strengthening and maintaining the *oikos* was the motivation behind much Greek family law and practice. The extended family (*anchisteia*) was a tightly knit unit that included cousins in the first degree, whether by blood, marriage or adoption, with a range of obligations, from dramatic events, such as prosecuting the murder of its members, to somewhat more mundane but socially significant responsibilities, such as arranging marriages, contributing to dowries, maintaining ancestral tombs and fulfilling burial rites. Each individual household was led by a male, who was the guardian (*kyrios*) of its interests, a role that was fulfilled by the father and spouse, with legal authority over his wife and children, and that, after his death, was assumed by his male heirs. The father/guardian oversaw the financial health of the household and his permission was needed for the buying and selling of property, issues of inheritance and legitimizing the marriages of the women in his care.

Marriage

Greek marriages were arranged, with the stability and financial success of the family the chief concerns. Overall there was a preference for endogamy, that is, marrying within the same kin group, although unions beyond the family (exogamy) were engineered if they were advantageous; at Athens, for example, wealthy families might choose a betrothed for the property that would be inherited or to form a political alliance. It is possible that a couple might have had little contact with each other before the wedding, but in most cases, and especially with endogamous unions, bride and groom would have had at least a passing acquaintance. At Athens, following a law initiated by the archon Pericles in 451 BCE, a child was deemed legitimate only if both parents had full Athenian citizenship, meaning that even exogamous marriages involved only fellow citizens, and were not permitted with non-Athenians, including metics (residents of Athens without citizenship). Although in Athens boys legally came of age at eighteen, men tended not to marry until around the age of thirty; since girls could possess (if not control) property at the age of fourteen, an age that would often coincide with menarche, it is probable that most girls in ancient Greece married at this young age. This form of 'Mediterranean' marriage, as anthropologists have called it, made normative a wide age gap between husband and wife that doubtless had ramifications for the emotional tenor of their relationship. In Xenophon's *Oeconomicus*, a didactic treatise on household management and agriculture, the wife of the gentleman farmer Ischomachus comes to him as a girl of fourteen, a *tabula rasa* ready for improvement at his hands (see also chapter 1):

> What could she have known when I took her as my wife, Socrates? She was not yet fifteen when she came to me, and had spent her previous years under careful supervision so that she might see and hear and speak as little as possible. Don't you think it was adequate that she came to me knowing only how to take wool and produce a cloak, and had seen how spinning tasks were allocated to the slaves?
> —Xenophon, *Oeconomicus* 7.5–6, trans. Pomeroy

The paternalistic dynamic that naturally arose from this age difference was reinforced by the highly sheltered upbringing of most girls, who were monitored lest their virginity, and thus the legitimacy of any offspring, be called into question. The wedding itself required only a few formalities. The intent to marry was established by a pledge (*enguê*), a marriage contract requiring witnesses by which the bride's father or guardian promised to transfer a women to another man; this was followed by the formal ceremony or 'handing over' (*ekdosis*) of the bride, and then the 'living together' (*sunoikein*), which implied not only cohabitation but also sexual intercourse with the goal of procreation. The orator Demosthenes sums up the Greek definition of marriage thus:

> For this is what living with a woman (*sunoikein*) as one's wife means – to have children by her and to introduce the sons to the members of the clan and of the deme, and to betroth the daughters to husbands as one's own. Mistresses we keep for the sake of pleasure, concubines for the daily care of our persons, but wives to bear us legitimate children and to be faithful guardians of our households.
> —Demosthenes 59.122, Loeb trans.

The wedding procession was a public affair with many witnesses, which formalized the marriage in the community (Figure 2.1). The bride's dowry was a key element in Greek marriage, and its contents were detailed, and thus safeguarded, in the marriage contract. Consisting of cash, valuables such as silver and gold plate, jewellery, furnishings and even land, the dowry belonged to the bride's natal *oikos* and was a kind of pre-mortem inheritance; it had to be returned upon divorce or widowhood so that she might use it to remarry, and it could be inherited by her children in the event of her death. The household was thus a mutable entity, altered by the deaths of its members but always with conservation as its chief concern. Marital disruption over adultery (*moicheia*) represented a special case, for in addition to harming the family honour, sex with a citizen woman created doubts in her own *oikos* about the legitimacy of any offspring, thus weakening the family's claim to citizenship. The need to protect the honour of the *oikos* and sustain it through the procreation of legitimate offspring made adultery a major matter of public, rather than merely private, concern. Divorce was possible, requiring for the husband only that he reject his wife and send her back to her father's house, while she had to apply in person to the archon. Both parties, however, had good reason to avoid divorce. The bride's dowry had to be returned to her birth family, and her husband's family finances would thus sustain a loss; in some cases, he might not have been able easily to repay it. For her part, a wife would be keen to protect her children and their interests, for, if she divorced, the children stayed with her husband's *oikos*, to which they legally belonged.

The Greek Heiress

The Greek custom of partible inheritance, whereby all children received a share of their father's estate, created a problem for the *oikos* when there were no

FIGURE 2.1: Wedding scene, red-figure *lebes gamikos*, 430–420 BCE. Credit: Metropolitan Museum of Art, New York (Open Access). Public Domain.

sons. A daughter could inherit property, but could not control it; by law, it had to fall under the supervision of a male relative. There was special word in Greek for a woman in this position: at Athens, she was called an *epiklêros* (literally 'attached to the estate') while at two other city-states, Gortyn on the island of Crete, and Sparta, respectively, the terms *patroiokos* or *patrouchos* (literally 'holding the father's estate') were used. All three terms are conventionally translated into English as 'heiress' and convey the same idea: that the girl and the estate constitute one indivisible package, and that a potential groom could not have access to the estate without marrying the girl. In theory, a single female with no male guardian was a threat to the stability of the extended *oikos*: if she had no children, the family line might die out, and if she married, her estate would go to her husband, thus decreasing the family wealth. As a way of protecting the family fortunes and future, the heiress's autonomy was strictly limited by Greek law, which stipulated that she had to marry the closest male relative of her deceased father, usually her father's brother or his son (i.e. her cousin). This legal requirement was a public matter, with the choice of groom needing formal approval by a special court procedure (*epidikasia*) and before witnesses, with the close circle of family members fully informed. The legal ramifications of this unusual practice could be severe for other members of the *oikos*. For example, if the most obvious candidate for groom was already married, he could be pressurized by the *anchisteia* to divorce his wife, an option that might even be attractive if the heiress's estate was substantial; if the heiress herself was married at the time of her father's death and had no son who could inherit, she had to divorce her husband and marry her kinsman. Alternatively, if there was no likely candidate, her male relatives could identify another man from outside the family to fill the role, while they would have to furnish her with a dowry from family funds. In such cases, and if her father were still alive, this external groom was often adopted by the heiress's father, so that he became a member of the family and legal heir to the estate.

While many details of the epiklerate system at Athens are murky, evidence indicates that women could not be full legal owners of property: a widow with a young son, for example, would have to give up all ownership to him when he came of age, with the advantage that she would not have to remarry, since she could pass the inheritance to her son and not disperse it beyond the family. The practice appears to have been widespread in ancient Greece, but was not uniform. The situation was somewhat different at the town of Gortyn, where were found the remains of a local law code. Here, despite highly prescriptive instructions about whom she must marry, the heiress was in fact allowed to own property, while at Sparta any woman, not just a single daughter, had legal ownership of the property given to her in her dowry. The regional distinctions in the rights of the heiress in ancient Greece indicate that each *polis* made its own rules; however, the existence of such practices in different places and in diverse societies illustrates how deeply embedded was the impulse to protect the financial interests of the *oikos* even at the expense of the freedoms of its members, male as well as female.

The Greek heiress has traditionally been viewed as a singular creature, but more recent demographic studies suggest that she was probably not uncommon; it is estimated that 20 per cent of Athenian households had no sons, but only daughters. Moreover, given the high mortality rates in the ancient world, it is thought that around 17 per cent of households were probably childless. Adoption was the solution for households with no natural sons who could inherit the family property, and in such cases there was a strong preference that the adoptee, perhaps a nephew, come from the *anchisteia*, thus stabilizing the family fortunes and protecting them from outsiders.

The Family at Home

In the eyes of the law, Greek men were in charge of the house; yet, as Xenophon indicates in the *Oeconomicus*, the house was not where they spent much of their time:

For the woman it is more honourable to remain indoors than to be outside; for the man it is more disgraceful to remain indoors than to attend to business outside.

—Xenophon, *Oeconomicus* 7.29–30; trans. Pomeroy

The division of labour between spouses reflects these innately gendered differences, with property brought into the house 'through the exertions of the husband, but . . . mostly dispensed through the housekeeping of the wife' (*Oeconomicus* 3.15, trans. Pomeroy). The all-male drinking party (symposium), with musicians, dancers and courtesans brought in for the occasion, took place in the houses of the elite, and a special room (the *andrôn*) was reserved for this use. In general, however, the house was under the purview of women: women were responsible for food preparation and wool-working, whether at their own hands or through the supervision of domestic slaves (Figures 2.2 and 2.3). Status distinctions made a difference, since working women were out in the world as they had to be, selling wares in the agora, for example, as Aristotle laments ('for how is it possible to prevent the wives of the poor from going out of doors?', *Politics* 1300a7, Loeb trans.), but the social ideal, set and practised by the elite, was that women stay home as much as possible, serving, in the words of Demosthenes quoted above, as 'faithful guardians of the household'.

FIGURE 2.2: Women working at a loom, *lekythos*, 550–530 BCE. Credit: Metropolitan Museum of Art, New York (Open Access). Public Domain.

FIGURE 2.3: Women folding cloth and spinning wool, *lekythos*, 550–530 BCE. Credit: Metropolitan Museum of Art, New York (Open Access). Public Domain.

But there were circumstances where even elite women would venture forth. In the legal case recounted by Lysias (see chapter 1), the wife of Euphiletos was spied by her future lover Eratosthenes when she was in a funeral procession, and women also participated in public rites at family tombs. Daily visits to public fountains to fetch water (Figure 2.4) afforded an opportunity to meet with other women to exchange family news and local gossip, and to enable important family decisions such as matchmaking. Responsibility for household affairs meant that women were also knowledgeable about family finances, and the sources demonstrate that women were often consulted and might be heavily involved in dotal and testamentary decisions. In the legal case of Polyeuktos, for example, which involved the recovery of funds from a dowry, a woman was sent to represent her husband and consulted her own financial records (Demosthenes 41.9, 17–19, 21), while in another suit a condemned man gives his wife specific instructions about how to dispose of his property after his death (Lysias 13.42). The assumption in both cases is that women not only had knowledge of, but were also expected to have some capability in, managing household finances. The orators also depict a home with normal bonds of affection among its residents. When Apollodorus is forced to be away on military duty for longer than normal

FIGURE 2.4: Women at fountain house, black-figure *hydria*, 510–500 BCE. Credit: Metropolitan Museum of Art, New York (Open Access). Public Domain.

and seeks financial restitution in the courts, he appeals to the jury on an emotional level by citing his love for his family:

> how do you think I must have felt, and how many tears must I have shed, while I reckoned up my present troubles and was longing to see my children and my wife, and my mother whom I had little hope of finding alive? For what is sweeter to a man than these, or why should one wish to live, if deprived of them?
>
> —Demosthenes 50.60–2, Loeb trans.

Even if this is a mere rhetorical flourish, its appearance in a forensic speech demonstrates that such an appeal had some force in the cultural context; every jury member might sympathize with a man missing his family. It is therefore clear that, despite the formalized nature of marriage and clear strictures for male and, above all, female behaviour, the Greek family functioned in to us customary emotional terms. A water jug (Figure 2.5), now in the Harvard museum, depicts a happy family tableau: a seated woman hands over a male infant to a nurse, while her husband stands behind her watching with approval;

FIGURE 2.5: Family scene, red-figure *hydria*, 440–430 BCE. Credit: Harvard Art Museum.

a loom to the left signifies her domestic competence. The vessel was not for household use, however, as revealed by the small hole in the base; rather, it was probably a grave good or used in the Greek funeral ritual of pouring a libation over the grave. Given her prominence, it is probable that the young woman was the deceased, and the key elements of her domestic existence – husband, child and home, as symbolized by the loom – convey her lifetime achievements. The family scene is idealized in nature, as is characteristic of commemorative evidence, but this should not lead to its dismissal. On the contrary, the funerary context, in which the most important cultural ideals are expressed, reveals the importance of family life for the young wife and mother, but also for her husband, who was probably the person who chose the scene as a memorial for his spouse.

The household identity was strengthened by regular devotions to domestic cults that were practised in the home under paternal supervision, with spouses sacrificing together (Xenophon, *Oeconomicus* 7.8). Zeus, most powerful of Greek deities and in effect himself the father of the Olympian gods, was worshipped in several guises in the home: as protector of household property (Zeus Ktêsios) and of the 'enclosure' (Zeus Herkeios, literally 'god of the fence') at altars located in the storeroom and in the courtyard, respectively. Hestia, goddess of the hearth, represented the religious as well as the physical focus of the home, and at the domestic ceremony of the *Amphidromia*, to which family and friends were invited, the week-old newborn was carried around the hearth to introduce the new addition to the household gods and to signify membership into the family. Proper burial and annual sacrifices to dead ancestors were woven into the fabric of household life in rituals such as the *Kathedra*, a family feast that occurred in the house a month after the death of a family member. Perpetuation of the memory of ancestors was in effect perpetuation of the family itself, and was an obligation of their descendants. In an inheritance dispute over the legality of an adoption, maintenance of family memory at the tomb is identified as one of the goals of having children in the first place:

> My opponent wishes now to deprive me of my father's estate, and to render the deceased childless and nameless, so that there may be no one to honour in his place the family cults and perform for him the annual rites, but that he may be robbed of all his due honours. It was to provide against this that he adopted a son, so that he might secure all these advantages.
> —Isaeus 2.46, adapted from Loeb translation

Sparta

The household at Sparta, the Greek city-state famous for its militaristic character, was different from all others in Greece, yet in many ways it was also quite similar. Sources for Sparta are small in number and contain many gaps and contradictions; as with all city-states, there was also variation over time. Xenophon's account is perhaps the most valuable, based as it is on his own experience at Sparta while in exile from Athens, while Plutarch's biography of the legendary Spartan lawgiver Lycurgus, which has shaped much of the popular wisdom about Sparta, was composed in the mid-second century CE and must therefore be viewed with some caution. Moreover, Sparta's reputation in the rest of the Greek world as a unique society defined by its difference from Greek norms might mean that many of the more unusual aspects of Spartan life are exaggerated for rhetorical effect or political purposes. The Sparta described here dates roughly from the sixth to the fourth century BCE, that is, from the so-called constitution of Lycurgus to the decline of Sparta as a military force following the Spartan loss to the Thebans at the battle of Leuctra in 371 BCE, after which it never regained its former military primacy.

A summary of Spartan society is essential for understanding the Spartan household. Sparta was made up of a relatively small number of citizens (Spartiates, or *homoioi*, 'the peers') who were thought of as social equals and who lived in several small villages; beyond this core lay a significant territory which was farmed by two classes of people: *perioikoi* ('dwellers around'), who were free, and helots, unfree people whom Sparta had conquered and subjected, and who also performed domestic tasks in Spartan households. The land itself was owned by citizens, who, according to the traditional Lycurgan system, received a portion (*klêros*) at birth, which produced food for their sustenance; since *perioikoi* and helots did all the agricultural work, citizens could devote themselves to the demands of the military state. Originally, upon his death a citizen's *klêros* returned to the state, although at some point in time citizens were allowed to keep their property and to will it to their descendants, thus bringing Sparta closer to practices in the wider Greek world. Spartan women inherited half the amount of their brothers, which was considerably more than the one-sixth share usually received by Athenian women. If she was an heiress (at Sparta, as we have seen, called a *patrouchos*), a Spartan woman could inherit all of her father's property; more importantly, and in contrast to Athens, it does not seem that she was required to marry within her *oikos*, although there might have been pressure to do so in order to perpetuate her father's line. Most significantly, however, Spartan women not only owned the land they inherited (rather than merely keeping it to pass on to sons), they also controlled it, a significant distinction from what was permitted to other Greek women; Aristotle (*Politics* 1270a3–4) complains that women at Sparta owned two-fifths of the land, a situation that he deemed an excessive liberty for the female sex. It seems that the early ideal of Spartan equality gave way to a more stratified economic order, with some families, and some women, owning more property than others, and thus accruing more social status.

It is unclear, however, whether land ownership in itself brought much of a practical advantage to Spartan women, who still lived within the very particular confines of their cultural context, for the military nature of Spartan society had significant consequences for the household. The family was the vehicle for the production of the next generation of soldiers, and all aspects of household life were structured around this goal. A council of state elders (the *gerousia*) decided the viability of each male infant; if he was not exposed, the child's father was required to raise him at home until the age of seven, at which point all boys were removed to military barracks for their education and training, remaining there until the age of thirty. Spartan boys underwent a rigorous programme (the *agôgê*), designed to make them the best warriors, that included physical fitness, endurance and hunting, as well as dancing and singing. At age twelve, this training incorporated a kind of formalized pederasty, as each boy entered into an erotic relationship with a young man (aged twenty to thirty), who served as a mentor as well as lover, shaping him into a suitable member of the Spartan army (Xenophon, *Constitution of the Lacedaimonians* 2.13; Plutarch, *Lycurgus* 16–21). Among the most important Spartan social institutions was the *syssition*, the dining club, which every male citizen aged twenty had to join and to attend each night. These dining clubs, for which each member had to contribute an allotment of food, were important male bonding units, and fulfilled a pseudo-familial function, with elders instilling appropriate behaviour in junior warriors.

This structured mode of living fashioned a Spartan man into a soldier, but by grounding his identity and every aspect of his daily life in the communal military context, the process must have also alienated him to some extent from the family of his birth, and defined his idea of home life as one lived separately from women. This fundamental separation of the sexes at Sparta is also evident in its marriage patterns. Compared to the rest of ancient Greece, marriage at Sparta occurred at different points in the life course, with both men and women marrying at around the age of twenty; according to traditional Spartan thinking, coeval spouses were believed to produce healthier children. Spartan marriage, like all Greek marriage, was geared toward reproduction, for according to Lycurgus, Spartan children 'did not belong to their fathers, but were the common property of the state' (Plutarch, *Lycurgus* 15.8, Loeb trans). The Spartan wedding ceremony was odd, to say the least: the bride, 'captured' from her home and taken to the house of her groom's family, was shorn and dressed in men's clothes, and made to lie in a dark room until her groom arrived in stealth to consummate the marriage (Plutarch, *Lycurgus* 15.5–7). While the historicity of this custom is unreliable, it is suggestive of several Spartan realities: young men had little contact with women, and were accustomed to life in male barracks, with homosexual involvements part of normal practice. The ritual transvestism of the bride, even if more a fiction than a reality, can be interpreted as a *rite de passage*, and a recognition of the stark differences of marriage for a young man separated from his own household for most of his life, and with little experience of women. Furthermore, sources indicate that husband and wife lived apart for the first decade of their union, since men had to remain in their barracks and were allowed only discreet nocturnal visits to their homes for the purposes of procreation. The hidden aspect of the Spartan wedding and the consequent separation between spouses can also be read as a form of trial marriage, lacking the witnesses of the more public and noisy Athenian wedding procession which helped to confirm its legitimacy. At Sparta, abetted by the partners initially living apart, infertile marriages could be easily dissolved and other unions arranged in the hope of producing children, and, as long as both partners agreed, arrangements of wife-sharing were countenanced for barren marriages. Unlike most Greek women, Spartan women received a food portion equal, if not superior, to that of men (Xenophon, *Constitution of the Lacedaimonians* 1.4) and they also received a formal, public education that included traditional Greek subjects such as music, singing and choral dance, but also a physical curriculum that included running, wrestling, strength trials, throwing the discus and javelin and even horseback riding, all aimed at improving the quality of their offspring.

Spartan women were not encouraged to stay indoors, nor were they shielded from the gaze of men outside their own family, as was the case for most Greek women. The Spartan household was famed for its simplicity. Since men ate most of their meals away from the home, there was no domestic entertaining and thus no need for displays of wealth in the form of silverware. The labour of helots and *perioikoi* provided food and fulfilled the normal tasks of a Greek household such as weaving and cloth production so that Spartan citizen women could focus on child-rearing. Thus, as in other Greek states, the home was populated mostly by women, with all male children over seven living in barracks and Spartan men, like other Greek men, expected to pass the day outside the house and dinnertime at their *syssition*, in the company of other men. Moreover, the frequency of Spartan military campaigns must have led to households with relatively little male presence for long periods of time. The distinctiveness of Spartan practices, however contrived and arcane they seem, did not therefore lead to households that were so very different from those in the rest of ancient Greece.

THE ROMAN FAMILY AND HOUSEHOLD

In the Roman era, much as in the Greek, the family was the institution that formed the framework for the social order. The word in Latin for the physical house (*domus*) was also used to refer to the people who lived in the house, which included parents and children as well as other dependants of lower social status, such as the slaves (*servi*) who performed the household chores and potentially freed slaves (*liberti*) who owed a set of obligations to their former owners. In Latin, the word *familia*, from which we derive the word for 'family' in English, is applied to all people and property belonging to an estate in the legal sources, but beyond the narrow juridical context, *familia* is most frequently used of household slaves, who dwelt in close proximity to their masters and who performed a plethora of household tasks. The presence of a large body of slaves, which was certainly the case among the Roman elite, marks one of the key distinctions between the Greek and Roman households. While domestic slaves are referred to in Greek sources, they were fewer in number than in the Roman, and are not portrayed as supplying the same kind of specialized labour. While a Greek man might host a symposium in his home, the Greek house did not play as prominent a role in social relations as it did in the Roman era. The Roman house had a more public dimension to it, especially among the elite; Roman domestic space was therefore more clearly articulated to meet its more complex social functions. Key social rituals took place in the house, including the morning call (*salutatio*), when clients paid their respects to their patrons, and the dinner party (*convivium*), an important occasion for social interaction as well as the display of personal wealth. More than the Greek, the daily rhythms of the elite Roman household were shaped by these external cultural factors, with the rich planning their day around an influx of guests; the households of the poor, who had less reason and less time to participate in such customs, instead devoted their time to economic survival.

The paterfamilias

The hierarchical structure of Roman society at large was writ small in the household. The head of the Roman household was the father, or *paterfamilias* (literally, 'father of the family'), a stern cultural archetype with complete legal power over his wife (*materfamilias*) and children. The authority of the *paterfamilias*, which was codified in Roman law under the legal right of *patria potestas*, or 'paternal power', was considered extraordinary by ancient Greeks, and even Romans themselves:

> The Roman lawgivers also ordain that the children are subjects and slaves of their fathers, and that power over the children's property belongs to the fathers and not the children, until the children have obtained their freedom.
> —Sextus Empiricus 3.211, cited in Saller 1994: 102–3

> Also in our *potestas* are any of our children who are the offspring of a lawful marriage. This right is peculiar to Roman citizens, for there are virtually no other peoples who have such power over their children as we have.
> —Gaius, *Institutes* 1.48, trans. Gardner and Wiedemann 1991: 5

Paternal power extended to the right to kill a wife or child (*vitae necisque potestas*) if the *paterfamilias* judged it appropriate. However, as Richard Saller has shown, the vast legal scope of *patria potestas* was undermined both practically and in terms of commonly held attitudes to appropriate familial behaviour. Rather than being dominated by the notional control of the *paterfamilias*, the dynamics of family life were shaped by a number of equally important cultural forces. First, although the law endowed the *paterfamilias* with exceptional power over his wife and even his adult children, lower life expectancy meant that the death of many a *paterfamilias* cut short the exercise of this extraordinary power, since at his demise his children became legally independent (*sui iuris*) and were no longer under the threat of his *patria potestas*. Secondly, the description of family life that emerges from the sources reveals that key decisions were made not unilaterally by the head of the household, but more collectively and in consultation with his wife and other significant family members such as uncles, aunts and adult siblings. This group of elders formed the family council (*consilium*), part of the extended family who also had a vested interest in protecting shared wealth, property and reputation, and who could restrain any abuses of *patria potestas*. Most importantly, however, the normal bonds of affection within the family were reinforced by *pietas* ('dutiful affection'), a fundamental concept that underlay Roman family life as well as Roman society more broadly. In conforming to *pietas*, proper filial regard for parental authority was answered with genuine loving care. The fearsome stereotype of the Roman father was thus counterbalanced by the competing ideology of family unity. With *pietas* as the dominant family value, it was incumbent upon all members – the *paterfamilias* included – to behave in a mutually loving and respectful manner, in order to protect the family interests and reinforce family identity.

Founding a Household: Roman Marriage

If the family was the core of Roman society, marriage (*conubium*) was the core of the Roman family, the vehicle by which the family itself was reproduced and family property was maintained and enlarged. In effect, every marriage was also the creation of a new household, with the husband as *paterfamilias* and his bride as *materfamilias*. The arrangement of marriages fell to the head of the household, who took advice from his wife and members of the family council. Seeking out an appropriate betrothed for sons, daughter, nieces and nephews seems to have fallen above all to female family members, who as a result probably played a particularly influential role in marital matchmaking. In contrast to the Greek model, the Romans had a preference for exogamy over endogamy, and while marriage between first cousins was not illegal and did occur, it does not appear to have been the norm. Marrying outside the kin group expanded the opportunity for family wealth but also for social connections, an important consideration in status-conscious Roman society (Shaw and Saller 1984). Marriage was a family affair, needing only paternal permission and intent by the two partners for it to be legal, with no oversight by the Roman state. Girls generally married between the ages of twelve and seventeen, with a tendency towards the later age, while men did not marry until they were at least twenty-five (Shaw 1987; Saller 1987). Much as in Greek marriages, it was therefore often the case that husbands and wives were from different generations, with perhaps a decade or more difference in their ages. There were restrictions on marriage on the basis of status: non-citizens could not marry Roman citizens, and senators and their daughters could not marry former slaves. Although no ceremony was required by law, by tradition there were rituals of betrothal and marriage that formalized the union in the eyes of the community and helped forge bonds between the two families (Hersch 2010). The bride's dowry (*dos*), which comprised to some extent the anticipated portion of her inheritance from her father, was agreed upon ahead of time by legal contract (*pacta dotalia*) and functioned as a sort of savings account for her. Her husband was responsible for protecting and maintaining the value of the dowry and she could sue him for negligence if he embezzled from it or made risky investments. Although legally the dowry belonged to the husband, his rights were conditioned by the popular perception that it still belonged to the wife, and she reclaimed it from his estate when he died or after a divorce.

There were two major forms of marriage, each with significant ramifications for the bride. In the republican era, a woman left her father's paternal power and, in legal terms, entered into the authority (*manus*) of her husband; this is referred to as *cum manu* (with *manus*) marriage. The bride was no longer a member of her natal family, but became a member of her husband's agnatic family and under his legal power. Her share of the family wealth went with her as her dowry (*dos*). When her husband died, she gained her legal independence (*sui iuris*) and could control her own property and wealth. By the first century BCE, however, this form of marriage was replaced by *sine manu* (without *manus*) marriage, in which the bride stayed within the legal control of her father's *patria potestas*, rather than falling under her husband's. Legally, she thus remained a member of her natal family and did not belong to her husband's. More importantly, however, she stayed under her father's legal authority, rather than her husband's; since fathers tended to die before husbands, she was thus likely to achieve her legal independence sooner than had she married *cum manu*. In a *sine manu* marriage, the bride's share of her inheritance was not transferred into the ownership of her husband, but was maintained as part of her birth family's holdings. As a result of this shift in marital practice Roman women could exercise control over their property and had the freedom to write wills, and although this was most relevant to women of means, it also applied to women of lower status, who might, for example, have had an interest in a small business.

The Romans also had institutionalized guardianship (*tutela*) for children whose fathers died while they were young. These male guardians, who were often a close relative such as an uncle or adult brother, were responsible for protecting the child's inheritance until they came of age. For girls, however, guardianship lasted a lifetime, or until they married *in manu* and passed into the legal control of their husband. Women could petition to change their guardian, or could gain their legal independence by having three children (four for former slaves), or, for the elite, by applying pressure to influential friends. The system of guardianship for women demonstrates the Roman impulse to protect family wealth, and springs from the idea of female incapacity in matters of finance. By the late second century CE, however, even Roman jurists such as Gaius recognized the anachronism of such attitudes:

> There appears to be hardly any worthwhile argument for women of full age being in *tutela*. The common belief, that because of their instability of judgment they are often deceived and that it is only fair to have them controlled by the authority of tutors, seems more specious than true. For

women of full age manage their affairs themselves, and in certain cases the
tutor imposes his authority as a matter of form and often is obliged by the
praetor to give his authorization even against his will.
—Gardner 1986: 21

Despite the law of male guardianship and in contrast to her Greek counterpart, an adult Roman woman, freed from paternal control by her father's death, had relative freedom over her property. Both *sine manu* marriage and guardianship helped to contain the dispersal of family property, demonstrating the supremacy of family interests above all others. The enhancement of female agency that arose from *sine manu* marriages and women's ability to subvert their guardian's control was an unintended consequence, and the system of guardianship over women was never abandoned, despite the open admission of female competence from legal experts such as Gaius. The jurist's comment makes it clear, however, that, regardless of the law, most adult women had free reign, with Roman officials such as the praetor even overriding a guardian's concerns.

Since Roman marriages were arranged, they were companionate, rather than love matches, but the unromantic genesis did not mean a lack of emotional attachment; the expectation was that genuine mutual affection and respect would grow, lead to the procreation of children and foster a satisfying home life (Figure 2.6). Funerary epitaphs commemorating deceased spouses reveal the chief conjugal values of Roman marriage – harmony, fidelity and kindness – that appear with particular prominence on the memorials of married woman (*matronae*). The modest epitaph for a woman named Amymone, set up by her husband Marcus, encapsulates the idealized behaviour of the Roman *matrona* in a series of adjectives:

Here lies Marcus' (wife) Amymone, the best and most beautiful,
Busy at her wool-working, devoted, modest, thrifty, chaste, happy to stay at home.
—*CIL* VI 11602 = *ILS* 8402; trans. Gardner and Wiedemann 1991: 52

The descriptors *lanifica* ('wool-worker') and *domiseda* ('homebody') declare with pithy economy an idealized vision of the *materfamilias*, content to stay at home (rather than venture outside with any frequency), and busy herself with the proverbially female household tasks of weaving and spinning for her family. While the poor probably did engage in such tasks out of economic necessity, the elite relied on the household slave workforce; yet the cultural ideal of the married woman who made her family's clothing with her own hands was so deeply embedded in the Roman mentality that Augustus himself supposedly wore only clothes made by his womenfolk (his sister, his wife Livia or their daughter or granddaughter; Suetonius, *Augustus* 73) and insisted that his

FIGURE 2.6: Roman funerary altar with wedding scene, 40–50 CE. Museo delle Terme, Rome. Credit: DEA/G.Nimatallah / Getty Images.

daughter and granddaughters be taught how to spin and weave (ibid.: 64). However improbable the story, it does reflect the model of retiring domesticity that framed women in the household.

Supporting Family Values: The Augustan Social Legislation

The emperor Augustus brought in legislation that supported the family in several ways, some positive, some punitive in nature (see above ch.1). The laws tried to control marriage between groups of different social status while encouraging marriage in general and the procreation of legitimate children, especially among the elite. The scope of the legislation was significant and intrusive, with a plethora of injunctions. The *Lex Iulia de maritandis ordinibus* (18 BCE), with amendments made by the *Lex Papia Poppaea* (9 CE), forbade intermarriage between members of the senatorial order (not only senators themselves but members of their families) and freedmen or actors, and while daughters of freedmen could marry senators, the sons of freedmen could not marry senatorial daughters. Instructions in wills that made marriage difficult in order to inherit were declared illegal, and men who married were exempted from the usual age requirement of thirty if they wanted to run for the office of quaestor. Penalties on inheriting were imposed on the unmarried by the age of twenty-five for men and twenty for women; widows were given one year (later changed to two years) to mourn before being required to remarry, while a divorce required remarriage after only six months (later changed to eighteen months). Limitations on inheritance were placed on those without children, while women who bore three children (four for freedwomen) were rewarded with legal independence from their father.

The emperor's reach even extended to the sex lives of married couples with another law (*Lex Iulia de adulteriis coercendis* of 18 BCE) that criminalized adultery, dividing it into two kinds of offence based on the marital status of the woman; the man's marital status did not matter. An affair with a married woman was true adultery (called *adulterium*) and was the more serious crime, while sex with an unmarried woman (*stuprum*) was a lesser transgression; there was no penalty for sex with a prostitute. The law was heavily prescriptive, forcing husbands both to divorce and then to prosecute their wives if they were discovered in an adulterous act or risk being charged themselves with procuring. A woman found guilty of adultery lost a portion of any property, plus half of her dowry, and was exiled from Rome; similar penalties applied to men convicted of the crime. Moreover, a husband could kill his wife's lover in certain circumstances: if the lover was of sufficiently low status and if the two were found in bed and in his own house. In the same vein, a father too could kill both an adulterous daughter and her lover if he discovered them in the act in either his house or her husband's house. The severity of the punishment permitted to husband and father reflects a highly traditional and arguably old-fashioned view of the house as an almost sacred space whose violation by illicit acts deserved the most extreme response. It also reinforced the traditional notion that it was male authority figures – father and husband – who were responsible for safeguarding the honour of the family and household against women who brought it harm by their immoral conduct. Subsequent emendations to the laws indicate that they were not repealed; yet it is unclear that they made any significant demographic impact (Tacitus, *Annals* 3.25). Augustus did, however, succeed in putting restrictions on women's sexual behaviour by making public matters that had previously been managed privately within the household. Indeed, under Augustus' successor Tiberius, some elite women tried to open a loophole in the law by registering as prostitutes, thus putting themselves beyond the law's reach (Suetonius, *Tiberius* 35), an act of protest that was stopped by a new law forbidding women of senatorial families from enrolling as prostitutes (Tacitus, *Annals* 2.85).

Divorce

Although the marital ideal at Rome was a stable and lasting union, the practice of arranged marriages and the generational difference between spouses meant that sentiment played a reduced role when marital problems emerged, rendering divorce a relatively uncomplicated matter. Divorce, like marriage, was a private rather than a civil matter, and was obtained without great difficulty, as long as there was agreement among the families concerned. Either spouse could initiate proceedings by lodging a notification of intent, without laying blame, although the Augustan legislation on adultery brought a new dimension of moral culpability when the law was applied. Potential causes included infertility (which was generally blamed on the woman), infidelity or, for the political elite, the desire to establish a new alliance through marriage. Wives recovered their dowries, but any offspring remained with their father, and under his legal control. But while there was no public censure in most divorce cases, there was social pressure for both parties to remarry and regroup in a new household, ideally one that produced legitimate children. The regularity (if not frequency) of divorce combined with the higher mortality rates of the Roman era meant that families might form and reform again, as spouses, whether divorced or widowed, created new households and children found themselves with a stepparent and siblings a generation older or younger than they were.

A Special Case: Egypt

For most of the Roman Empire, historical texts and funerary commemoration provide the basis for understanding household composition. Roman Egypt, however, is exceptional in the kinds of evidence available. While there are few conventional historical accounts for the region, there is instead a unique set of sources preserved on papyri that are specific to Egypt and especially relevant to family matters, including letters, wills and contracts. Most important among these papyri are census returns that record the makeup of Egyptian households and reveal aspects of family life. Two features that seem unique to Roman Egypt emerge from this evidence. One is the phenomenon of brother–sister marriage, a controversial subject that is still debated by scholars. Greek sources of the Classical period refer to brother–sister marriage as a peculiarity of pharaonic Egypt, and the practice was adopted by the Ptolemaic dynasty that assumed power after the death of Alexander the Great. Yet the widespread cultural taboo against incest and the genetic problems of inbreeding have kept this assertion under discussion. It has been suggested that names in the census reports that appear to reflect brother–sister marriage are in fact cases of the adoption of sons-in-law by fathers with no sons of their own, a strategy by which men could be incorporated into the family of their wives to enhance family bonds and to protect family property. These adopted sons, having changed their names and been received as 'sons' in the census, are recorded in the census as brothers to their wives, daughters of the family to which they now belonged. While the argument over brother–sister marriage persists, a second feature of family life particular to Roman Egypt and diverging from practices in the rest of the Roman Empire is household composition. More than in other parts of the Empire, households in Egypt most often had multiple families, often intergenerational, with a couple and their adult married sons, spouses and children occupying the same home; another variation on this same theme saw married brothers and their families cohabiting in one household (Huebner 2007: 203). Egypt seems to have been the outlier in maintaining deeply ingrained, pre-Roman social customs, a situation attributable to its role as an important grain-producing region, as imperial authorities, keen to preserve its stability, kept control of immigration and emigration to the province.

Children in the Roman Household

The procreation of children allowed the continuation of the name and bloodline, the support of parents in old age, the performance of burial rituals and the maintenance of wealth within the family. Children were thus the focus of expectations and the embodiment of hope for the future and greater prosperity. High rates of child mortality doubtless created a different emotional landscape, as parents could not be free from the anxiety over unexpected death. It is estimated that over 50 per cent of children did not survive until the age of ten (Saller 1994: 25), a startling figure that has prompted social historians to question the degree of emotional investment placed by parents in children (Golden 1988). The law limited mourning for children who died over the age of six at one year, under the age of six at one month (Paulus, *Responsa* 1.21.2–5), and there was no mourning period at all for child who died before the age of one year (Plutarch, *Life of Numa* 12). The Stoic philosopher Seneca, with characteristic severity, berates the mourning of a friend whose small son has died (Seneca, *Epistles* 99.2), and Cicero evinces a somewhat callous response to the premature labour of his daughter Tullia (*ad Atticum* 10.18), referring to the infant as 'it', rather than 'he'. Yet Cicero was inconsolable at the death of Tullia herself at the age of thirty-three. The grim demographic reality in the ancient world and the clear possibility that a child who survived being born might succumb to a multiplicity of illnesses, from a minor infection to a quickly spreading epidemic, puts into perspective the emphasis on the procreation of children, including the Augustan social legislation, that emerges from the sources. Monuments to deceased children offer snapshots of family life (Figure 2.7).

Adoption and fosterage were acceptable alternatives for the childless who wanted to form a family of their own. As an inheritance strategy, the adoption of children from the same bloodline was preferred by the elite, and in the absence of an available relative, those lower on the social ladder might turn to foundlings (*alumni*), children abandoned by parents out of impoverishment or illegitimacy. An infant abandoned at birth and with no legally acknowledged parentage automatically became a slave; if the child survived long enough, he might be found and raised by a childless couple who could subsequently free him and then adopt him. Less fortunate foundlings might simply have been kept as slaves, to be added to the household workforce.

FIGURE 2.7: Sarcophagus for a child, 120–130 CE. Credit: Soprintendenza per i Beni Culturali e Ambientali, Agrigento.

Slaves in the Household

The normative nature of slavery at ancient Rome meant that anyone who could afford to own slaves did so. In Roman culture, the mere possession of slaves in great quantity was in itself a mark of status, and their deployment in the house, often in colourful livery and on display to guests at formal occasions such as banquets, was a visible sign of wealth and social power. Slave labour in the Roman era was not merely economically productive, but had a currency of its own in the social sphere that was most effectively demonstrated in the domestic context. With no legal status and few protections under the law from an owner's cruelty, slaves in the household performed all manner of tasks, ranging from menial jobs such as cleaning to positions of considerable responsibility that might include overseeing domestic accounts and childcare.

Masters and slaves often lived together in close quarters, slaves sleeping in work areas such as kitchens and stables or outside their master's bedroom door. This mix of physical proximity and unambiguous status distinction was the norm in households small and large, and contributed to the dynamics between slave and slave-owner, among members of the master and his family, and among the slaves themselves. Slaves often formed their own quasi-marital relationships (*contubernia*), which could, however, be broken up if the slave-owner decided to sell one of the partners, since slaves had no rights under Roman law. Good slave management favoured these informal unions, however, for the stability they brought to the household and the loyalty they engendered in slaves. The offspring of such relationships were slaves, since the legal status of the child was taken from that of the mother, and a male slave who was fortunate enough to be freed might buy his slave partner and child and then free them, thus forming his own legitimate family and household. House-born slaves (*vernae*) are often referred to in the sources as favoured slaves, partly because their origins were

FIGURE 2.8: Funerary relief of the Vettii, 20 BCE. Museo delle Terme, Rome. Credit: German Archaeological Institute.

not in doubt: an owner could raise such children along proper Roman lines, and even fetch a higher price at the slave market should he decide to sell them. Some house-born slaves were doubtless fathered by the slave-owner himself, given that the sexual use of slaves by their masters was common. Slave families who did remain intact and were lucky enough to be manumitted by their masters took particular pride in the achievement, as shown by the numerous funerary markers with family groups (Figure 2.8). Identifying themselves as Roman citizens with legitimate families of their own, these successful freedmen and women demonstrate the high valuation put on the family and reflect the social power attached to the family in the Roman mentality.

CONCLUSION

Family and household in the ancient world were not one and the same, and there were differences between the Greeks and Romans. Yet in both societies, family was positioned at the centre of social structure and values, and was bolstered by law and deeply embedded custom. Family composition was remarkably stable, given the long timeframe involved, and although the makeup of individual households changed with births, deaths, marriage and divorce, the household as a cultural entity remained the focus of the most important human interactions.

CHAPTER THREE

The House

LISA NEVETT

This chapter explores the character of ancient Greek housing between *c.* 800 BCE and 600 CE – that is, over the period of approximately 1400 years, from the Early Iron Age and Archaic periods which saw the growth of villages into flourishing urban communities, through the time when those communities had been an integral part of the Roman Empire for several centuries, to late antiquity. While the start of this process predates the earliest known alphabetic texts from the Greek world, and cannot therefore be researched extensively through written sources, literary works do survive from the later eighth century BCE onwards, their numbers increasing through time. These are useful in general terms as sources of information about the nature of Greek society, although it is only in a small minority of them that houses and households can be perceived, and then only dimly as backdrops against which the action takes place. Therefore, while various genres of text (many of them from Athens and dating to the fifth and fourth centuries BCE) provide a context for some of the discussion here, we must rely primarily on the physical remains of the houses that have been discovered and excavated since the mid-nineteenth century. A further aid to interpreting them is the iconographic evidence from painted pottery, mostly from the sixth, fifth and earlier fourth centuries BCE, and again, much of it from Athens and Attica. Although these images cannot be understood as literal representations of social life, they must have made some kind of sense to ancient viewers and they may therefore suggest a possible range of activities and associations between artefacts, activities, members of the household and (occasionally) architectural settings.

As this chapter shows, the archaeological remains offer a rich database which reveals a variety of aspects of the social and economic lives of the households once occupying the houses. They also provide insights into the wider communities and societies of which those occupants were a part. An individual house represents – through its size, architectural features, layout and furnishings – something of the values of the community to which its owners belonged, and by whose norms their lives must have been influenced. Furthermore, changes made to the appearance or the organization of a house may indicate shifting social and cultural norms, as well as adaptations made to accommodate smaller scale changes – in the size, composition or preferences of the occupying household.

As a source of information, archaeology has the advantage that it includes a large and diverse body of evidence which covers a long period of time, a wide group of geographical locations and a diverse social spectrum. At the same time, like any other kind of evidence, the physical remains of houses require careful interpretative work if they are to be used to address the sorts of questions raised above. A first consideration is the level of preservation, which is in part determined by the construction materials. In some locations, such as the mountains of Epiros or the island of Delos, the walls of a house were constructed of stone blocks. Such examples are rare, however: more typically a stone wall-base or socle supported a superstructure of sun-dried mudbrick. The roof above normally made use of a timber framework which supported either thatch (during the earlier period) or (by Classical times) terracotta tiles. Through most of the period under consideration here the majority of floors were made of clay or beaten earth, with (again, by Classical times) some use of cobbles, paving, mosaic or mortar. By the Roman and late Roman periods such durable materials came to be used more commonly. The surviving remains of most houses when they are excavated consist of a floor together with stone wall socles which are overlain by any preserved roofing materials, mixed with dissolved mudbrick. The layout of the house can therefore often be reconstructed, but it is frequently difficult or impossible to say much about the superstructure.

Relatively few fixtures survive from domestic interiors to give an indication of how different spaces were used, although the numbers of such features (like the size of the houses themselves and the numbers of different spaces they contained) tended to increase through time. During the earliest period discussed here, the Early Iron Age, features are limited to pits which may have been used for storage or for refuse disposal, bases or holes for vertical wooden posts that supported the roof, platforms or benches for sitting or for placing objects, and hearths for fires used for heating, lighting and cooking. By the late Classical period, however, these are sometimes supplemented by additional elements such as wells or cisterns, drainage pipes, terracotta bathtubs or stone slabs which formed bases for flights of stairs. Although these features provide useful information, understanding what the original occupants did in any one room – or even within the house as a whole – is still a challenge, and such an understanding is only a first step towards addressing more complex questions, such as the roles played by different categories of individuals (for example, men, women, children or slaves) within the household. One strategy pursued increasingly since the 1990s has been to look at the range of artefacts remaining in the different rooms as a guide to understanding what activities may have taken place in them and, by extension, who might have used the space. But while artefacts offer a good starting point, they clearly have their limitations. One problem lies with the nature of ancient society and domestic life, in which (compared with the contemporary West) people had relatively few possessions: items may have been used and reused many times, as indicated by (for example) the mending of pottery, and the apparent continued use of damaged ceramic vessels, or even parts of broken vessels. The purpose an individual object served may therefore have changed through time. Interpretation of its significance is also complicated by the fact that it may typically have had multiple uses, or uses that cannot today be discerned with ease or precision. Other complications are that many domestic tasks will have involved items made of organic materials which have not survived; some artefacts may have been moved and/or removed at the time a house was abandoned, and others (especially items of waste) may have been left in the abandoned structure as a means of disposing of them. Finally, earlier excavators focused mainly on the architecture of the houses they uncovered, recording few or none of the artefacts they found. All of these considerations mean that, while artefacts potentially offer some information about domestic activity, they are not always as helpful as one might hope.

Geographically, the focus of the discussion in this chapter is on housing in and around the city of Athens. Continuous habitation here over the entire period discussed, together with intensive archaeological investigation, provides a substantial database of physical remains on which to draw, and the written and iconographic sources offer important contextual information which originated in the same time and space. While the remains of the Athenian houses themselves are not always well preserved or published in great detail, they can be understood more fully when viewed as part of a long series and when compared with those from other ancient communities which are sometimes better preserved or have been documented in greater detail.

PRELUDE: EARLY COMMUNITIES: THE ATHENIAN AGORA

The hill that later became the Athenian Akropolis is known to have been a stronghold during the Late Bronze Age (Figure 3.1). The area to its northwest – which later became the Agora, a public square – has also yielded evidence of activity during the Bronze Age, including elite tombs. From the Early Iron Age, scattered traces of small clusters of housing have been found there. Most of the

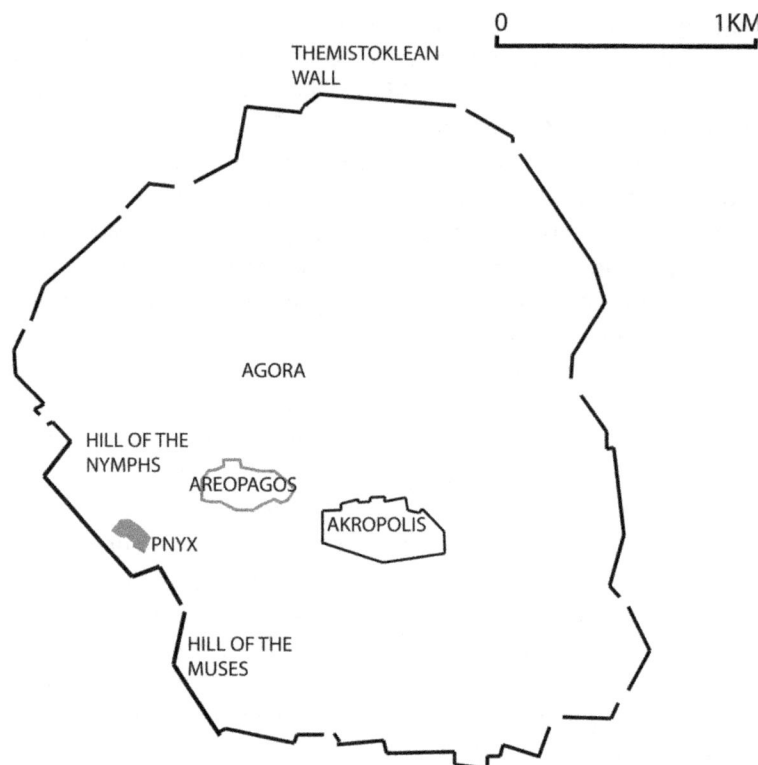

FIGURE 3.1: Sketch plan showing the topography of ancient Athens in relation to the Classical city wall Credit: Lisa Nevett.

buildings themselves were destroyed by later construction activity, leaving only the wells associated with them, fallen into disuse and used as dumps for pottery. But the original character of the structures here in this period is suggested by the fragmentary remains of an oval structure measuring about 11 x 5m that was located on the north slope of the Areopagus (Burr 1933). It had a low stone socle and a floor laid using beach sand. It appears to have been oriented approximately east–west. The excavator, Dorothy Burr Thompson, noted that the interior was filled with carbonized organic material, and this may have been the remains of a thatched roof. A burned area of floor towards the centre of the building may have been a hearth, and two stone constructions may have been partitions that split the interior into separate sections or rooms. At the eastern end lay a granite quern for processing grain, and two more were found just outside. Thompson says that this building was probably one of several that were packed closely together next to an outcrop of rock, the others represented at the time of the excavation only by concentrations of domestic pottery lying where they once stood. The nature and distribution of the associated artefacts suggest that the activities carried out in and around these dwellings included the preparation and consumption of food and drink, but their fragmentary and disturbed character means that it difficult to say more about how the inhabitants lived their lives. Similar communities have been found elsewhere on the Greek mainland, for example at Nichoria in the southern Peloponnese, where one structure, known as Unit IV.1, was relatively well preserved (Mazarakis Ainian 1992, with earlier references). It was slightly larger than our Athenian building and the interior was partitioned into a porch, a main room with a central hearth and a round stone platform, and a small apse room. Finds of large ceramic storage vessels and pits containing grain, together with cups, jugs and spindle whorls for cloth production, indicate that a variety of subsistence activities were carried out by the inhabitants. Both the apse space and the front porch seem to have been used for storage.

What must life have been like in one of these houses? In contrast with many modern Western homes, they would have afforded little privacy: there are no bedrooms and each one of the small number of separate spaces must have been used for a range of different activities – either simultaneously, at different times of day or in different seasons of the year. These included tasks that might, today, be classed as more typically non-domestic, such as cloth production or bulk storage of agricultural goods. At the same time, cooking, eating and drinking are also well represented, in parallel with today's domestic kitchens and dining areas. The use of space seems to have been relatively unspecialized, with a similar range of artefacts in each area. Every space was utilized – even the front porch.

THE FIFTH AND FOURTH CENTURIES BCE: EVIDENCE FOR URBAN ATHENIAN HOUSES IN THE AREA SURROUNDING THE AGORA

By the Classical period the Agora had become an open space, cleared of the houses that were located here in Geometric and earlier Archaic times. But to its south and west densely settled neighbourhoods had grown up in which the dispersed groups of free-standing, curvilinear structures like the oval house had been replaced by closely packed rectilinear houses bordered by a dense network of famously irregular streets. The mudbrick superstructures of these buildings do not survive, but there is sufficient evidence of the stone socles for their layouts to be reconstructed (summarized in Thompson and Wycherley 1972: 170–85; Graham 1974; Tsakirgis 2009). Their variously shaped plots make them appear to have been a rather heterogeneous group, but upon closer inspection there are a number of similarities between them which point to common patterns in the lives of their occupants.

Most of these houses would have appeared relatively modest from the exterior and they seem to have had only a single street entrance. Early work

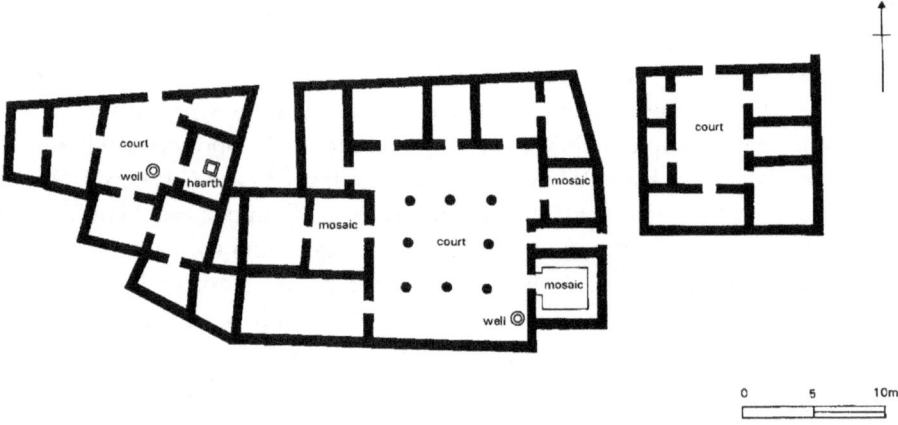

FIGURE 3.2: Plan of three Classical Houses from the Areopagus. Credit: Lisa Nevett.

suggests that there were a number of small houses with a courtyard, three rooms on the ground floor and sometimes also an upper storey (summarized by Orlandos 1991) but these are not well preserved and are difficult to date. A variety of larger structures have been investigated more extensively: these featured a single entrance which often opened into a lobby or corridor (e.g. Figure 3.2, central house). This provided a buffer between the interior and the street: even when the front door was open, a passer-by could see little of the inside of the house. Once through the lobby or corridor, however, a visitor would have entered an unroofed courtyard. The courtyard was generally at the centre or south of the house and dominated the plan, since most of the interior rooms were reached from here or from the portico that generally occupied one or more sides. Anyone entering or leaving the house or moving between rooms would have had to pass through here, and would have been visible to the house's other occupants – whether from an interior room or from the courtyard-portico area itself. There would therefore have been the potential for quite high levels of surveillance. A variety of Athenian texts also suggest that such social control was a feature of domestic life during this period, betraying a certain level of anxiety about the safekeeping of material wealth, the reliability of slaves and the faithfulness of the wives of citizen householders. Separation of the interior of the house from the street and the necessity of walking through a common area to get from one room to another would have been a practical way of addressing such anxieties.

The central courtyard area in a house like this would have been the main source of light and air, since in many cases party walls were shared with neighbouring buildings, which meant that the opportunity for external windows was limited. The courtyard-portico area seems to have been an important place for domestic tasks: often a well or cistern was located here. The portico, in particular, would also have provided a shady but well-ventilated place to spend time during the warmer months, but it is difficult to know exactly what took place here.

Houses with a similar pattern of organization and from roughly the same time period have been found widely across Greece (Nevett 1999). In cases where the artefacts found in the courtyard and portico area have been published, such as the cities of Olynthos and Halieis, these have consisted of a wide range of table and storage pottery as well as loom weights for textile production (Cahill 2002 and Ault 2005, respectively). Small domestic altars are sometimes found here as well. The interiors of courtyard houses like these are likely to have been used in a flexible way, depending on the season and weather: the lack of good artificial lighting and heating meant that residents had to adapt to the conditions outside, changing their location in order to remain comfortable. This was easier than it would be in a modern Western house since the number of built-in features was very limited. At the same time this very lack of features makes Greek houses more difficult to understand today, since there are frequently a variety of rooms where the only aid to interpretation is a mixed assemblage of artefacts suggestive of a range of different household activities. Nevertheless, several characteristic rooms can be recognized although they are not all found in every house and they occur with varying frequency in different communities.

Perhaps the most striking and easily identifiable of these spaces is the one known by archaeologists as the *andrôn* (related to the Greek word for 'man' – *anêr*), which features a durable floor consisting either of plain cement that was sometimes coloured red or yellow, or of a cement border surrounding a central mosaic which usually had a figurative or geometric design (Nevett 2010: 43–62). Where evidence survives of the walls of such rooms, the socle is sometimes more substantial here than in other parts of the house (Nevett 2009). In the House of the Parakeet Mosaic, on the slopes of the Areopagus, for example, large, cut limestone blocks would have made the room stand out to a visitor, even from the exterior (Figure 3.3). The door was also normally off-centre, suggesting that the room was organized to accommodate couches arranged continuously along the walls. Surviving Athenian texts describe a symposium or male drinking party, in which participants reclined on couches in a manner also depicted on a range of painted pottery. The features of the *andrôn* seem to fit it to be the location of this kind of occasion (indeed this name is derived from the one sometimes given to the location for such activities in the ancient texts). Couches would have been placed around the plain borders and an asymmetrical doorway would have enabled them to be arranged continuously. An anteroom sometimes provided a buffer between the *andrôn* and the courtyard, and this might support the impression created by both texts and

FIGURE 3.3: Photograph of the House of the Parakeet Mosaic, showing the walls of the *andrôn*. Credit: Lisa Nevett.

images, that symposia could sometimes get quite riotous if large quantities of wine were consumed. Although our evidence about the symposium comes mainly from Athens, the *andrôn* occurs widely in houses across the Greek world and in fact is more common among the excavated houses of cities outside Athens, such as at Olynthos and Halieis. In those cities, such rooms were embellished not only with pebble mosaic or coloured mortar floors, but also with walls enhanced with red, yellow or white painted plaster. The residents of properties that lacked an *andrôn* were nonetheless apparently not excluded from holding a symposium: close scrutiny of the textual and iconographic sources suggests that other spaces may also have been used for this kind of gathering, particularly the courtyard, where participants might have reclined on cushions on the ground. Of course, they would then have been at the centre of the house, on view to all of its occupants including any women in the surrounding rooms. We do not know whether, without the kind of isolation that a dedicated *andrôn* and anteroom would have provided, such parties had a different atmosphere, but this seems likely.

Some of the texts mentioning the *andrôn* also make reference to a space known as the *gunaikôn* or *gunaikônitis* – related to the Greek word for woman (*gunê*). But the word seems not to have had a consistent use – in one (Classical) text it represents the location where the lady of the house slept; in another it was the quarters allotted to female slaves; in a third (Roman) text it was where the women of the house spent their time (Nevett 1999: 17–19). Traditionally such references have been taken to imply that Classical Greek houses were divided into two areas to be used separately by men and women. In practice, however, as we have seen from the excavated evidence, the plan of the house was an integrated one with the rooms arranged in a radial pattern around the courtyard. While it is possible that the two words refer to upper and lower storeys (as one of the texts, the speech of Lysias discussed in chapter 1, implies), many houses lack evidence that they had more than one storey. What, then, might explain the heterogeneity of the texts and the apparent lack of fit with the archaeological evidence? It is worth keeping in mind that the references we have are very few in number and are all by male authors. At the most basic level it seems that the *gunaikônitis* is a place in the house where women are present. Studying the distribution of artefacts associated with activities that the literature and iconography represent women carrying out reveals their presence throughout the house, with the possible exception of the *andrôn* (which usually contains few objects anyway). It therefore seems likely that *gunaikônitis* was not a single specific room, but rather the domestic quarters where women were present, contrasting with the *andrôn* or *andrônitis*, where male visitors were entertained. It is likely that the location of the *gunaikônitis* was fluid, changing according to who was present in the house at any particular time and which spaces they were occupying. Even the *andrôn*, which can be identified archaeologically in some houses, may have been defined in a similarly flexible manner in others (Nevett 1999: 68–74).

In addition to the *andrôn*, a further prominent aspect of the houses surrounding the Athenian Agora is that residential accommodation seems to have been combined with workshops: evidence for various trades has been found in different cases, including marble-working and shoemaking (Tsakirgis 2005). Residues from other productive activities taking place in domestic contexts have also been found in various Classical Greek communities, including the manufacture of terracotta plaques or the processing of agricultural goods such as olives and grapes. Vessels for bulk storage of agricultural produce are also a common feature of houses and usually take the form of large, coarse ware jars or *pithoi* – like one that was found in fragmentary form in the northwest corner of room S in the House of the Greek Mosaic, a neighbour of the House of the Parakeet Mosaic. Given the range of artefacts and facilities included in residential structures of this period it seems that many households aimed to be self-sufficient in a range of goods such as foodstuffs and textiles, while buying in other more specialized products, such as pottery, as a supplement. Some also engaged in specialist manufacture of products of their own, mainly for the market.

In most Athenian houses the other rooms appear to have been relatively undifferentiated. Information about the artefacts associated with them is currently available only at a general level. A wide variety of slipped and unslipped ceramic vessels have been recovered from the general area of the Agora, and many of them must originally have come from houses. They reveal the range of activities carried out, with specialized items ranging from spouted vessels that look like feeders for children or invalids, to small, portable terracotta ovens (Sparkes and Talcott 1970). The large number of slipped shapes for serving and consuming liquids seems suggestive of the importance of wine consumption, when taken in the context of the evidence for symposia, touched on above (Lynch 2011).

Beyond Athens, numerous houses follow a similar pattern of organization to that just described, but there are some additional characteristic architectural installations: at Olynthos, for example, there is sometimes a domestic complex consisting of a large main room (sometimes with a hearth at the centre), leading to two smaller rooms. The floor of one of the smaller rooms is frequently composed of waterproof mortar, and in a number of instances a small terracotta hip-bath was set into this floor. The second small room often contained ash, bones, broken pottery and other debris, suggesting that it was used for accumulating rubbish. Together this suite of three rooms seems to represent the major domestic part of the house, combining facilities for heating, cooking and warming water for baths (Mylonas 1946). At roughly 290m^2 the Olynthian houses are generally significantly larger in ground area than their contemporaries excavated at Athens, perhaps suggesting that the households occupying them had higher living standards, or at least the luxury of more space to spread out. (This figure includes the central courtyard but excludes the upper storey we know that many of them had, since in some cases the bases for stone staircases have been found; by contrast the Athenian houses vary in area between about 100m^2 and 400m^2).

In sum, this evidence suggests that during the Classical period Athenians, and also residents of other communities, placed an emphasis on the isolation of the interior from the street outside. Once inside, though, individuals would have been very aware of each other's movements into, out of and around the house. While much of the interior was used in a flexible manner, specific rooms were sometimes provided for entertaining male guests and, more rarely, for domestic tasks such as preparing food and bathing. The range of activities encompassed by the house also includes small-scale craft production that would not necessarily be considered 'domestic' in modern Western society. While such conclusions can be drawn, it is dangerous to generalize too much: the Athenian evidence shows that there was considerable variation in house size and in the range of facilities provided. The smallest houses there have only three rooms. Such properties are rarely found elsewhere, suggesting that the houses of the poorest households may often be missing from the archaeological record because their size, and perhaps less sturdy construction, make them more challenging to detect archaeologically. The diversity in the housing stock that can be observed in its physical remains may to some extent be connected with an underlying diversity in the population, which literary and epigraphic sources show encompassed not only citizens' households but also those of metics or resident foreigners. Such social distinctions were surely paralleled by economic ones, if differences in house size can be taken as a measure of inequality – albeit a crude one. Our picture becomes still more diverse if we widen the scope of our discussion to include Attica, Athens' rural territory.

RURAL COMMUNITIES: THE ATTIC DEMES

The rural hinterland of Athens was so large that it encompassed a network of villages or deme centres. The sites of some of these have been engulfed by the expansion of the modern city, but excavation of a few has revealed that the houses of their inhabitants were sometimes somewhat different from those of their urban contemporaries. Two such settlements that have seen relatively extensive excavation are Thorikos and Ano Voula (Nevett 2005). In each case the community was composed of winding streets with blocks of residential properties between. The sizes of the houses were comparable to those of the urban houses from Athens itself, discussed above, and there was some resemblance in plan, with space organized around an unroofed central court. There were also some significant differences, however: there seems to have been less emphasis on the creation of a private environment in the interior, with fewer measures taken to separate it from the street, and on occasion a single property was also equipped with more than one street entrance, as in house 1 at Thorikos (Figure 3.4). In addition, although occasional evidence of decoration is found – such as red wall plaster in a room in the same house – *andrônes* resembling those of Classical Athens or Olynthos are almost never

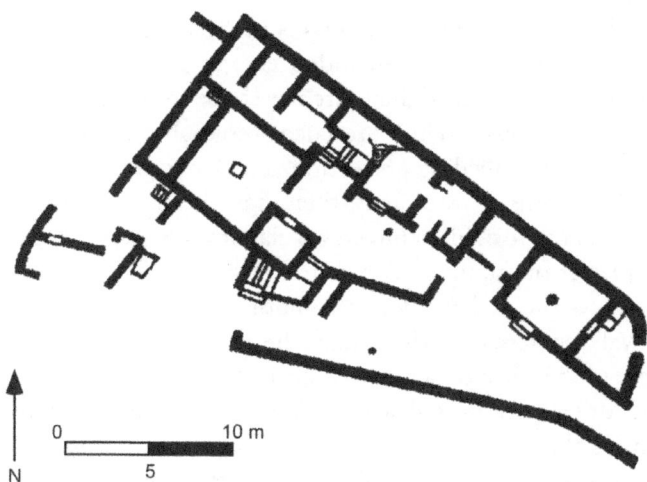

FIGURE 3.4: Plan of House 1 at Thorikos. Credit: Lisa Nevett.

found in such communities. It seems possible that households in these villages had different relationships with their neighbours from those of their urban contemporaries, involving more freedom of movement into and out of the house, and possibly less formality in entertaining. It may be that because there were fewer inhabitants in these villages, most people would have known and trusted each other, so that there was felt to be less need to secure the house from unknown, and possibly undesirable, passers-by.

One striking feature that has been identified in some of the deme houses is a circular tower that is integral to some other houses at Thorikos and also some structures at Ano Voula. Such towers must have been prominent features of the built environment in these communities – their circular shape contrasts with the orthogonal design of the surrounding buildings, and they may also have risen higher than the remainder of the structures to which they were attached. Their function has been debated. One suggestion is that towers such as these were used for locking up slaves outside work hours (S. Morris and Papadopoulos 2005). Thorikos was an unusual settlement in that many of its households seem to have engaged in mining and processing silver ore, and may have kept slaves who were involved in this work. At Ano Voula such mining activities are not known, and the settlement seems to have been a small, agricultural community. Although its residents were perhaps using slaves to farm, it is also possible to associate towers with a more generic use – perhaps as locations to secure a range of different valuables such as agricultural produce as well as slaves. Why this should have been particularly necessary in these deme centres rather than in the city itself is an interesting question. One possibility is that the owners of such properties had periodically to spend time away, perhaps conducting business in the city, and therefore felt a need to secure their property. Another is that in these smaller communities personal property was more subject to banditry and theft. At the same time towers may have come to represent status symbols since they must have demanded energy and resources to construct (including tricky integration of their circular shape into the orthogonal plan of the remainder of the house). Their presence presumably also implied ownership of the kind of valuables needing protection, and hence perhaps helped to confer a certain level of status. Towers may, then, have been an alternative means of asserting status to the formal architectural elaboration seen in the mosaic floors and painted plaster of the urban Athenian houses.

In addition to these deme villages, both excavation and surface survey (systematic walking across fields to map the residues of ancient settlements – usually visible in the form of scatters of broken pottery) show that parts of the landscape of Attica were dotted with isolated farmsteads. In many ways these houses resemble those of the city of Athens itself: they normally have a single entrance, central courtyard and colonnade, with rooms entered individually from this space (Nevett 1999: 95–8). While in some cases attempts have been made to identify an *andrôn* there are no mosaic floors and the rooms so labelled do not conform to the configuration seen at Athens and elsewhere, so that the identification seems doubtful. Such houses differ from their urban counterparts. First, they generally have larger courtyards, presumably partly because space was at less of a premium than in a built-up urban centre, and also perhaps because a greater variety or larger quantity of agricultural produce and/or equipment was kept here. Second, there is often one room in which the socle is thicker and more substantial than the others, suggesting that it supported multiple storeys and may represent the remains of a square or rectangular tower. Such a structure may have been important in the rural setting, either for security or as a lookout point, or both.

A question arising from the small number of excavated examples of these farms is how representative they may be of the range of isolated farmsteads occupied during the Classical period. One suggestion is that they may have been the property of relatively wealthy individuals. Smaller, more ephemeral farmsteads belonging to subsistence farmers may have existed alongside them but left only more limited archaeological traces in the form of scatters of pottery and/or associated facilities such as pressing equipment for wine or olive oil, or paved threshing floors for processing grain. Traces of such agricultural installations have been detected, for example, at the southern tip of Attica, and also in the territory of the ancient deme of Atene, where intensive survey revealed terrace walls attesting to intensive cultivation during the late Classical period. A second question is whether such isolated farmsteads were typically inhabited throughout the year, or whether they represent buildings belonging to owners who were normally resident in the city or in a deme centre, perhaps staying in them only at peak times of agricultural activity, such as the harvest. It is difficult to answer this definitively, and it seems likely that rural houses were used in contrasting ways in different places and at different times. (For discussion of these and related issues, see most recently McHugh 2017.)

CHANGING STYLES: ATHENIAN HOUSES IN THE LATER HELLENISTIC AND ROMAN PERIODS

Like the Athenian democracy itself, the Classical-style courtyard house seems to have been a relatively short-lived phenomenon. The Hellenistic and especially the Roman period witnessed dramatic changes in housing which correspond to the broader political, social and economic changes taking place in the Greek world in general. Some of the houses of Classical Athens continued to be inhabited or rebuilt over several centuries, into the Roman period. Nevertheless, evidence for Hellenistic housing is scarce at Athens itself. The housing of the Hellenistic period is therefore best studied on the island of Delos, which coincidentally came under Athenian domination between the mid-second and mid-first centuries BCE, and gained wealth and notoriety as a free port and trading centre. The town and its houses are spectacularly well preserved, owing to their construction from stone, and to the abandonment of the island during the Roman period with a lack of substantial subsequent settlement. About ninety separate dwellings have been excavated over a long period beginning in the late nineteenth century (summarized in Trümper 1998). These houses were typically built into *insulae* or blocks comprising a number of different properties, with multiple storeys. A wide range of sizes have been identified: the smallest units have a ground area of less than 100m² comprising only two or three rooms and a small courtyard, with few architectural or decorative features. While many covered about 150–300m², the largest examples range up to (in one case) over 800m². Some of these houses have two street entrances, or even three, which would obviously have reduced the potential for the kind of social control noted above for Classical Athens. While they retain the courtyard plan of their predecessors, in many of the larger buildings the courtyard has become an elaborate peristyle, with columns on all four sides, as is the case in the House of Dionysus (Figure 3.5, top). A sunken, mosaic-paved area at the centre drained rainwater into a cistern beneath, from which water could be drawn via a well-head in the courtyard or portico. The courtyard still served as a light-well and as a route by which to access many of the different rooms, but the level of decoration suggests that it may have lost some of its role as a functional space, with domestic chores relocating to a closed internal area. At the same time there were often several decorated rooms ranged around the peristyle. On occasion a second courtyard was included, which at least sometimes seems to have resulted from the amalgamation of two smaller courtyard houses (e.g. Nevett 2010: 63–88). In such cases there may have been functional differentiation between the two courtyards and their adjoining rooms, although information is rarely available about the artefacts associated with the different spaces, so it is hard to investigate this in any depth. Other spaces found in these houses include not only cooking areas and terracotta bathtubs (in parallel with their Classical predecessors) but also, on occasion, latrines.

There has been some speculation concerning the status of the occupants of a number of the larger houses: did the wealthy merchants whose names have been found on multiple inscriptions across the city live in the town all year round, or did they leave slaves or servants in charge of their luxury residences and visit only occasionally (e.g. Rauh 1993)? As with the question of who lived in the Attic farmsteads, there is unlikely to be a single definitive answer: again, the situation may have varied household by household, and changed through time according to political and economic circumstances as well as personal preference. What does seem certain is that the wealthiest households during this period saw a rise in their standards of living as compared with those of Classical times (I. Morris 2005: 107–23). Not only was there an increase in the

THE HOUSE 73

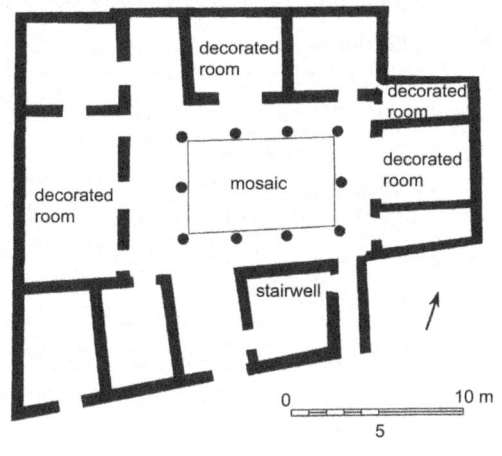

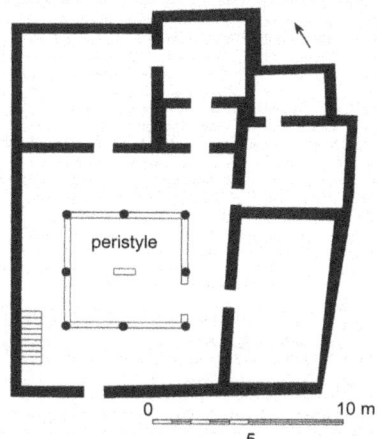

FIGURE 3.5: Plans of House of Dionysus, Delos (top) and the early Roman house from the northwest shoulder of the Areopagus (bottom). Credit: Lisa Nevett.

size of the largest houses, but also decoration became more and more lavish, with mosaic floors or sculpture in a variety of different rooms and sometimes also in the courtyard as well. The same is true for wall painting: the plain colours of the *andrôn* and portico in the Classical house were replaced by painted panels designed to resemble large stone blocks, which adorned the walls of the peristyle and multiple interior rooms. At the same time sculpted marble figures – often representing deities such as the divine huntress, Artemis – became part of the decor of the most elaborate properties and were placed in prominent locations so that they would catch the eye of visitors, or even of passers-by in the street. Property owners therefore seem to have been presenting themselves in a new light, inviting the gaze of visitors where before an effort had been made to exclude it. The role of the house in receiving guests also seems to have been enhanced within, with the multiple decorated rooms perhaps serving as dining or reception rooms. Although some of them retained the mosaic floors of a Classical *andrôn*, they were often rectangular rather than square and were arranged so that the occupants reclined around three, rather than all four, sides, suggesting a change in dining or drinking practices. It has been argued that, whereas in the Classical period Athenian citizens were expected to be politically active within the city (rather than spending time at home), by the Hellenistic period the house had assumed a more important role as a location where the householder would spend time, since the city had lost its independence to Macedon and its civic institutions were therefore diminished in importance (Walter-Karydi 1998).

These features, seen in the upper end of the housing stock at Delos, are paralleled by some of the houses found at Athens dating from the Roman period. The few complete published examples fall into the same size range as the mid-sized Delian houses (Thompson and Wycherley 1972: 183–5). Again, these Roman Athenian structures were built around a single central courtyard that provided light and air, and continued to be the main route for communication around the house. Unlike some of the Delian ones, they seem to have retained the traditional single-entrance, single-courtyard layout. In one house of about 350m^2 from the north shoulder of the Areopagus (Figure 3.5, bottom), a comparable layout was adopted to that seen in earlier periods, with a single entrance leading into a central courtyard. That courtyard had become more elaborate, however, with a decorated peristyle containing a small water basin at its centre. At the same time a few of the rooms were interconnected, forming suites and reducing the importance of the courtyard as a route for moving around the house. A rectangular room in the southeast corner was floored with marble chips and perhaps represents a reception room. A second example (House N, on the northwestern edge of the Areopagus, not illustrated), which was built in the first century CE, was similar in scale but somewhat closer in form to the earlier structures. A dog-leg passage led into the central court which was surfaced with marble chips although no trace of a colonnade was found. Elaborate dining areas continued to be used in houses of this date, and indeed in some cases where an old house was occupied through many generations, earlier floors were replaced with more fashionable mosaic designs (as in the House of the Parakeet Mosaic mentioned above, Figure 3.3). Interestingly, while the characteristic feature of the late republican to early imperial house of southern Italy, the *atrium* or covered hall with an opening in the roof and rain pool or *impluvium* below (see Introduction, Figure 0.2), has been identified in some locations in Greece (such as at Eleusis in northwest Attica), examples of such buildings do not generally come to light in the city of Athens itself

(Papaioannou 2007). It seems as if the *impluvium* is most commonly found in communities that were re-founded as official Roman *coloniae* or colonies, and settled with veterans from the Roman army, as at Corinth. There seems, then, to have been some difference between these new settlers and their hosts in terms of how the house was used to express status, with the *atrium* providing a theatrical backdrop against which the master of the house could appear in some, while in others it was the decorated dining room that was the centre of attention. Indeed some Roman authors highlight differences between Greek and Roman practices, for example in the way members of the two cultures arrange themselves in their dining rooms, or in whether the respectable women of the house are included in elegant dinner parties (Dunbabin 1998).

Just like the home of today, the ancient house was a product of the culturally determined expectations and practices of its occupants. It must have been a location where norms were reinforced through the ways in which daily activities were performed. Houses may also have been loci where contrasting cultural practices came into contact with each other. Perhaps they were contested here or new ones were created which reflected the diversity of the population of Roman Greece and the roles played by its individual inhabitants in a social, political and economic system that had to some extent been transformed by the advent of Roman rule. Just how far down the social scale these changes reached is difficult to say since, as with the houses of earlier periods, the smallest and least substantially built structures are likely to be missing from the archaeological record, so that our evidence represents the experience of elite households.

THE TRANSFORMATION OF THE HOME IN LATE ROMAN ATHENS

The lives of socially and economically advantaged groups continue to dominate our picture as we move into the later Roman period. But whereas in Classical and Roman times there is strong evidence for the continuation of earlier house forms, by the fourth century CE houses built and rebuilt after the city was sacked in the mid-third century CE look very similar to houses from other parts of the Roman Empire. Three relatively well-preserved examples on the lower slopes of the Areopagus, both built during the later fourth century CE and occupied for a period of 200 years, offer a picture of the domestic surroundings of comfortably-off households in the city during this time (Frantz 1988: 34–48) (Figure 3.6). These buildings all retain the courtyard arrangement of their predecessors. House A covers about 650m². As reconstructed its fourteen rooms are arranged around a central peristyle. The entrance is placed in the centre of the northern facade and opens through a lobby into the peristyle. Immediately opposite it is the most elaborate room of the house – an apsidal space entered via a smaller anteroom. Three niches in the apse may once have been adorned with sculptural

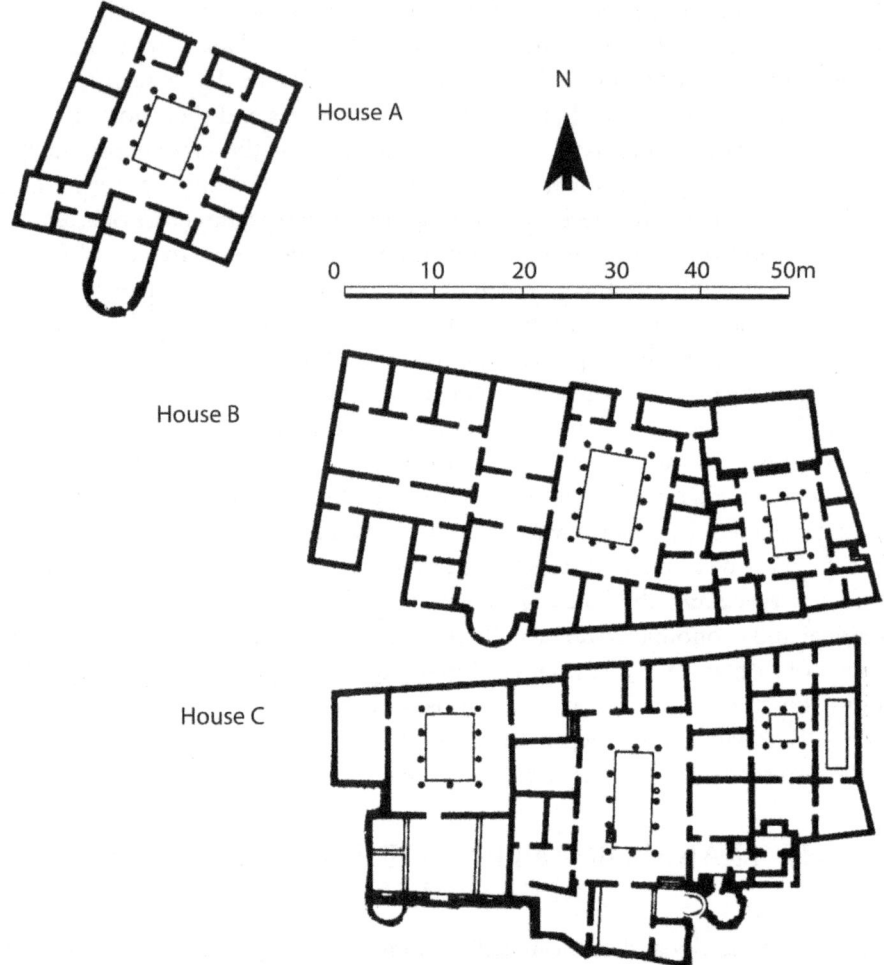

FIGURE 3.6: Plans of later Roman houses from the Areopagus. Credit: Lisa Nevett.

decoration. Such apsidal rooms are a characteristic feature of two of the three other houses in this neighbourhood and indeed of larger houses in other Roman provinces as well. In at least some instances such rooms were furnished with curved couches and seem to have been used for entertaining visitors in a manner similar to the Classical *andrôn* or the banqueting room of the Hellenistic and earlier Roman periods.

Two further houses excavated nearby, Houses B and C (the latter sometimes also referred to in the literature as the 'Omega House'), are far larger in area than House A or indeed than anything we have seen in previous periods, each covering a total area of around 1800m². In order to maintain access to light and air for the interior rooms, space is arranged around three different courtyards.

The multiple-courtyard arrangement was adopted in larger houses of Roman and late Roman date throughout the Roman world. Although in House C these all take the form of peristyles, more often a single peristyle is supplemented by one or two simpler courtyards with no portico, or with a portico on only one side (as in House B). At Rome itself and in the towns of southern Italy such as Pompeii, during late republican and early imperial times, a partially covered *atrium* replaced one of the courtyards. The overall effect of such arrangements is a somewhat modular plan, and indeed in some cases the layout can be shown to have been the result of combining what were previously separate, single-courtyard properties. Nevertheless, the arrangement meant that individual rooms had access to light and ventilation through these open courtyard spaces, and that there were a variety of different environments that could be used by the inhabitants at different times of year according to the weather.

House C seems to have been particularly elaborate, possessing features designed to create a luxurious environment and enhance the status of its occupants. In the southeast corner of the peristyle lay a small, mosaic-paved dining room with an adjoining apsidal pool with a flight of steps leading down into it, which was fed by an adjacent spring house and by springs further up the Areopagus. This area not only provided an intimate, decorated dining space but the water feature would also have had a cooling effect in the hot summer months. The presence of such an amenity was an expression of wealth – which was necessary to support the abundant use of this important commodity, and it echoes the use of such features in dining contexts in elite houses from other parts of the Empire, such as the North African provinces. While moving through the peristyle was an important way of getting around this house, the individual rooms also fall into clusters or suites of intercommunicating spaces which would have enabled individuals to move from room to room without necessarily using the peristyle.

There has been some debate about the range of roles played by these and other domestic structures in this neighbourhood of Athens during the later Roman era. The city had shrunk in size relative to its earlier extent. During the fourth century CE it does not seem to have played a major economic role in the region. Nevertheless a range of surviving literary sources suggest that it had significant cultural capital: in particular Athens was famous for its philosophers, who attracted pupils from across the Empire. There has been some speculation that the buildings of this neighbourhood, including those just discussed, may have housed such philosophical schools. Such a use is entirely possible, although their close resemblance to contemporary houses from other provinces suggests that a large part of their role was residential. (Fragmentary remains of even larger, more elaborate residences have been found elsewhere in the city.)

CONCLUSION

Although the archaeological record is unlikely to represent households at all socio-economic levels, this long-term overview reveals the way in which the physical house provides a barometer of some of the broader social, economic and political changes affecting Athens, and the wider Classical world, over a period of more than a thousand years. Basic trends include a rise in standards of living, from small structures like Nichoria Unit IV.1 (which had limited living space and few material goods), through to large buildings like the later Roman houses on the Areopagus (which had multiple interior rooms and decorative architectural features). Some aspects of the earlier houses, such as the free-standing location and apsidal end, were superseded as settlements became larger and more densely occupied, requiring houses to share party walls. Similarly, new technologies were developed, such as tiled roofs, which replaced the previous, thatched ones. Other features stood the test of time: for example, the same basic materials – stone socles and mudbricks – continued to be used for wall construction throughout the period covered by this chapter. In the same way, the courtyard, once it was introduced, remained the most practical way of lighting and ventilating the interior rooms, particularly when houses were built in blocks or *insulae*, or when they covered a large area.

Practical considerations were not the only ones governing continuity and change in house design. Another long-lived element was the decorated *andrôn* or dining room, which survived from the Classical period down to the apsidal dining rooms of the fourth century CE and beyond. While such rooms must have created a pleasant environment for members of the household, they surely also reveal the role of the house as symbolic capital – evidence of the wealth of the householder, and more particularly, of the elite drinking and dining culture in which he participated (or perhaps, wished to be thought to participate). The symbolic role played by the house seems to have increased through time into the Hellenistic and Roman periods, to judge by levels of investment in larger, more elaborately decorated buildings. These changes must surely have been accompanied by a dramatic growth in levels of inequality, materialized in the contrast between the smallest and largest of the houses found around the Athenian Agora, the range of housing stock on Hellenistic Delos and the enormous size of some of the late Roman houses on the slopes of the Areopagus.

Finally, it is clear that personal wealth and elite status were not the only qualities that a house owner communicated through the architecture, organization and decoration of his home. The inclusion of a feature such as an *atrium* is likely to have signalled other information, such as cultural affiliation. In the same way, other features such as the general accessibility of the interior or its pattern of organization may have expressed the householder's conformity or otherwise with the values of the wider community, as with the screening of the interior of the urban Classical house from the street and the arrangement of its interior to facilitate surveillance. The contrast between the houses around the Classical Agora and those from the outlying deme villages and farmsteads of Attica suggests another kind of cultural difference, this time between city dwellers and those from the countryside, which may point to underlying alternative patterns of social life in smaller communities to the better-documented ones of urbanites. While this chapter has taken Athens as a focus, similar patterns in the use of domestic space and comparable trajectories of change have been detected in other areas of the ancient Mediterranean. In all these cases, while the study of housing reveals interesting details about the buildings themselves, it is equally important for the variety of questions it opens up concerning the changing social and cultural lives of the ancient households who once lived in them.

ACKNOWLEDGMENTS

I am grateful to David Stone for assistance with the illustrations, and to the editors for their patience in awaiting this contribution.

CHAPTER FOUR

Furniture and Furnishings

JOANNE BERRY

Scholars today would agree that houses are built to address the social and cultural needs of different peoples – this is why they are different the world over, both geographically and chronologically, from Navajo hogans in America to terrace houses in Britain (e.g. Parker-Pearson and Richards 1994; Kent 1984 and 1990). This was clearly the case in the ancient world, too. The plan of the ancient Greek house, for example, seems to have been designed to monitor contact between visitors and members of a household (Walker 1983; Nevett 1994; above, chapter 3). There were different concerns in the Roman world, as can be seen in the writings of the architect Vitruvius, who claimed that houses needed to be suitable for their inhabitants. Poor Romans had no need for large apartments and prestigious decoration, since they would visit their patron, not receive clients into their own houses; the houses of the social elite, however, could be elaborate display areas that communicated wealth and status to the onlooker (Vitruvius, *On Architecture* 6.5.1–2; cf. Saller 1996: 92–3; Wallace-Hadrill 1994; Hales 2003).

The fixed architectural design of a house is clearly important, therefore. But the domestic environment or home is more than just a collection of fixed features (buildings, floors, walls); it also consists of semi-fixed features (furniture and furnishings) and non-fixed features (people and their activities and behaviours) (Rapoport 1990: 13). These semi-fixed features, the moveable and semi-permanent contents and fittings of the home, both useful and ornamental, are crucial for the interpretation of the function and importance of particular spaces and rooms. Beds, couches, tables, benches, chests and cupboards, whether free-standing or set in alcoves, marble furniture, portable hearths, lighting equipment, and soft furnishings such as curtains, carpets and bedspreads fundamentally shape the use of each room. Furniture and furnishings are an easily changed (or quickly damaged) feature of a house, and may vary in different periods according to fashion or financial situation. Therefore they are more likely to shed light on the actual condition and domestic organization of a house at a particular time than the architecture and decoration alone. Although often influenced by architecture, it is these semi-fixed features that have the potential to transform a space.

This is exactly what we see in a wall-painting from the House of the Chaste Lovers in Pompeii (Figure 4.1). It shows scantily clad men and women reclining on substantial wooden couches covered with coloured cushions and woven bedspreads. Curtains hang between columns, and a three-legged wooden table holds drinking vessels. The scene is vivid and busy – a colourful party in progress, with male diners, courtesans and slaves. The furniture and furnishings are an integral part of the room, transforming it from an empty architectural shell into the luxurious setting of a Greek symposium. Furniture is not strictly necessary to human life, so its presence indicates specific social and cultural activities (Lucie-Smith 1994: 7). In the case of the symposium, it was used to create a specialized environment that allowed normal social rules to be transgressed, alliances between elite families to be built and aristocratic power

FIGURE 4.1: House of the Chaste Lovers (IX.12.6), Pompeii. Credit: Domenico Esposito, with permission of the Parco Archeologico di Pompei

to be bolstered (Nevett 2010: 43). Wealth and social hierarchies are on display. The wall-painting also reveals that the Romans themselves understood the importance of semi-fixed features and how they could shape the use and interpretation of a space and the activities within it.

We ought to expect, therefore, that the range and distribution of furniture and furnishings in ancient houses will shed light on the organization of domestic life and the cultural needs and aspirations of their inhabitants. It should tell us about the desire (or not) for privacy, the display of social status, the control of visitors to the house, the protection of household goods and valuables, the role of domestic religion and so on. For example, can the location of beds shed light on the desire (or not) for privacy while sleeping? In general, we would know a lot more about the social and practical uses of space in the ancient world if we restored furniture and furnishings to the houses that have been excavated. What activities occurred habitually? Were rooms always used in the same way or did their function change over time, for example in response to daily needs or seasonal changes? Can the things found inside the houses, and in particular the furniture and furnishings, tell us about how people lived, and their everyday activities and concerns? We should also consider how easily particular items of furniture could be moved, and their potential to transform the appearance and use of a particular room or space.

Unfortunately, the nature of the surviving evidence does not allow us to answer these questions fully. For the vast majority of excavated ancient houses across the Greek and Roman world, only the floor plan or architectural shell survives, and the household contents are mostly missing because they were removed in antiquity, destroyed or left to decay slowly. This is particularly true of furniture and furnishings. Bronze and marble items were usually recycled or salvaged in antiquity, and items such as beds, couches, tables, cupboards, shelves and textiles were made of perishable, organic materials that have survived rarely and only in particular circumstances. Elements of wooden furniture have been found occasionally, for example in the dry conditions at Karanis in Egypt and in waterlogged sites such as Vindolanda in northern Britain. These solitary finds are interesting, but they fail to give us information about how furniture was used in everyday life because there is little understanding of their wider domestic context and relationship to other objects. Only at Pompeii, Herculaneum and the other Roman sites of the Bay of Naples is there enough evidence to get an idea of the domestic assemblage of a house at one particular time, but even here the record is not perfect.

This means that in most cases we have to turn to literary descriptions, inscriptions, funerary goods and visual depictions on friezes, in Greek vase-paintings and in Roman wall-paintings, to get an idea of the range of furniture used in antiquity. Until recently, modern scholarship focused on describing this literary and visual evidence and tracing the development of furniture from the fourth millennium BCE through to late antiquity, with little acknowledgment of the problems inherent in this evidence (Andrianou 2006a discusses the problems in using literary and iconographic depictions of ancient furniture). Thus we know a great deal about the most important, prestigious and luxurious forms and materials of furniture, and how it was made, but until the work of Mols on Herculaneum in the 1990s, there was little discussion of any furniture that might be considered part of a normal household assemblage – the wooden pieces that undoubtedly made up the majority of the furniture used on a daily basis (Mols 1999). Today there is greater acknowledgement of the potential importance of this type of evidence, and increased discussion of how to reconstruct the furniture and furnishings of ancient houses (Nissin 2015 and 2016; Andrianou 2006a, 2006b, 2007, 2009).

This chapter will give a brief overview of the literary, archaeological, epigraphic and visual evidence for Greek and Roman furniture, and discuss the range and significance of furniture and furnishings in Greek and Roman houses. It will examine the problems encountered when trying to reconstruct the extent and use of furniture in the house, and will conclude with a case study from Pompeii, one of the few archaeological sites where furniture has actually been found in situ.

FURNITURE IN THE GREEK WORLD

The earliest evidence for furniture in the area that would become the Greek world comes from the Neolithic period (6500–3000 BCE) and consists of terracotta figurines sitting on seats and miniature objects such as stools and tables. These presumably depict real pieces of wooden furniture, and have many similarities to Near Eastern examples (Baker 1966 discusses Near Eastern furniture). More is known about furniture from the Bronze Age (third to second millennia BCE). Cycladic sculptures depict chairs with distinctive designs and forms, and fine ivory fittings that once adorned furniture have been found at Minoan and Mycenaean sites. Linear B tablets from sites such as Pylos give inventories of palace furniture that include tables, chairs and footstools of stone, wood and ivory, adorned with ebony, ivory, gold and silver, that confirm the sophistication of some furniture in this period (Baker 1966: 246–53). Homer's descriptions of furniture in the *Odyssey* may also shed light on this period. For example, he describes a beautiful bed (10.347), a chair decorated with silver nails (10.314–15), and silver tables and banquet furniture (10.352–67) belonging to the witch Circe. Penelope has a chair that is inlaid with silver and ivory, made by a famous craftsman called Ikmalios (19.55–8), and Odysseus himself constructs his matrimonial bed around an olive tree (which becomes the headboard) and adorns it with gold, silver and ivory (23.166–204; cf. Baker 1966: 253).

Little is known of the furniture used in the Dark Ages (1150–800 BCE), but from the eighth century BCE chairs, stools, footstools and beds, often in the context of a funerary procession, begin to be depicted on Greek vases (Baker 1966: 253). Miniature models of items of furniture such as chairs and beds have been discovered in graves from this period, and some fragments of furniture, such as small wooden stools (most likely footstools) decorated with carved figures, have been found in permanently waterlogged earth in and around wells at the archaic Sanctuary of Hera on Samos (Baker 1966: 251–2; Kyrieleis 1993: 141–5). By the sixth century BCE, a fairly canonical range of furniture was depicted on Greek vases and on stone funerary reliefs, including portable three-legged tables, thrones, chairs and, as the custom of reclining to dine grew, banqueting couches. For example, the famous grave stele of Hegeso (*c*. 400 BCE) depicts a young woman seated on an ornate chair with a footstool, inspecting jewellery from a box (Figure 4.2).

Other types of furniture are known from literary texts, although texts that describe furniture in any detail are rare. Pausanias, for example, describes a

FIGURE 4.2: Stele of Hegeso, National Archaeological Museum of Athens. Credit: Mansell/Getty Images.

folding stool supposedly made by Daedalus that was exhibited in the Erechtheum on the Acropolis, and the lost chest of Kypselos at Olympia, and there are other examples in the ancient literary texts of donations to the gods of furniture that had belonged to mythical figures (Pausanias 1.27.1, 5.17–19; Andrianou 2009: 115; Shaya 2005). Inscribed temple inventories, such as those found in Athens, Eleusis and Delos, also document, albeit incompletely, expensive and ornate pieces of furniture made by specialists that were dedicated to the gods or given to temples for safekeeping or display (Andrianou 2009: 116–21). In the case of Athens, the Parthenon frieze depicts men and women carrying musical instruments, ritual objects, metal vessels and furniture – all of which are mentioned in the temple inventories (cf. Lapatin 2015: 12).

All this evidence suggests that there was a limited number of types of furniture in the Greek world, which were developed and improved over the years so that there were many variations of detail but not form (Mols 1999: 10; Richter 1966: 3; Baker 1966: 285). Study of the development of these types has traditionally dominated modern scholarship, although the recent work of Andrianou has shed light on the archaeological and epigraphic evidence for furniture in domestic contexts (see Andrianou 2006a, 2006b, 2007, 2009).

To what extent, therefore, do the expensive and ornate pieces of furniture depicted on vases and funerary *stelai* and described in temple inventories and literary texts represent those used in an everyday context by the ancient Greeks? The elaborate items described by Homer are outnumbered by the simple, ordinary items of furniture that form a backdrop to the action of his stories, but that are not described in any detail (Laser 1968; Pritchett 1956: 226; Mols 1999: 9). Images on vases provide an idea of how furniture was used by the ancient Greeks, but the furniture depicted was not necessarily customarily used in the home (Andrianou 2006a: 222). Similarly, temple inventories document prestige furniture used in sacred contexts, not everyday furniture, and inscriptions have been found that explicitly forbid the use of this furniture outside a sanctuary (see Andrianou 2009: 118 for examples of relevant inscriptions).

A better source of information about everyday household goods and furniture are inscribed records of confiscations, such as the Attic *stelai*, a group of carved gravestones from the fifth century BCE, found in and around the Athenian agora. These record the sale of personal property confiscated from Alcibiades and others after they were falsely convicted of mutilating herms throughout Athens and profaning the Eleusinian mysteries during a drunken rampage in 415 BCE (Plutarch, *Alcibiades* 19–20; Pritchett 1956: 178). Despite his wealth and prominence, Alcibiades' furniture, and that of his companions, was mostly made of wood and consisted of chairs, chests and boxes, couches and beds, doors and tables, plus furnishings such as rugs, blankets and bedspreads, cushions and mattresses, curtains and hangings, and painted picture-boards

(Pritchett 1956: 210–54). It has been claimed that this simplicity may be explained by a general distaste for exhibiting private wealth in fifth-century Athens (Pritchett 1956: 211). Luxury goods had been unfashionable since the time of the Persian Wars since they were associated with kingship and tyranny (Lapatin 2015: 2). Sumptuary laws were enacted against conspicuous consumption in this period, and elaborate furniture may well have fallen into the category of unnecessary luxury (see Andrianou 2009: 123 for further discussion). There is even a comedy by Menander, dating to the late fourth century BCE, that depicts household members borrowing furniture from their middle-class neighbours when they were expecting guests for a symposium because they did not have enough appropriate furniture in their own home (*Dyskolos* 920–45; cf. Andrianou 2006a: 221). This does not mean that Athenians ceased to find luxurious items desirable or that the elite did not display them – there is certainly evidence of fine imports and well-crafted goods. In the fourth century BCE, Demosthenes claimed that his father owned a furniture workshop that used approximately two *minai* worth of ivory every month, an imported luxury used to decorate the furniture (*Against Aphobos* 27.1.9–10; cf. Lapatin 2015: 174). But these items were probably not in general use. It appears that ornamental furniture was fairly rare and not usually intended for domestic use in Classical Greece; instead it was more commonly intended for display in sanctuaries and temples.

It is often claimed that furniture became more ornate and luxurious during the Hellenistic period, as the display of wealth became more common (Mols 1999: 11; Reincke 1935: 505). The extreme wealth generated by Alexander's conquests was used deliberately by Hellenistic rulers as part of a calculated political strategy to increase their prestige and highlight their divine right to rule. For example, Athenaeus records that in 279 BCE Ptolemy II Philadelphus inaugurated a festival in Alexandria and dedicated it to his parents. For this festival, he constructed a banqueting pavilion that held chryselephantine (i.e. gold and ivory) couches for 100 people, each of whom had their own golden table and golden place setting. The pavilion was decorated with purple curtains, paintings, sculpture, exotic animal hides, tapestries and golden tripods (*Deipnosophists* 5.196A–203B; see Rice 1983 for discussion of this event). In fact, literary descriptions abound of banquets and luxurious palaces, with golden tables and ornate couches. It is unclear to what extent such descriptions by Greek authors are intended simply to express distaste for kingship and its association with tyranny, but there is some archaeological evidence to support the existence of luxury furniture, since the gilt-ivory appliqués from wooden furniture have been found in Macedonian royal tombs (Lapatin 2015: 174). But again, we are left with the question of whether these items of luxury furniture were used by people beyond palace circles in the wider Greece world, or just the political and social elite (Andrianou 2006a).

There is little excavated evidence of furniture from domestic contexts, beyond a few examples of metal-sheathed legs or appliqués for wooden beds, and in fact it is impossible to know how much perishable furniture was used in daily life (Andrianou 2006a: 224; see Andrianou 2009 for a catalogue of the fragmentary furniture found during excavations of urban sites such as Olynthos and Delos). It is also important to remember that there would have been regional variations throughout Greece due to the availability of materials: wood is abundant in Macedonia, for example, but not on Delos (Andrianou 2006a: 259). Thus overall it is impossible to give more than general conclusions about the nature and extent of furniture in the Greek world.

§§ THE EVIDENCE FOR ROMAN FURNITURE

Finds in seventh-century BCE graves at Verucchio near Rimini give us some information about early Italian furniture, including three-legged tables with round tops, footstools and chairs with back rests (cf. Gentili 1987; Richter 1966 and Steingräber 1979 discuss the influence of Greek furniture forms on Etruscan furniture, particularly from the sixth century BCE). But in general, Roman furniture appears to have developed from, and elaborated on, Classical and Hellenistic Greek forerunners, and it is generally agreed that the Romans had only a few original innovations to make (Richter 1966: 117; Moss 1988; Budetta and Pagano 1988; Pernice 1932). It seems also to have been fairly uniform across the Roman Empire, although within the main types of furniture there seems to have been a good deal of variation in design and decoration. Varro, for example, claims that 'identical rooms are ornamented in unlike manner, and couches are not all made the same in size and shape' (Varro, *Lingua Latina* 8.32, Loeb trans.). He goes on to say that these differences give pleasure and should not be avoided. Nevertheless, it is also generally claimed by scholars that Roman furniture was more strictly connected to function than is the case today, and had very specific uses (Mols 1993: 492).

There are many images of beds and couches, chests, cupboards, chairs and benches, and tables in visual representations in Roman wall-paintings and on funerary reliefs. However, these images often depict scenes of Greek, not Roman, mythology and culture (Mols 1999: 16). An example from the famous House of Menander in Pompeii (Figure 4.3) depicts the Greek poet Menander, seated on a high-backed chair that looks very much like a throne and resembles chairs depicted on Greek vases and in reliefs. This also highlights another problem: the furniture depicted is often high-status or ceremonial. Thus the bench depicted on the Tomb of Navoleia Tyche at Pompeii is a *bisellium*, an honorary chair associated with magisterial authority, and is an explicit reference to the public office once held by her husband rather than an illustration of a typical item of everyday furniture (Figure 4.4). Indeed, this was a significant

FURNITURE AND FURNISHINGS 89

FIGURE 4.3: The Poet Menander, from the House of Menander, Pompeii. Credit: Domenico Esposito, with permission of the Parco Archeologico di Pompei.

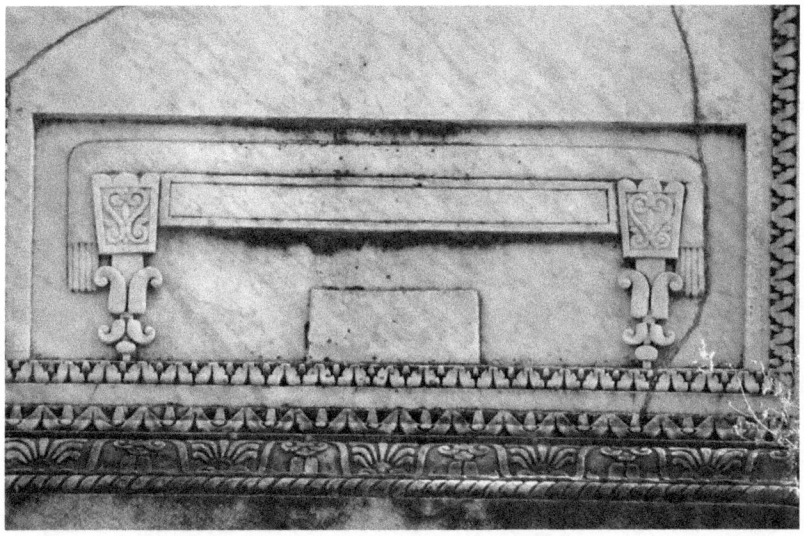

FIGURE 4.4: Bisellium depicted on the Tomb of Navoleia Tyche at Pompeii. Credit: Domenico Esposito, with permission of the Parco Archeologico di Pompei.

symbol in Roman politics. Julius Caesar, for example, was condemned for sitting on a golden chair that looked like a throne on the rostra to address the Senate. This was a step too far because it held allusions to kingship and despotism (Cassius Dio 44.11; Schäfer 1989). After his murder, Octavian minted a coin that depicted Caesar's golden laurel wreath lying on an empty *sella curulis* with the legend CAESAR DIC[tator] PER[petuus]. It is clear that furniture could take on a symbolic role.

In Roman literature, the word *supellex* is used to describe an assemblage of household objects rather than specifying individual objects. The following comment by Cicero is typical of how it is used: 'The spoils won from the enemy, the memorials of our commanders, the ornaments and decorations of our temples, will hereafter, when these illustrious names are lost, be reckoned in the furniture and appointments (*supellectile*) of Caius Verres' (*Verrines* 2.4.97, Loeb trans.). When individual items are described by Roman authors it is because they are particularly valuable, luxurious or unusual, including unusually simple. To quote Cicero again:

> In truth, Sthenius from his youth had collected such things as these with more than ordinary diligence; elegant furniture of brass, made at Delos and at Corinth, paintings, and even a good deal of elegantly wrought silver ...
> —*Verrines* 2.2.83, Loeb trans.

Livy provides more details about the wealth of furniture that was imported into Rome from the second century BCE. He claims that:

> the beginnings of foreign luxury were introduced into the City by the army from Asia. They for the first time imported into Rome couches of bronze, valuable robes for coverlets, tapestries and other products of the loom, and what at that time was considered luxurious furniture – tables with one pedestal and sideboards.
> —Livy 39.6, Loeb trans.

From sources like this, we know that luxury furniture became an essential part of elite houses, and a byword for elite extravagance, particularly during the republican period, and that much of this furniture was used to display the social status and wealth of Roman families and statesmen, often in a competitive way. Valuable woods, such as citrus, and marbles and rare materials, such as ivory, were sought out and used by wealthy Romans in their desire for luxury goods (for example, Pliny, *Natural Histories* 13.29.91; Cicero, *Verrines* 2.4.17.37). Elaborate and ornamental tables, couches and beds were particularly sought after, no doubt because they could be displayed to guests in the context of a banquet.

The most luxurious items of furniture seem to relate to dining and to the formal display of authority. These are contexts in which the utilitarian purpose of furniture may have been secondary to its potential for social and psychological manipulation. We can look to other cultures and chronological periods for support for this idea. Furniture has played an important role in studies of consumption and social emulation in other historical societies. It has been demonstrated, for example, that in nineteenth-century America furniture and related artefacts were used deliberately 'as props for the drama of life' (Ames 1981: 215–18). A study of hall furnishings in this period showed that the position and ornamentation of a piece of furniture need not have anything to do with its function. Items of furniture instead became symbols of status or authority and, as such, were used deliberately to create a particular impression. To understand furniture, and its role within a particular society, we need to know something about the places in which it was located, whether these were passageways or activity areas, communal or private areas (Ames 1981: 212). The visual impression or importance of a piece of furniture will obviously change according to the place in which it is located, and the household artefacts that are associated with it. In this respect, the size and quantity of furniture is important, as is the repetition of particular types or the combinations of particular types. This will be explored further in the case study below.

Despite references to luxury furniture and furnishings in the ancient literary sources, they are not usually described for their own sake; rather they are used to articulate particular points, often moral ones. Suetonius used furniture to illustrate the simplicity of Augustus' life: apparently this could be seen 'from couches and tables still in existence, many of which are scarcely fine enough for a private citizen. They say that he always slept on a low and plainly furnished bed' (*Augustus* 73, Loeb trans.).

This can be compared to Nero's bedroom, which, according to Suetonius, contained statues of Nero as a lyre-player (*Nero* 25). Horace commented on the simplicity of his own household too:

> If you can recline at my table on couches made by Archias, and are not afraid of 'a dinner of herbs' only, from a modest dish, I shall expect you, Torquatus, at my house at sunset.
> —*Epistles* 5.1, Loeb trans.

Archias was apparently a maker of unpretentious furniture: according to the scholiast Porphyrio, his couches were small ones (although the fact that the name of the maker of these small couches is known suggests that they were not as simple and inexpensive as Horace would have us believe).

There are many other throwaway comments, particularly in works by writers such as Plautus, where items of furniture form an incidental background to the action, but there are no detailed descriptions unless they are expensive and particularly luxurious. A more comprehensive account of the *supellex* of a working farm can be found in the treatises of Roman agricultural writers. According to Cato, for example, an olive-yard of 240 *iugera* should have (among other things) thirteen people, one small table, two tables, three large benches, one bedroom stool, three stools, four chairs, two armchairs, one bed in the bedroom, four beds on cords, three common beds, eight mattresses, eight coverlets, sixteen cushions and ten table covers. A smaller (but more intensive) vineyard of 100 *iugera* should have sixteen people, four beds, one bench, two tables, one small table, one clothes chest, one wardrobe, six long benches, four mattresses, four coverlets, six cushions and six table covers (*On Agriculture* 10–11). It is interesting that a small vineyard was thought to require more furniture than a larger olive-yard, which leads to questions about who was allowed to use the furniture (for example, did slaves have the same access to seating and mattresses for sleeping, or was this reserved for the landowner or overseer and his family?). In addition, it is questionable whether the requirements of a rural farm were the same as those of an urban house, and thus on the basis of literary evidence it is almost impossible to form an idea of what average urban houses should contain. One thing is certain, however: expensive luxury furniture must have been out of reach for most people. It was also unnecessary since most Romans would not have thrown large dinner parties, held magisterial office or had many visitors to their houses.

THE ARCHAEOLOGY OF THE BAY OF NAPLES

To get a better idea of what furniture and furnishings were like in normal houses, we have to turn to archaeological evidence. Unfortunately, as we have seen, most sites do not yield this kind of evidence, and wooden furniture in particular is systematically under-represented in the archaeological record. Yet wood would have been used for floors, doors, windows, balconies and staircases, as well as for much furniture in houses, shops and public places (Mols 1999: 1). This is clearly illustrated at the archaeological sites of the Bay of Naples, and at Herculaneum in particular, where wood was carbonized during the eruption of Vesuvius in 79 CE. The furniture from Herculaneum was studied by Stephan Mols, who described the various types of furniture, but also attempted an interpretation of their function through their position in the house (Mols 1993, 1994). He claimed that wooden furniture had a practical use in daily life and that marble and bronze furniture was intended for display and placed in the most public and open rooms of the house. He also concluded that more wooden furniture was found in smaller houses, which were not designed to receive or impress guests, and that wooden furniture was hardly ever placed in a room simply to show the social status of the homeowner (Mols 1994: 286). Finally, he concluded that wooden furniture was far simpler than the expensive bronze and marble pieces that

FIGURE 4.5: Carbonized wooden table from Herculaneum. Credit: Andrew Wallace-Hadrill, with permission of the Parco Archeologico di Ercolano.

feature in the literary sources, although some of the wooden pieces clearly still had a decorative element, as in the example of the wooden stool/table with beautiful inlay work illustrated (Mols 1994: 54; see Figure 4.5). However, the lack of systematic excavation reports for Herculaneum, the carelessness of the excavators more generally and the fact that there was no means of preserving excavated wood before the 1920s mean that Mols's study was based on just thirteen beds, nine tables, three benches, one stool and fifteen pieces of storage furniture found in the twentieth century throughout the *Nuovi Scavi* of Herculaneum (i.e. on forty-one pieces of furniture found in seventeen houses) (cf. Mols 1994: 1; Ruggiero 1885 discusses the earliest finds of furniture at Herculaneum). These items are unique and quite diverse in form, but must be merely a fraction of what was actually in use in 79 CE. Indeed, a more recent study by Laura Nissin has identified beds in twenty-seven houses in Herculaneum, based on the evidence for fragments and fittings of beds in addition to the wooden beds themselves (Nissin 2016). To get a better picture of the range and extent of furniture in Roman houses we can turn to the neighbouring site of Pompeii and an examination of some of the excavation reports from the twentieth century.

A CASE STUDY: *INSULAE* 7, 8 AND 9 OF REGION 1 OF POMPEII

The area in the southeast of the city designated as *insulae* 7, 8 and 9 in Region I of Pompeii (Figure 4.6) was excavated from the 1910s to the mid-1950s, and

FIGURE 4.6: Plan of Region I, *insulae* 7, 8 and 9 at Pompeii. Credit: Joanne Berry.

overall the quality of the excavation reports is reasonably good (cf. Laidlaw 2007 for a summary of the documentary sources and problems related to them). These *insulae* contain a range of different sizes and types of houses, from the grand House of Paquius Proculus (I.7.1) and House of the Ephebe (I.7.10–12) in *insula* 7, to the smaller, non-atrium houses in the south of *insula* 9, and the shops and bars mainly along the Via dell'Abbondanza. There is plenty of evidence for wooden furniture – not usually the wood itself, but the iron nails and studs, and bronze and ivory fittings and ornamentation that were used to construct and adorn the furniture. In addition, the excavators found the impressions of items of wooden furniture in the hardened ash deposits and were able to make plaster casts of some of them in some of the houses. Finally, marble tables and the single-legged tables known as *monopodia* were also found in these *insulae*, adding to the overall impression of furniture in use in 79 CE (Moss 1988; Cohon 1984).

The semi-fixed nature of furniture means that, unlike other categories of household object found at Pompeii and Herculaneum which were easily moved and not necessarily stored where they were used, the find-spot of each item is likely to be its actual position in 79 CE. There is evidence of building work and restoration in many of the houses (a consequence of ongoing seismic activity in the region in the years before Vesuvius erupted), which suggests normal domestic organization was disrupted to a certain extent (Allison 2004; Berry 1997a, 1997b). Nevertheless, some patterns emerge that shed light on the most common forms of furniture in use in 79 CE, its distribution and location.

Storage Furniture

It is hardly surprising that the most common items of furniture in these houses and shops related to storage (chests, cupboards, shelving and household shrines or *lararia*). Wooden chests were the most common: evidence of forty chests was found in sixteen houses and shops. The ancient literary sources suggest that strongboxes were located in the *atria* of Roman houses (Servius, commentary on Virgil, *Aeneid* 1.730, 9.648), and these have occasionally been found at Pompeii and elsewhere in the Bay of Naples, for example in the *atrium* of the House of the Vettii at Pompeii, and in Villa B (Villa of Lucius Crassius Tertius) at Oplontis. However, from the evidence here, this does not seem to be the case for the majority of houses: only five chests were located in *atria*, and only one of these is likely to have been a proper strongbox: a chest in the House of the Beautiful Impluvium (I.9.1) which contained over 300 silver coins. In fact, chests were found throughout the houses, in open areas such as *atria*, courtyards and porticos but also in enclosed rooms. The remains of cupboards were found in ten houses and one shop, occasionally positioned next to chests, and more frequently located in *atria* and porticos.

Unlike chests and cupboards, evidence for wooden shelving was found in only six houses, and was usually found in small rooms, unless it formed a *lararium*, such as in the house annexed to the House of the Ephebe (I.7.19), or as in a shop. The artefacts found fallen from shelving were generally small commonware vessels, although they could also include tools, kitchen vessels and tableware. The implication is that none of these artefacts were valuable enough to be shut away in chests and cupboards. It is also clear that, with the exception of the *lararium*, shelves were utilitarian spaces and not used for display (see Kastenmeier 2007 and Cova 2013 and 2015 for further discussion of storage solutions in the Roman house).

However, chests and cupboards were not used just to store the more valuable household objects. A total of 1,069 artefacts were found in or in association with chests or cupboards, a fact that demonstrates their utilitarian function. These artefacts were made mainly of bronze (118), glass (83) and terracotta (151). Of these the largest number of artefacts were vessels (181), jewellery (118) and tools (113), with a limited number of lamps and gaming counters. The vessels consisted mainly of tableware, particularly jugs and bowls, with some plates, beakers and pans, and more rarely cups and ladles. Perfume bottles were also fairly common. In contrast, kitchenware and larger storage vessels were only rarely found in chests or cupboards, presumably because they were too big.

Most cupboards actually contained a mix of different types and category of artefact, although vessels usually predominated. Even chests that contained extremely rare artefacts, such as a crystal bowl and ladle found in the House of Fabius Amandus (I.7.3), also contained other forms of artefact (in this case a pair of tweezers, a commonware jug, two perfume bottles and a bronze pan). The chest and cupboard found together in the *atrium* of the House of the Beautiful Impluvium (I.9.1) contained, in addition to the 300 silver coins, a bronze lamp, jewellery (two gold bracelets, a gold ring), a silver mirror, a pumice stone, parts of a set of scales with relevant weights, two pairs of tweezers and a lead weight; many vessels made of silver, bronze and glass; and terracotta commonwares and finewares, including bowls, beakers, jugs, a bucket and four glass perfume bottles.

This is also seen in chests and cupboards discovered elsewhere in the town in other periods of the excavations (Mols 1994: 284). For example, during the excavations at the Villa Pisanella at Boscoreale, Pasqui reports that that two chests were discovered, one containing various types of glass bottle, and the second containing many glass vessels, four terracotta bowls, a couple of bronze pans and some toilet and surgical instruments (Pasqui 1897: 411–15, 477).

To summarize, storage-related furniture predominated in these Pompeian houses and was found throughout the houses and shops. In addition, we should remember that other means of storage, such as baskets, were probably used but have rarely survived. The contents of chests and cupboards were nearly always mixed, and they did not always contain valuable objects. This is not surprising – storage was obviously a major function of furniture, but it is interesting that much of this storage furniture was decorated or ornate in some way, whether with inset wood or carved bone fittings and appliqués. For example, decorative pieces of bone and bronze and a key were found with the cupboard in the portico of the House of Paquius Proculus (I.7.1); the chest in the *atrium* of the house annexed to the House of the Ephebe (I.7.18) had gilded bronze studs and a key. This is a utilitarian piece of furniture, unlike the elaborate items described in many literary sources, yet it was often located in open areas of the house where it would have been seen by both inhabitants and visitors to the house. This suggests that it was also one of the elements of the house that was intended to be on display and could add to the impression of the wealth or status of a house.

Beds and Couches

Beds were the next most common item of furniture. Mols (1994: 280) identified three types of bed at Herculaneum: beds for sleeping, couches for dining and cradles/cots for children (no cots or cradles have been found at Pompeii). In *insulae*

7, 8 and 9 at Pompeii, the remains of twenty-seven wooden beds were found in sixteen properties (fourteen houses and two shops/workshops). In ten cases the evidence consisted of the negative imprints of beds in the volcanic ash; in seventeen more cases only the metal and bone fittings of the beds were found. From these remains, it is impossible to tell whether these beds were used for sleeping or eating, or whether they were used for both these activities. However, most were found in small rooms, which may support Nissin's claim that beds were used primarily for sleeping rather than daytime use (Nissin 2016). In addition, the frequent discovery of associated bone or ivory ornamental plaques and fittings as part of the remains of wooden beds suggests that they were often ornate.

Groups of wooden beds were rare, and were clearly related to dining activities. The remains of two wooden beds, including a beautiful and expensive silver armrest (*fulcrum*), were found in the indoor *triclinium* of the House of the Ephebe (I.7.10–12; see Mols 1994: 280). This house also contained a unique set of bronze statuettes, the so-called *placentarii*, 'pastry cooks' holding serving dishes (Maiuri 1925; Vanesse 2016), which were all found packed away in chests (which can probably be explained by the extensive evidence for building work going on in this house), and also some marble statues and the bronze statue of an ephebe that gave the house its modern name. The statues might have been used to adorn the *triclinium*, but were more probably used to decorate the outdoor *triclinium* found in the peristyle of this house. This consisted not only of masonry beds and table, all covered in marble veneer, but also a *nymphaeum* and fountain, a pergola and a number of statue bases, with nearby a circular marble seat and marble table (Barrett 2017; see Figure 4.7). Evidence that similarly elaborate settings were created in other houses can be seen in the peristyle of the House of Paquius Proculus (I.7.1), where the remains of wooden *triclinium* beds were discovered along with a fountain and basin, in the garden of the so-called Writers' Workshop (I.7.15/16/17) where, on a less expensive scale, a masonry *triclinium* was painted to imitate marble, and in the peristyle of the House of Vetutius Placidus (I.8.9), which was half-covered in marble slabs.

Tables

Evidence of only two wooden tables was found: the decorative fittings of a small three-legged table in the House of Paquius Proculus (I.7.1) and the fragmentary remains of a table in the House of Ceres (I.9.13), but it is likely that there were more simple wooden tables that did not survive the eruption of Vesuvius. Indeed, marble and travertine single-legged supports (*monopodia*) without tabletops were found in nine houses and one shop. The tabletops were probably made from wood, and thus also perished during or after the eruption (Pernice 1932; Moss 1988: 96; wooden tabletops are also described in the literary sources, e.g. Martial 9.22.5; 14.90). In contrast, eleven marble tables

FIGURE 4.7: Garden *triclinium* in the House of the Ephebe (I.7.10–12). Credit: Joanne Berry, with permission of the Parco Archeologico di Pompei.

were found in eight houses. In general, the heavy marble or travertine *monopodia* and tables would not have been easily moveable; they were found predominantly in open areas such as *atria* and peristyles where they could have been used both for practical purposes and to display objects. In at least one case, the House of Vetutius Placidus (I.8.9), a travertine *monopodium* supported a marble tabletop upon which was set an Egyptian vase.

Seating

Seating was surprisingly rare in these Pompeian houses. Partly this may be because the habit of reclining on couches to eat, standard for formal entertainment in the elite and well beyond, meant that there was less need for chairs for entertaining, but other types of seating are missing too. Evidence for wooden stools was found in only one house (the House of Fabius Amandus, I.7.3 *atrium*) and two shops (I.7.5 and I.9.2). There was only one marble bench, which was found in the garden of the richly appointed House of the Ephebe (I.7.10–12). The literary sources tell us about many different types of chair, stool and bench. We know that there were benches in public places, for example, and we have representations of chairs and stools in wall-paintings and on reliefs, relating mainly to scenes of luxury or of work. But at Pompeii (and Herculaneum, where only one wooden stool has been found) the evidence is scarce. It is certainly possible that this type of furniture simply did not survive the eruption (for example, wooden benches located in peristyle gardens would have been buried in the layers of *lapilli* and thus decomposed), or that the excavators did not record it, but it remains surprising that there are only three examples of seats in this sample. There are other possible seating arrangements, however. The inhabitants of the houses may have sat on chests or on beds, and an ornate bed could easily have served a formal purpose – it could have functioned as a substitute for a chair, for example, during the morning *salutatio* (Nissin 2009: 97; Nissin 2015: 98). A small number of beds were found in areas such as *tablina* in some atrium houses. But even if all houses had beds, and beds were also used for sitting, it is important to note that not all inhabitants of the houses may have been able to use them. Slaves, for example, were surely not allowed to sit on elegant pieces of furniture. Furthermore, we can question whether all inhabitants of ancient houses actually needed seating. An examination of the skeletal evidence from Pompeii revealed evidence of lateral squatting facets on the tibia of a large proportion of the population. This is a modification of the ankle that is thought to be caused by habitual squatting, and thus it may well be that many of the inhabitants of Pompeii and other ancient towns habitually squatted to work, eat, play games and so on, and that the ability to be seated on a chair or bed was a marker of high status (Lazer 2009: 244–5; Dunbabin 2003: 80–5).

Finally, I want to pull this discussion together in a single example, the House of Ceres (I.9.13), which was excavated in 1951. This was a fairly standard medium-sized *atrium* house, which was at least 100 years old in 79 CE and in fairly poor decorative condition. The excavation reports are detailed for this house, which may explain the surprisingly large amount of evidence for wooden furniture that was found inside it, including the fittings, fixtures and ornamentation of beds and cupboards, plus a small wooden table. In particular, the excavators were able to make plaster casts of six items of furniture in four different rooms, which helps us to understand how the space was organized in 79 CE. As can be seen in Figure 4.8, furniture was found in almost every room of the house. Chests and cupboards dominated the space, and were filled with a mixture of domestic artefacts, which emphasizes the importance of storage in the house. These chests and cupboards were not all hidden away in closed rooms; four were clearly on display in the *atrium* and garden portico. Similarly, four beds were found in smaller rooms, but there was also one in the open *tablinum*, which was probably not for sleeping but may have been used for seating or for eating. With the exception of the beds, there was no evidence of seating. Evidence of ivory and bone plaques and ornate bronze studs suggests that much of this furniture had decorative features and was intended to be seen. The marble table in the atrium might have had a practical purpose, but potentially it was also an item of display furniture. Taken as a whole, the range and extent of furniture in this house reveals that furniture was ubiquitous, that

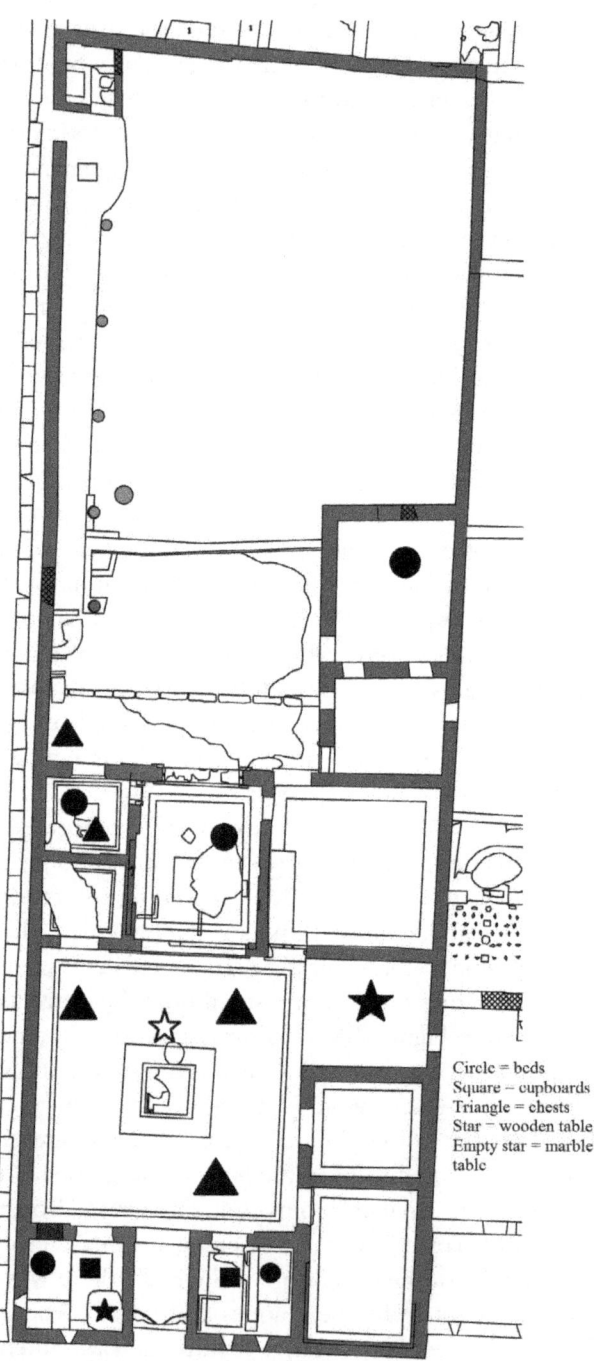

FIGURE 4.8: Plan of the House of Ceres (I.9.13). Credit: Sophie Hay (British School at Rome/University of Reading Pompeii Project).

cupboards, chests and beds were the most common types used in the home, and that these semi-fixed features were not simply utilitarian but may have been intended to be on display.

CONCLUSION

The evidence from *insulae* 7, 8 and 9 in Region I of Pompeii corroborates Mols's claim that there was more furniture, particularly wooden furniture, than expected in the ancient house, and that it was distributed across houses of all sizes. It is important to remember that the evidence from Pompeii does not represent a complete record of everything in use in 79 CE, so probably there was even more wooden furniture at that time. This must have been the case in other parts of the ancient world too, both Greek and Roman. Although the literary and visual sources tell us about elaborate and expensive items of furniture, the majority of furniture in use was probably fairly simple and utilitarian. Most people would not have had expensive furniture in their houses. At the same time, there is evidence that even simple wooden furniture had the potential to be used to display wealth or aspirations to visitors to a house. Wood might be elaborately decorated with carvings and inlay, or with bone, ivory and bronze fittings, and marble tables and *monopodia* could be used to add elegance to the home as well as having a practical domestic use. Although this evidence is missing from the majority of ancient houses, it is clear that semi-fixed features had the potential to have a profound impact on the articulation, use and display of different areas in the house, from creating particular settings for dining and entertaining to impress visitors to highlighting social differences between members of the household (for example, who had access to cupboards and who was permitted to use a bed). Thus furniture and furnishings were multifaceted tools that were essential to the everyday functioning of the ancient home.

ACKNOWLEDGMENTS

I'd like to thank Molly Swetnam-Burland, Sarah Bond, Mark Humphries, Maria Pretzler and Stephen Harrison for reading and commenting on the first draft of this chapter.

CHAPTER FIVE

Home and Work

NICOLAS TRAN

This chapter aims at exploring some of the manifold relations between home and work in the Classical world. Strictly speaking, it does not focus on the most frequent work relationship, which concerns the work of domestic staff. During the entire period of Greek and Roman antiquity, aristocratic households represented workplaces, for male and female servants who were often – but not always – slaves. The readers of the *Odyssey* internalized this model during the whole Classical era. Most of the time, those domestics lived and worked at the same place, assuming more or less specialized and skilled tasks. Inscriptions from large funerary monuments, built in Rome at the beginning of the Principate, and called *columbaria* by historians, reflect such a division of labour. For example, bedchamber servants (*cubicularii*) shared the intimacy of their masters, while cooks (*coci*) and their assistants sustained them. Servants were sometimes so numerous that they were divided into *decuriae*, at least according to Petronius (*Satyricon* 48), in a fictional and humorous context. But as impressive as they are, *columbaria* should not obscure the fact that even humble households included a few servants. Even if he lived in a very modest *casula*, the Italian peasant of the *Moretum* – a Latin poem attributed without certainty to Virgil – houses an African slave woman (*Moretum* 32, 61 and 67). Among novel characters, even the worst miser, the pawnbroker Milo created by Apuleius in his *Metamorphoses*, possesses a female servant, although he chose to live in a tiny house (*Metamorphoses* 1.21). In sum, anyone who could afford it was served, in his home, by domestics.

Moreover, work in and for the household was not confined to personal service, house maintenance and supply. Very often and during the whole of antiquity, manufacturing activities took place in household contexts. Typically, spinning and weaving were reserved to free or slave women, in the Greek *gynaecium*, in particular. Nevertheless, this textile production is interesting, in more ways than one. Indeed, archaeologists are sometimes impressed by the abundance of its remains, when they find far too many loom weights for a production and consumption restricted to an *oikos* or *domus*. A specific form of 'domestic' labour, broadly defined, can be distinguished. It corresponds to independent work, accomplished by all or part of the household, undertaken for private customers. It is this that forms the specific topic of this chapter. It deals with urban contexts, where domestic spaces are also workplaces occupied by craftsmen and/or shopkeepers. These men and women produced and/or sold goods consumed outside the household.

Prima facie, such an approach can seem quite narrow, but it is not so limited, for several reasons. First, recent studies have revealed how frequent this form of labour was during antiquity. This emerges in particular from research into craftsmanship and trade in the Roman cities of the Vesuvian area. Specialists have long claimed that those towns had very singular characteristics in the decades prior to their destruction. Indeed, one should avoid over-generalization, produced by tacking realities specific to Pompeii and Herculaneum onto other contexts. Such methodological cautions are useful. Yet material remains and textual evidence reveal that ancient houses developed manufacturing and commercial activities centuries before and after the eruption of 79 CE. Furthermore, the study of those dwellings contributes to the understanding of several important topics. On the one hand, it helps to visualize in a different way, and in all its diversity, the place of crafts and trades in ancient towns, just as with the place of craftsmen and retailers in Greek and Roman societies. On the other hand, it underlines the extent to which domestic spaces had many functions and were not only residential.

A LONGUE DURÉE PHENOMENON: LIVING IN THE WORKPLACE IN ANCIENT GREECE

Sometimes called 'mixed units' by archaeologists, houses including workshops are now better understood as an architectural form combining residence and labour in the ancient Greek world (Hellmann 2010: 118–27). Pottery ovens and metallurgical installations are already attested in eighth-century BCE housing, in Attica and Euboea. Nevertheless, for two decades and sometimes on the basis of older excavations, Classical and Hellenistic Greece has been the subject of the most numerous and innovative investigations. They highlight houses with working areas more or less separated from residential parts, in diverse regions of Greece, from the fifth century BCE to the imperial era (see Bonini 2006: 105). The southern edge of the Athenian Agora, in the district of the Areopagus and the surroundings of the Pnyx, provides much evidence. A few fifth-century BCE houses, among the dozen excavated by American teams from 1931 onwards, present 'a dual purpose of living and working' (Nevett 1999: 90). In the second half of the fifth century BCE, a cobbler seems to have occupied the so-called 'House of Simon' (Tsakirgis 2005: 70–5). Nothing proves that he bore that name, which is engraved on a cup discovered near – but not inside – the building. It consisted of at least two rooms opening onto a courtyard, where archaeologists have found hundreds of small nails and bone eyelets. Some blades and a needle tend to confirm the type of work practised here. Nearby, on the slopes of the Areopagus, is the district conventionally defined as the Street of the Marble Workers (Lawton 2006: 17–20). Such professionals lived in the House of Mikion and Menon, as shown by the discoveries of debris of raw material, of an unfinished statue, and of specific tools, in particular in the street-facing rooms. As a matter of fact, Athenian evidence suggests that openings onto public space and courtyards were used to welcome customers.

These houses of Athenian artisans were located in residential and densely populated neighbourhoods. They were hardly distinguishable from the other dwellings, even if their occupants gave themselves the means to work there. Well integrated into the urban landscape, craftsmanship does not seem marginal at all. Textual evidence from the fourth century BCE confirms that houses with a workshop opened onto the streets. At Piraeus, a stele engraved in the last quarter of the century (*IG* II^2 2496, esp. lines 9–11) provides evidence of a lease of an atelier (*ergastêrion*) adjoining a dwelling (*oikêsis*). Aeschines may allude to such a spatial organization in 346/5 BCE, in his speech:

> For it is not the lodgings and the houses which give their names to the men who have lived in them, but it is the tenants who give to the places the names of their own pursuits. Where, for example, several men hire one house and occupy it, dividing it between them, we call it 'apartment house', but where one man only dwells, a 'house'. And if perchance a physician moves into one of these shops on the street, it is called a 'surgery'. But if he moves out and a smith moves into the same shop, it is called a 'smithy'; if a fuller, a 'laundry'; if a carpenter, a 'carpenter's shop'; and if a pimp and his harlots, from the trade itself it gets its name of 'brothel'. So that you made many house a brothel by the facility with which you have plied your profession.
> —*Against Timarchus* 1.124, Loeb trans.

Outside of Athens and Attica, Olynthos, before its destruction by Philip II of Macedon (in 348 BCE), sheds an exceptional light on Greek houses at the end of the Classical era. In this Chalcidian city, about a quarter of homes have provided hints of manufacturing activities (Cahill 2002: 236–65; 2005: 54–60). And this rate must be considered as a minimal reflection of reality, because excavators have long neglected this kind of find. For instance, 300 loom weights come from two rooms of House A viii 7/9. Given that, depending on its size, a loom required between twenty and thirty weights, the presence of seven to fifteen looms is probable. This gives an indication of how many individuals worked in this single house and it is sufficient to demonstrate that their production was destined for sale. Here, the number of artefacts determined the identification of a 'mixed unit'. The situation is sometimes much less obvious, because it is difficult to define a threshold beyond which production for sale is certain. In other cases, the presence of more or less important equipment or of diverse tools is noticeable. There was a cistern and a basin suitable for washing clay in House B i 5. This raw material and the thirteen moulds discovered in the same building were used to make figurines. Finally, unfinished objects found in other houses reveal manufacturing activities too. As in Athens, craftsmanship is not marginal. Houses with workshops are in the city centre and their production often takes place in the heart of the domestic space. Some of them transformed commodities produced in the countryside. For example, a miller probably occupied House A 6. Indeed, twelve millstones were in the courtyard, which involves the use of a quite abundant workforce.

During the Hellenistic era, the Ionian city of Priene gives evidence of about 500 houses, among which more than thirty incorporated workshops in their frontage. In addition, a number of smaller towns allow case studies and shed light on the domestic and professional environment of Greek artisans. In the late fourth century or the early third century BCE, a coroplast from Halos, in Thessaly, lived in a 200 m² house (on the ground floor), divided into eight rooms (Reinders and Prummel 2003). In the eastern part, an area opening onto the street was devoted to work, as shown by the numerous figurines and moulds discovered here (Figure 5.1). The living rooms were in the western part. However, Delos represents the Hellenistic city the houses of which are the best known. Research has long focused on the richest households, but more recent studies have explored modest housing (Trümper 1998, 2003, 2005). These houses indicate that work was integrated into the city in very diverse manners. Small rooms that had wide openings onto the street – a sort of Delian counterpart of Italian *tabernae* – were an important component of the urban landscape. It is often impossible to determine if they served as dwellings or not, but a few walls are still well enough preserved to reveal beam holes, thus providing traces of habitable upper floors. These remains recall the 'small upstairs rooms' (*hyperôia*) mentioned by inscriptions from the island (Hellmann 1992: 423–6). Rental contracts for the properties of the great sanctuary of Delos confirm relations between *ergastêria* and *oikia* emphasized in archaeological reports. Other shops formed part of buildings which could cover areas greater than 60m², without having the shape of proper houses.

Finally, houses were provided with premises for sale or manufacture. An original feature of Delos, compared to Pompeii, is that such spaces were absent

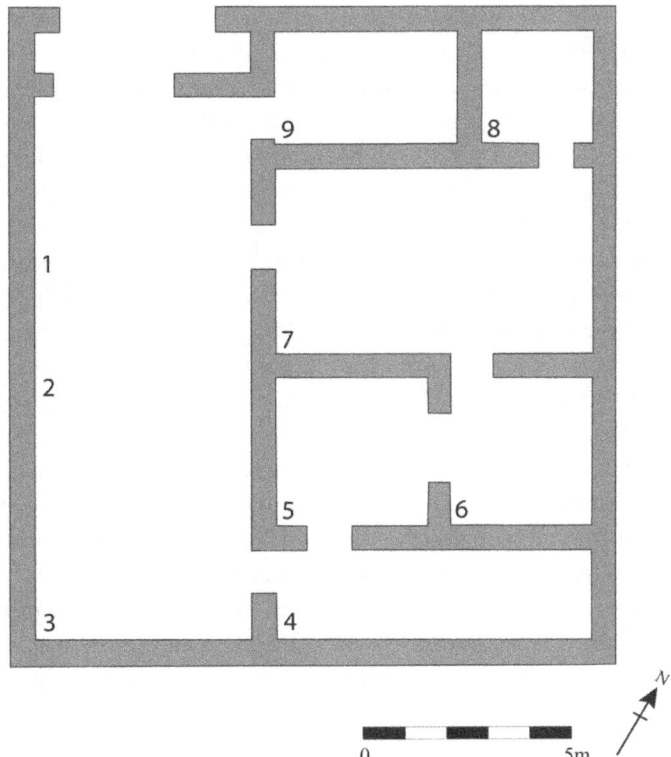

FIGURE 5.1: Plan of the Coroplast's House, Halos. Credit: Sophie Hay after Hendrik Reiners.

in four out of five elite dwellings. Thus, this phenomenon was typical of buildings of low or average social standing. In the *Quartier du Stade*, House I B accommodated a perfumery, built around 100 BCE (Brun 2000: 287–90). Excavations carried out in 1997 demonstrated that not only two olive press beds but also four furnaces were tied to this activity. Furnaces and cauldrons were used to mix hot oil and aromatic substances. In short, domestic spaces closely linking home and work pertained to a phenomenon of *longue durée*, which was both coherent and very diverse in its forms, in Greece as well as in Rome.

TABERNAE AND *DOMUS*: DIVERSE LIVING AND WORKING UNITS IN THE ROMAN WORLD

In Rome and in the Empire, not all the artisans and retailers inhabited their workplace, but such was the way of life of at least a significant proportion of them (Tran 2013: 317–19). One cannot quantify this phenomenon, but it was important enough to mark urban landscapes deeply. *Tabernae* were a characteristic element. From a material point of view, they were located on the frontage of diverse buildings (houses, private or public buildings of any kind), and opened onto the street through wide thresholds and were shuttered with planks of wood (Montcix 2010: 42–6). Some of them had a back store and/or an upper floor, which consisted of a *pergula* (when it covered the entire floor space) or a more basic mezzanine (Pirson 1999: 19–20). Hence, a famous painted inscription mentions the rent of *tabernae cum pergulis suis* in the Pompeian *Insula Arriana Polliana* (CIL IV, 138; see Pirson 1997).

In Roman cities, tenants often inhabited their *tabernae*, except the smallest ones. Clear evidence is available, even if ancient texts are sometimes very allusive. During the late republican era, Cicero described the modest living conditions of Roman shopkeepers. Catiline's supporters made trouble around shops (*concursare circum tabernas*) and prompted *tabernarii* to join their insurrection. Yet these agitators failed eventually, because shopkeepers prioritized their concerns about the safety of their workplaces (*operis et quaestus cotidiani locus*), where their bed (*cubile ac lectulum*) was (Cicero, *In Catilinam* 4.8.17).

A case study offered by the jurist Alfenus Varus, who lived during the first century BCE, implied too that *tabernarii* often slept in their workplaces (*Digest* 9.2.52.1). A thief awakens a shop tenant in the middle of the night, they fight and the stealer loses one eye:

> One night a shopkeeper had placed a lantern above his display counter which adjoined the footpath, but some passer-by took it down and carried it off. The shopkeeper pursued him, calling for his lantern, and caught hold of him; but in order to escape from his grasp, the thief began to hit the shopkeeper with the whip that he was carrying on which there was a spike. From this encounter, a real brawl developed in which the shopkeeper put out the eye of the lantern-stealer, and he asked my opinion as to whether he had inflicted wrongful damage, being in mind that he had been hit with the whip first.
>
> —trans. Watson

The best-preserved *tabernae* in the cities around the Vesuvius also provide archaeological evidence of their use as dwelling. Beds were found in two shops of Herculaneum. One of them was a wine shop (*Insula Orientalis* II.9–10). In Pompeii, where the eruption destroyed most wooden furniture, beds disappeared, but alcoves designed to accommodate them remain in several back shops. Other equipment, such as cisterns or latrines, confirms that *tabernae* were conceived as living places. And beyond the most material aspects of existence, some *lararia* and niches for statuettes imply that occupants considered their shops as their home. A painted inscription discovered in a Pompeian *taberna* located on the Via dell'Abbondanza (IX.11.2) illustrates such a feeling. Indeed, it proclaims that 'A good god lives here, in the house of Actius' (*CIL* IV, 8417: *Bonus deus hic [h]abitat, in do/mo / Act[ii]*).

Nevertheless, the *taberna* as a conventional designation and the generic description introduced previously are partly misleading. Indeed, they tend to give a too homogeneous image of accommodations and workplaces. In Pompeii, much larger units than ordinary *tabernae* have been classified in the same category, whereas they possessed at least three rooms besides their shop. Other towns in Italy, such as Ostia (Girri 1956; Schoevaert 2018) or in the provinces, such as Volubilis, in Mauretania Tingitana (Étienne 1960), bear witness to the same diversity, even in rows of *tabernae*, which are not as uniform as one could expect. The presence of technical equipment or, more generally, the practice of a specific craft explains the size of some premises. For instance, the workshop of Mustius, a Pompeian fuller, was centred on a room open to the street, in the back of which a small basin, three vats and a storage space were located (Pompeii VI.15.3. See Flohr 2013: 192–4; and Figure 5.2). Two small rooms surmounted by an upper floor might have been used for technical purposes too. Conversely,

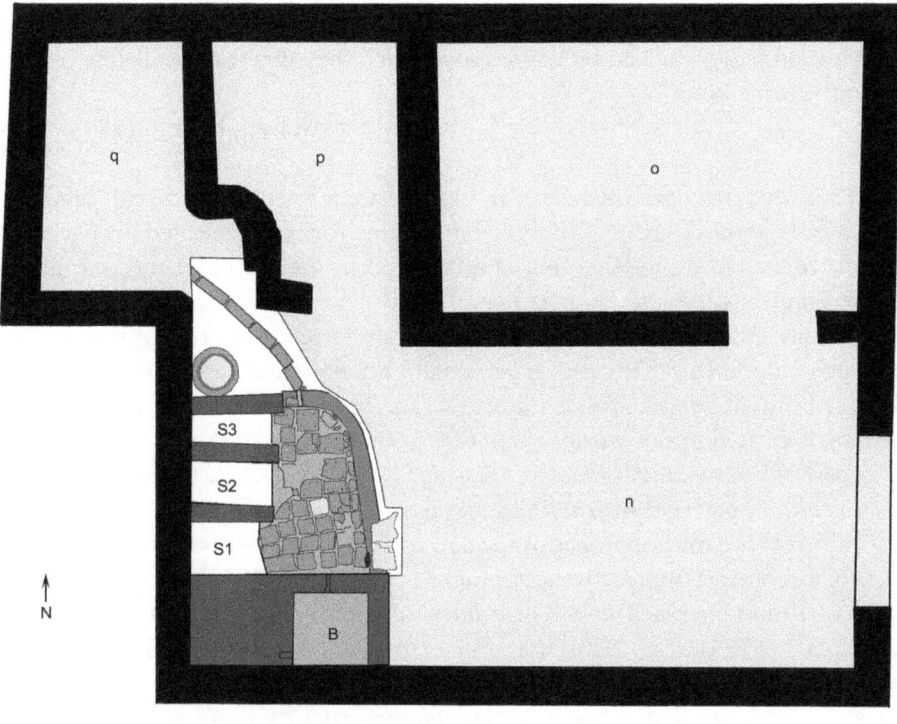

FIGURE 5.2: Plan of the fullery of Mustius, Pompeii. Credit: Miko Flohr.

the room the entrance of which was just to the right of the threshold looks like a residential space. Wall-paintings and terracotta, representing a chariot race of Cupids, decorated it. Quite elegant objects – bronze vessels and fineware pottery – were also found there. In Herculaneum, a *bottega con abitazione* (V.10–11) had two entrances and its plan shows a relative separation between commercial work and home (Monteix 2010: 300–12). It was a grocery shop, where customers could buy cereals, stored in a *dolium* embedded in a counter. A narrow door gave access to the residential part. It had not only a *cubiculum* (with a bed located in a recess), latrines and a *lararium*, but also a large living room decorated with a beautiful fresco. Through its size and layout, this kind of building corresponds to hybrid forms, between large *tabernae* and small *domus*.

Many Roman *domus* with *atria* had functions other than residential, because they welcomed retailing or manufacturing activities. This may surprise us, because we are used to a clear distinction between economic and residential functions in modern towns. Yet, as Wallace-Hadrill has underlined, this separation did not exist in antiquity:

> We distinguish the commercial from the residential; shops, workshops, offices, and factories from houses. The Roman town draws the lines elsewhere, and though spatial, architectural, and decorative contrasts were constructed between petty trade and dignified sociability, they might nevertheless coexist in the same house.
>
> —Wallace-Hadrill (1994: 118)

Nevertheless, beyond this general observation, an impression of diversity prevails. In some cases, economic activity seems very concentrated in space. So, in accordance to a model common at the end of the Republic and during the early Empire, *tabernae* flanked many house entrances (Gros 2001: 30–92). Shops and small workshops were sometimes related to the rest of the *domus*, through a door. In other cases, *tabernae* did not communicate directly with the house. Both situations are well attested. For instance, in Pompeii, one of the *tabernae* located in the *insula Arriana Polliana*, in front of the Via delle Terme, was part of the so-called 'House of Cuspius Pansa' (VI.6.22). It was linked with a *cubiculum* open to the *atrium* that the tenant might have used as a back store. By contrast, the four other shops located to the west only opened to the street. A similar contrast appears on a fragment of the *Forma Urbis*, the great marble plan of Rome engraved at the beginning of the third century CE (Rodriguez-Almeida 1981: 108, pl. XX). In the first situation, a member of the household would have exploited the *taberna*. Letting to a third party, who could be the master of an appointed slave (*seruus praepositus*), is more probable in the second case. Nonetheless, it would be vain to suppose a systematic correspondence between architectural structures and forms of management. In any case, house owners made a profit on the specific relations between their property and the work achieved by someone else. At least in the cities of the Vesuvian area, the real estate at issue was very diverse, which suggests that incomes from *tabernae* concerned several social groups.

When a workshop was included in a *domus* with *atrium*, its technical equipment could cover an area so great that archaeologists have questioned the existence of a residential function. Pompeii and Herculaneum concentrate a significant part of evidence of this phenomenon (Wallace-Hadrill 1994: 136). Consequently, researchers have wondered if the Vesuvian cities were an exception or not in the Roman Empire as a whole. According to Maiuri, who was in charge of those sites for decades, Pompeii and Herculaneum changed very specifically between the earthquake of 62 CE and the volcanic eruption of 79 CE. Elites, according to this thesis, would have fled to the countryside after the first event, while master craftsmen (members of a mercantile class) would have benefited from this situation to develop their activities in the vacant residential spaces (Maiuri 1942: 162–3, criticized e.g. by Wallace-Hadrill 1994: 122–3).

Yet archaeologists do not support this thesis anymore. Many houses with workshops did exist in Pompeii long before 62 CE. Above all, manufacturing activities took place in houses apart from Pompeii and Herculaneum, far beyond 79 CE. In the early third century CE, jurists dealt with structural changes that a usufructuary was not allowed to make in a *domus*. For example, a full owner could install a fullery inside, but a usufructuary had no right to do so (*Digest* 7.1.13.8; Modestinus, *Excuses* 4). Likewise, according to Severan jurists, a husband made a useful outlay when he built a bakery in a house belonging to his wife's dowry (*Digest* 25.1.6; Paulus, *Ad Sabinum* 7):

> [Useful expenses are ones which the husband usefully incurs and which improve the wife's property; that is her dowry,] for example, where a new plantation is established on the land, or where the husband adds a bakery or a shop to the house, or teaches the slaves some trade.
> —Paulus, *Ad Sabinum* 7, trans. Watson

Running a workshop and teaching slaves a trade, as Paulus envisages in this passage, could be very complementary activities (see also *Digest* 50.16.79.1; Paulus, *Ad Plautium* 6). In fact, in the third century CE, jurists considered as common buildings that comprised residential as well as productive spaces. These architectural forms seem very close to *domus* observed by archaeologists in Pompeii and Herculaneum.

Like *tabernae* and other premises studied before, houses with workshops appear quite diverse in the Vesuvian area. The House of the Labyrinth (Pompeii VI.11.8–10) is remarkable for its great size and its luxury. During the last decades of Pompeii, four rotating millstones and an oven – that is to say a bakery – were installed inside. This equipment was suitable for a much more copious production than any domestic consumption. P. Sextilius Rufus, a great Pompeian notable, probably owned the *domus*. The bakery exploited by his slaves would have completed his income, though he might have lived elsewhere (Capanna et al. 2012: 308–9). However, this house is the exception rather than the rule, insofar as most of the workshops took place in much more modest buildings. Archaeologists sometimes define them as 'average houses', which amounts to considering – more or less consciously – that their occupants belonged to the 'middle classes' of society. The House of the Fullonica of Herculaneum seems typical (Gros 2001: 83–4). Its stalls, its low walls and its vases, which could have contained fuller's earth, leave no doubt about the presence of a manufacturing activity in the final phase of the building. It was long and narrow and this layout allowed a clear separation between an economic space (a *taberna* and a storage room at the front) and a residential space (consisting of four rooms opening on the second *atrium*). The fuller and his family benefited from a quite neat decor, made of paintings designed before the creation of the workshop. In fact, architectural heterogeneity seems to result from a social and highly hierarchical organization of labour.

DIVERSITY OF HOME AND SOCIAL CONDITIONS OF WORKERS

Relations between home and work confirm that Greek and Roman craftsmen or traders formed a very heterogeneous category (Tran 2011, 2013). To admit this reality, we have to distance ourselves from a too binary vision of ancient societies, which tends to distinguish elites, on the one hand, from a undifferentiated mass of poor people, on the other hand. Yet it is not so easy to get rid of this simplistic view, because explicit testimony is lacking, and because distinctions to be perceived are quite subtle. The home belonging to characters of Apuleius' *Metamorphoses*, offering a detour through a fictional artwork, may suggest to us a helpful comparison.

In this mid-second-century CE novel, whose author transposes to Greece realities from his native Africa, a fuller and a baker come into play. Besides sharing the same destiny of cuckold, they belong to the same milieu. Nevertheless, a closer look shows that their homes and workplaces are different. Apuleius describes in a humorous way how tiny is the fuller's home. The craftsman is supposed to live with his wife in a *taberna* open to the street (*Metamorphoses* 9.25 alludes to the threshold of their shop, *limen tabernae*). And the discovery of his wife's adultery happens in a noticeable unity of place. He tells this story to his friend, the baker:

> She has been constantly meeting him for stolen embraces, and at the very moment when we came in for supper after our bath she and the same young

man were making love. Disturbed by our sudden arrival, she was forced into a hasty plan, and concealed him under a wicker cage formed of smoothly bent sticks rising to a narrow top, which was fumigated with white sulphur fumes to bleach the clothes hanging all round it. Since he was safely hidden, as she supposed, she confidently joined us for supper. Meanwhile the acrid, heavy odour of sulphur was eating into the young man. Overcome by the cloud of fumes, he began to grow limp from suffocation. Furthermore the sulphur, as is the natural property of that active chemical, caused him to sneeze repeatedly.
—9.24, Loeb trans.

The fuller dines in the immediate vicinity of his equipment and of the fabrics that he handled: he lived in his workshop. Apuleius invites the reader to imagine it as a single room, without any separation between technical and domestic spaces. This scheme does not correspond to a convention of writing, since a very different layout appears when the novelist describes the baker's house-workshop. He defines this building as a *domus*, after describing the fuller's dwelling as a *taberna*. This terminological variation coincides with two different forms of relation between work and home. Hence, the baker and his wife have a bedroom, near the workshop, where they can isolate themselves. The wife is able to order slaves to put Lucius – the narrator turned into a donkey – to work, without leaving her bed:

Such being the kind of woman she was, she persecuted me with extraordinary hatred. Even before dawn, while she was still in bed, she would shout out for the apprentice-ass to be yoked to the mill-wheel. Then the very moment she came out of her room she would insistently order me to be whipped over and over again while she watched.

—9.15

A little further in the story, the same *cubiculum* enables the baker to isolate himself from his workforce, with a magician who provokes his death:

This strange woman gently laid a hand on the baker's arm as if she had something to tell him privately, took him away to his own room, and remained there with the door shut for a very long time. But when all the grain which the workers had been dealing with was now processed and more had to be asked for, the slaves stood outside the door and called to their master to request a new supply to work on. After they had shouted several times at the top of their voice without any response from the master, they began to pound violently on the door. When they found that it was thoroughly bolted, suspecting that something was seriously amiss, they dislodged or broke the hinges with a powerful heave and finally forced their way in. The woman was nowhere to be seen, but they found their master hanging from a rafter and already dead.

—9.15

In short, the baker's house consisted at least of a room for the millstones, a stable, perhaps a dormitory for the slaves and certainly a bedroom for their master and his wife. There might be a reception room too, where the wife could dine with her friends (9.23). Anyway, this architectural image does not look like the fuller's *taberna* at all. This contrast is all the more interesting that the novel echoes archaeological evidence.

The tenants of the humblest Greek *ergastêria* or Roman *tabernae* literally lived 'in the middle of their work' (Flohr 2007: 142). Their material environment pointed not only their poverty, but also the centrality of work in their social existence. Domestic spaces were all the more confined in that craftsmen and retailers often lived in their workplaces with their family. To insist on the humble origins of Vatinius, a courtier of Nero, Tacitus calls him a *sutrinae tabernae alumnus*: he had grown up in a shoemaker's workshop (*Annals* 15.34.2). Likewise, in the *Satyricon*, Petronius makes Trimalchio – whose recent wealth was equalled only by his bad taste – pronounce this sentence: 'He who is born in a *pergula* does not dream of a palace', he says to his companion Fortunata (*Satyricon* 74.14). Furthermore, the lack of functional separation between work and residence, which was typical of modest *tabernae*, was a cause of discomfort. Indeed, artisanal production generated dirt, noise and bad smells. In sum, the social image of the shopkeepers was associated with poverty. To condemn the mischief of P. Clodius Pulcher, Cicero had some very harsh words to say about individuals who could have participated in riots provoked by this demagogic tribune, after closing their *tabernae*: they were nothing but a bunch of slaves, wageworkers, rogues and beggars (*De Domo Sua* 89: 'multitudo hominum ex seruis, ex conductis, ex facinerosis, ex egentibus congregatam'). Of course, the political and personal circumstances of his speech encourage Cicero to exaggerate: he is not an objective witness, let alone a sociological observer. Nevertheless, in a very different context, the poet Horace tends also to define *tabernae* as a living environment for the poor: 'pale death knocks alike at the shops of the poor and the towers of kings' (*Odes* 1.4.13–14: 'pallida Mors aequo pulsat pede pauperum tabernas regumque turris').

Following a logic already current in Classical Greece, some master artisans were well-to-do enough to be able to dissociate their family life and the exercise of their profession. The Campanian craftsmen who occupied *domus* with *atria* moved in environments that had little to do either with elite dwellings or with *tabernae*. Sometimes their houses reproduced the complementarity between shops and back shops, but at a very different scale. Technical and commercial installations were at the front, and residential spaces at the back. As in the case of the House of the Fullonica in Herculaneum, a Pompeian perfumery located on the Via degli Augustali (VII.4.24–5) had an elongated plan, because no lateral room opened to the *atrium*. Both houses also have in common the fact that artisanal activity was limited to their front part. The perfumer's workshop communicated with the street, through a *taberna* formed of two adjacent rooms (Brun and Monteix 2009: 123–8). Just behind, the Tuscan *atrium* was adorned by a fresco of Hercules. Between a *cubiculum* and the *tablinum*, a narrow corridor led to a kitchen, a painted *lararium* and latrines. From the *atrium* and the kitchen, one could reach a residential floor by way of stairs.

Beyond this division between front and back, Pompeian houses reveal other means to separate technical equipment from housing spaces. In the fullery of Lucius Veranius Hypsaeus (VI.8.20–1), a wall was built to hide artisanal activities, which occupied the western part of the peristyle (Flohr 2013: 207–8). So the latter could serve as a pleasant garden, adjoining the *domus* where the fuller and his family probably lived. Its entrance, upper floor and *atrium* were independent from the workshop. Yet the master craftsman may have used a large room located in the western part of the peristyle as a *triclinium* and his slaves may have slept in the *cubicula* open to the same courtyard. The famous painted pillar, representing the treatment of fabrics at its successive stages, reveals the fuller's mindset: his explicit attachment to a professional identity and the desire to live surrounded by elegant decor (Figure 5.3). These two

FIGURE 5.3: Painted pillar in the fullery of L. Veranius Hypsaeus, Pompeii. Credit: Fausto and Felice Niccolini 1854, *Le case ed i monumenti di Pompei*. DEA/ICAS94/Getty Images.

dimensions were not contradictory at all. Finally, few plans show a longitudinal separation between working and living spaces. It seems almost complete in the house of a baker, located on the Via dell'Abbondanza (I.12.1/2). From the sidewalk, visitors had access to an entrance hall and could reach either the residential part or the productive one. To the left, they entered a room with four millstones. Kneading and baking were done further south. The furthest independent rooms of this group might have served as dormitory for slaves. Placed on an axis with the entrance, the residential sector communicated with the bakery only through a narrow door of the *tablinum*. Nevertheless, not all the craftsmen settled in a house-workshop tried to isolate their living and reception places. Such a separation was only one manner among others to make a home pleasant and worthy of an honourable citizen.

Entrepreneurs pursued such goals by taking care of their home decoration. Again, they perceived no contradiction between an elegant environment and the existence of spaces devoted to economic activity. Such a combination already appears in the layout of Delian houses occupied by Italian businessmen. As Zarmakoupi (2015) has underlined, those interiors were arranged to satisfy economic needs as well as a desire for social affirmation. Indeed, in a few cases, workshops or storage rooms are on the ground floor, whereas the residential upper floor was adorned with care or even luxuriously. Moreover, facades with religious paintings, representing the worship of the *lares compitales*, drew attention to an Italian origin which was part of the occupants' professional identity. For instance, the House of the Seals received its conventional appellation after the discovery of 16,000 seals: most of them bear names of Italian families attested in Delos. While its ground floor was reorganized to welcome a workshop (maybe a mill), busts of the two owners decorated the upper floor (Brunet 1998: 686–7).

In Pompeii, the desire to live amid elegant decor, and to parade it to visitors, is obvious in the decoration of walls and floors. In the last years of the city, the jeweller Pinarius Cerialis lived in a house of 275 m^2 on the Via Nocera (Pompeii III.4.b). The discovery, in addition to few chisels, of a small box containing precious or semi-precious stones in different states of finish is linked with the craft of the last occupant. The courtyard was quite modest, in comparison to aristocratic norms, and the house consisted of six rooms, including a *triclinium*. One of the *cubicula* and an *exedra* had very beautiful frescoes, depicting mythological scenes. They count among the most refined examples of the fourth Pompeian style (*PPM* III: 435–77). Yet the other decorative schemes are more common, especially in the peristyle. This contrast tends to emphasize a division between economic activity and residential function, which the house plan does not indicate clearly.

The large tannery next to the city wall also had a pleasant reception space (I.5.2). In this summer *triclinium*, guests could admire a mosaic, famous for the representation of symbols of equality before death – a skull, a wheel, a butterfly, a coat, a bag and a stick useful for the great journey (*PPM* I: 185–92). This *emblema* in *opus vermiculatum* was probably an antique, made more than a century before. Wall-paintings participated in a same aspiration to domestic refinement. Nevertheless, the master artisan made his guests banquet in his workshop courtyard, with a view of the tanning installations. He can have felt neither embarrassment nor social awkwardness because of this plan.

To come back to the artisans of Apuleius' *Metamorphoses*, one great difference between the fuller and the baker consists in the presence of slaves in their home and workshop. The first unfortunate husband seems to possess no servant, while Apuleius mentions the baker's workforce several times (9.12, describing their tough working conditions). Where and how did the slaves of houses with a workshop live? It is difficult to answer this question, whether in general, or in the light of the archaeological traces. The quest for dormitories, in Pompeii or Volubilis for instance, leads to plausible hypotheses. But proofs are often lacking, because domestic spaces were multifunctional. Even so, houses with workshops deserve to be considered not only as architectural complexes, but also as social spaces, where employees worked under the orders of their master or his representatives (Nevett 2010: 90, à propos Wallace-Hadrill 1988).

The greatest 'mixed units' were probably based on servile labour, from Classical Greece onwards. Indeed, houses with workshops in Athens and Olynthos echo literary evidence. From his father, Demosthenes inherited a furniture workshop, which had been entrusted to a manager (27.18–26, 28.12). Twenty slaves worked and seem to have lived in it. In the *Quartier du Stade* of Delos, the perfumer settled in House I B could have employed several employees, unlike more humble professionals (Brun 2000: 285–7) – this perfumery was larger than the one installed in House III O, in the *Quartier du Stade*. However, apart from conjectures, the integration of servile labour into domestic spaces remains hardly discernible. It is not surprising, since this low visibility concerns all slaves, regardless of their activities: exceptions are rare. In Pompeii, the name of M. Terentius Eudoxsus was painted on the facade of a house, where a workshop was probably located (Pompeii VI.13.6.8–9; *CIL* IV, 4456). Eleven names – female, at least in most cases – were inscribed on a column of the peristyle. A weight indication and a word related to thread (*trama*, *statem* or *suptenem*) follow each of them (Monteix 2010: 175–6). Settled in a nice house, Eudoxsus probably employed spinsters (professional spinners). Nobody is able to determine if they lived here or not, but their presence made Eudoxsus' *domus* exceptional. Hierarchical work relations shaped socially this kind of house-workshop.

Before concluding, it is important to clear up a potential misunderstanding. The brief overview offered here has aimed to outline over the *longue durée* the architectural complexes defined as 'mixed' because they had a double function:

residential and economic. Such material structures existed in Greece and in the Roman Empire for nearly a millennium. An impression of continuity – from Olynthos to Pompeii and from Athens to Volubilis – could emerge. Yet the permanence of houses with workshops should not induce us to ignore the singularity of each historical context or to minimize changes. It would be presumptuous to judge that Maiuri and the scholars who support his theses were completely wrong, when they emphasized the urban and social specificities of Pompeii and Herculaneum, in the last decades of those cities. Yet their distinctiveness resulted from a particular combination of factors that did not come out of nowhere in 62 CE and did not disappear after 79 CE. Furthermore, the Greek and Roman 'mixed units' formed a very heterogeneous category, not only in time and space but also from a social point of view. The relations between 'home' and 'work' affected and linked different strata of ancient societies. The house with workshop, then, is not a constant. On the contrary, it reveals how diverse and complex were the social structures tied to Greek and Roman domestic spaces.

CHAPTER SIX

Gender and Home

KATE WILKINSON

'Home' and 'gender' appear obvious. They are not. Gender has a troubled history as an analytical category. Its contours are still under debate in feminist theory, the humanities and the social sciences. Since its introduction as a description for masculine and feminine roles as distinct from biological sex, 'gender' has won fierce defenders and detractors. Within academia, it is commonplace to distinguish sex and gender; in ordinary English conversation the two are used as synonyms. For the purposes of this essay, I will treat 'gender' as the ideology of masculine and feminine which maps, very imperfectly, onto biological sex. That all males count as men and all females count as women will not be taken for granted. 'Home' might not seem to be an analytical category at all, but once one tries to define it, the term also tends to reflect an ideology rather than an object. A home is not, after all, a house. The discussion of what counts as one's 'true home' is endless. Not all living spaces count as homes. Think of dormitories, prisons, military barracks, RV parks, nursing homes. Every one of the functions of a home – from sleep, to eating, to sex, to property acquisition, to child-rearing – can be done elsewhere. The ancient terms *oikos* and *domus* map reasonably well onto the current English usage of 'home,' but I will emphasize how both promoted very specific ideologies of social class, gender and citizenship.

While gender and home were (and are) ideas motivated by concerns of power and status, real sexed persons lived in real spaces throughout antiquity. How they truly lived their day-to-day lives is at least as important as the ideas about how they should have been living. Unfortunately, almost all of the remaining evidence points towards the ideal (or the worst-case scenario) rather than how people negotiated ideals in ordinary living. Moreover, the evidence is almost entirely produced by and for upper-class men. The thoughts of the majority of the population are simply unavailable or badly skewed to one particular geographical region. For example, nearly every piece of evidence from this very long time period indicates that upper-class citizen women should stay at home, but that there were some occasions for going out. Almost nothing can tell us how often 'seldom' was or what 'an appropriate occasion' might have been.

This chapter will be limited, very artificially, to Greek and Roman evidence. The many variations found within cultures under Hellenic and Roman rule would add to the richness of the discussion but would over-extend the capacity of this brief overview of an already complex topic covering a very long span of time and wide span of geography.

HOME AS REPRODUCTIVE AND EROTIC SPACE

The home, *oikos* or *domus*, was in antiquity, as it often remains, the privileged space for patrilineal reproduction and primary locus of heritable property. Both the Greek *oikos* and Roman *domus* included house, furnishings and persons, as well as land and animals in rural settings. A household might contain only a few persons or hundreds, in the case of imperial households, but the centre of the home was a single male lineage, father to son, if at all possible, but in practice including brothers, paternal relations and adopted sons from related families. This male lineage was, by definition, a lineage of free citizens. Status as a free person counted much more than wealth in the establishment of a home. Slaves in both the Greek and Roman contexts could accrue real wealth, but the legalities of inheritance and legal status of children of slaves made the patrilineal transfer of property nearly impossible. Male slaves who had been manumitted might set up a home and bequeath property to their children, but usually maintained close ties to the household of a former owner. Roman freedmen, for instance, set up funerary monuments for deceased former owners, suggesting they still considered themselves very much part of the former owner's *domus*. The emphasis on male-line inheritance does not mean that women could not or did not both inherit wealth and bequeath it at death. Law varied greatly from place to place within the Greco-Roman world and over time. Female inheritance, however, was never at the centre of the ideology of home. The key role of the free citizen woman was to assure the purity of patrilineal inheritance through her strict sexual fidelity to her licit husband. Semonides in the sixth century BCE pours forth a wave of misogyny on lazy, dirty, ugly, stupid, spendthrift, ill-tempered, gluttonous, crafty women and admits of only one sort of woman who will make a good wife.

> One sort is the bee woman: lucky the man who gets her! For to her alone no blame attaches, but life flourishes under her and increases. She grows old,

loving with her loving husband, and bears a fine and famous family. She is outstanding among all women, and godlike grace surrounds her. Nor does she take pleasure in sitting with women gossiping about sex. Zeus grants men such women as a gift, the best and the most thoughtful.
—Semonides 7.85–93; trans. Andrew Wallace-Hadrill

This emphasis on the reproduction of legitimate heirs to the masculine line never wavers. Roman tombstones praise women for producing children resembling their fathers. When later Christian moralists try to condemn divorce of legal wives for infertility, they are going against the grain, and likely failing. Indeed, the only acceptable cause for divorce among Christians was closely tied to patrilineal concerns. In the Gospel of Matthew, Jesus allows divorce only in the case of a woman's sexual immorality (Matthew 19.9). John Chrysostom, in the late fourth century CE, promotes the replacement of lewd singing at weddings (to encourage fertility) with a solemn clerical blessing, an innovation he promises will promote fatherhood and a prosperous family life. Despite the new anti-family tendencies in the Christianizing world, the reproductive goal of the home remains central.

A key function of the home was to assure and display the free citizen woman's fidelity. Authors from Homer up until the invasion of Roman territory by Germanic peoples agreed that the citizen woman's place was in the home. Authors claim that it was most suitable to their delicate nature. To describe a woman as 'white-armed' in the Homeric literature referred to her indoor life and avoidance of the sun. In Classical Athens, at least, men and women lived in separate quarters in the house. How strict was the seclusion of women and maintenance of separate living spaces? This seems to have varied considerably by time period and geography, not to mention degree of wealth. The very wealthy were in a much better position to guard free women in absolute domestic seclusion. Not all free women would have had access to the same numbers of male and female servants to send on errands. In Greece, carrying water from wells was female work that was ideally performed by servants, but some families could not have done without the labour of free women. Spartan girls were encouraged to do outdoor exercise, in order to improve health for child-bearing. Freeborn Roman women were much less secluded and segregated than their Greek counterpoints, although the ideal of staying at home remained paramount. *Domiseda*, literally 'stay-at-home', was a term of praise on one woman's funerary inscription (*ILS* 8402).

In addition to temporal and geographical variation, one must keep in mind that any ideal of free female domesticity was constantly negotiated. The straightforward imprisonment of wives and daughters was not practicable or praiseworthy. Many ethnographic accounts of the seclusion and/or segregation of women in contemporary societies note the importance of talking, and even arguing, about the correct way to enact seclusion and segregation on a day-to-day basis. A Muslim folk healer in Hyderabad, India, sees unrelated (and even non-Muslim) men in her house as part of her healing practice because the business functions as an extension of her domestic space. In another context, she would sit in another room or veil and recede from social interaction while her husband entertained the very same men (Flueckiger 2006: 52). Ethnographers also comment on the many ways men and women communicate across lines of separation while maintaining social honour. The same Muslim folk healer sits behind a dividing curtain, *purdah*, at a Sufi musical gathering and pulls and pushes the curtain where she wants it, complaining to her disciples on the other side, 'Don't you think we women want to see?' (Flueckiger 2006: 218). There are many indications that the seclusion and separation of freeborn women in antiquity was similarly flexible and open to discursive manipulation. When Christianity began to shift the language of marital fidelity to the 'brides of Christ', consecrated virgins, they also emphasized seclusion in the house while simultaneously noting the occasions and ways that this might be negotiated. Pelagius comments that the young senatorial woman Demetrias will already know, from her gentle and noble rearing, to leave the house rarely – except for visits to church and charitable visits, of course. He also suggests that she not allow *too many* visits from friends and clients in her personal bedchamber (*Letter to Demetrias* 22.2). In many ways, the woman's reputation for staying at home, and therefore for being chaste and securing the legitimate male line, was highlighted by carefully chosen outings and being *seen* to be at home.

If the home was meant to secure a free woman's sexual exclusivity, it was also the idealized space for fertile conjugal pleasure. While a freeborn husband was expected to show more respect to a wife than a slave or prostitute, he was also expected to enjoy sex with his wife and she with him. Erotic themes were common on household items such as vessels, lamps, mosaics and wall-paintings. Paintings in the conjugal bedroom sometimes showed the shy bride encouraged to join her husband in satisfying, and ideally fertile, lovemaking. In the *Oeconomicus*, written by Xenophon in the fourth century BCE, and again 500 years later in Plutarch's *Advice to the Bride and Groom*, wives and husbands are encouraged to solve disputes in the bedroom and come together regularly for mutual pleasure, not only for producing offspring. Free women's beautification routines were closely associated with conjugal pleasure and fertility. Although moralists inveighed against cosmetics, perfumes, jewellery, fine clothes and elaborate hairstyling, the tools of beautification were etched on women's funerary monuments, portraits celebrated wifely beauty, and ordinary correspondence listed beautification equipment along with household items and weaving tools. The Projecta casket, which was either commissioned by or later purchased by a Christian owner, shows a matron undergoing her beauty routine (Figure 6.1). She is aided by female attendants and the dolphins of

FIGURE 6.1: Projecta casket. Credit: The British Museum.

Venus/Aphrodite surround her. Her beautification for erotic ends is integral to her role as a successful wife and mother.

The expectation of conjugal pleasure in the domestic setting was not so much replaced as redefined in the Christian era. Worldly erotic pleasure was a forgivable sin, if practised within the bounds of marriage, but far better was a spiritual eroticism. The divine Bridegroom replaced the human husband for the female virgin – and the male celibate. The soul being intrinsically feminine in relation to God, both men and women could become 'brides of Christ' or fictive eunuchs. The domestic spaces evoked in the Song of Songs aided in the development of what one might call the spiritually erotic home. A scene from a martyrdom written sometime between the late fifth and seventh centuries CE, at a time when the *cubiculum* was starting to disappear from domestic architecture in the West, imagines a young saint and her bridegroom reinventing their wedding night as a chaste union between bride, groom and glowing angel, who crowns them with heavenly garlands rather than wedding wreathes (Sessa 2007: 195).

The goal of pleasure was offspring. Greeks and Romans did practise birth control, abortion and infanticide in cases where additional legitimate children, especially girls, would be economic burdens. Rates of infant mortality, and mortality in general, however, were high enough to keep fertility a perpetual concern. Augustus' family laws famously rewarded parents who bore three or more children by granting them *ius liberorum*, which gave preference to men in political appointments and women the right to function in legal affairs without the consent of a male guardian. The home was the idealized space for conception, birthing, nursing and child-rearing.

The home produced many more children than legitimate heirs. Xenophon's ideal householder, Ischomachus, notes that he bolts the door separating the men's and women's quarters to prevent slaves from reproducing without his explicit permission. The home was the space of reproduction for persons other than the conjugal couple, and slave reproduction increased (or decreased) the possessions of the free man and his lineage. Permission to form families within the master's home was a common incentive for good behavior throughout Greco-Roman antiquity, but slave marriages could also be forced by the owner and, of course, forcibly broken up. Slave children were identified by their mothers, and the paternal bond was largely ignored in recordkeeping and law. Any number of the children of slave women might have been fathered by the householder himself, his sons, male relations or free male guests, since slave women (and men, especially boys) were understood as sexually available by definition. As in American slavery, children followed the condition of the mother. Although no laws prohibited the forced separation of slave mothers and children, evidence over the timespan of antiquity suggests that a benevolent, gentlemanly master should not separate slave women and their children. Financial necessity, especially for less wealthy householders, however, outweighed delicate sensibilities every time.

The home in antiquity focused on the reproduction of the free male line. In this sense, the home was intensely masculine and devoted to freeborn masculine interests. The reproductive capacity and sexual fidelity of the freeborn wife functioned to secure the male line. In this sense, the home was intensely feminine. In order to protect the legitimacy of the male line, the freeborn woman had to stay at home. To announce that legitimacy to the wider public, she had to be seen to stay at home. Child-bearing, as women's work, was entirely homebound. It was also a key source of free women's honourable reputation and access to those social and legal benefits available to women. Free women depended especially on sons for advocacy and support in old age. For slaves, the home was also the space of reproduction, but their children were the heritable property of the master, not the heirs of their parents. Slave fathers may have felt strong bonds of attachment to their children, but they had no legal claim to them. Slave mothers relied entirely on the goodwill of their owners to continue ties to their children. As with the children of his wife, the master could always decide not to raise a slave child and have it disposed of through sale, infanticide or exposure. Exposed infants were regularly picked up by brothel-keepers or other persons willing to raise a child as a slave with a view to future profits.

As suggested above, reproductive sex was never strictly separated from sexual pleasure. The freeborn couple were assumed and encouraged to enjoy one another's company, although Greek and Latin literature are also full of tales of conjugal disaster. An expectation of pleasure in conjugal sex did not mean that sex between husbands and wives was not governed by a number of strong prohibitions. A free man was expected to have sex in an appropriately manly way; a freeborn woman in an appropriately feminine and respectable way. Even the great champion of sexual fidelity, Augustine, in *On the Goodness of Marriage*, agrees that some activities are more appropriately engaged in with a slave or prostitute, since they would violate the dignity of the freeborn wife. He seems to be referring to oral and anal contact. While masculine fidelity (or at least discretion) was advised by moralists long before Augustine and other Christian writers, it never seems to have become a cultural norm. John Chrysostom agrees with his opponents that male infidelity is only usually perceived as adultery when a free man violates the chastity of another free man's wife:

> I am not unaware that most think it is adultery only to violate a married woman. But I say that it is wicked and licentious to have an affair even with a public whore, a slave-girl, or any other woman without a husband ... Do not show me the laws of the outside world, which say a woman committing adultery is to be brought to trial, but that men with wives who do it with slave-girls are not considered guilty.
> —*Propter fornicationes* 1.4; trans. Harper

His objections are raised, quite clearly, against the more common state of affairs and public opinion. Adult citizen men were free to enjoy sex in the home with their wives and with female and male slaves, so long as they stayed within the bounds of appropriately masculine sexuality, that is, penetrative sexuality. To suggest that a free man had been penetrated, especially by a slave, was to call him no man at all. Invective against the 'bad' emperor Heliogabalus included the accusation that he purchased slaves with large members for the express purpose of enjoying the woman's role. This all took place within the imperial household and sullied the state, which was an extension, in many ways, of the emperor's *domus*. When Cicero condemned Marc Antony, he followed standard Roman invective practice and accused him of being the sexually receptive partner in a relationship with Curio:

> You assumed the *toga virilis*, which you at once turn into a prostitute's dress ... but soon Curio intervened, who led you away ... as if he had given you a bridal gown, established you in a fixed and steady marriage ... how many times his father threw you out of the house (*domus*), how many times he posted guards to keep you from crossing the threshold! But you, with night as your ally, your lust urging you on, and your payment compelling

you, were let down through the rooftiles. These shames the house (*domus*) could bear no longer.

—Cicero, *Philippics* 2.44; trans. Richlin 1992

The tainting of Curio's father's home is central to Cicero's condemnation. Freeborn men were able to take advantage of sexual opportunities outside the home, and since the age of marriage was often in the early thirties, non-marital sex was simply assumed for men in their teens and twenties. Freeborn daughters, as future wives, were off limits as sexual partners and seduction or rape of a daughter by another citizen male was a serious offence, though much more against her father or guardian than against herself. Freeborn adolescent sons occupied a more ambiguous role. At least in Greece, homosexual relations with freeborn adolescent boys could be tolerated, and even celebrated, under certain circumstances, although the home wasn't the only location for these affairs. Platonic dialogues show affairs being conducted in homes, apparently without real interference from the younger partner's family. The question of age was crucial; a young man faced serious social disabilities if he was rumoured to have been the *eremenos*, 'boyfriend' or receptive partner, past the appropriate age. In Rome, freeborn boys were not potential partners and seduction of a boy was *stuprum*, a sexual crime, in the same way as seduction of a wife or daughter. Within the home in antiquity, free men were free to have manly sex, free women were only free to have sex with husbands, and all others were more or less free for the taking. Or not so free: masters often pimped out slave girls and boys or charged their male slaves a fee for sexual access to female slaves.

Sex was not restricted to the home by any means in antiquity, but both Greeks and Romans assumed that it was a common setting for both licit and illicit encounters. The forms of sex and the relative social status of the participants were as important as the gender of the participants. Indeed, the kind of sex one had, and with whom, produced gender as much as it was determined by gender. Sex could make a freeborn man either more or less manly or a freeborn woman more or less womanly. Male homosexual sex within the home was allowable or forbidden depending on the relative social status and sexual role of the participants. This is one area where the Christianization of the empire did change law and much public opinion, if not practice. Christianity condemned all homosexual activity, regardless of sexual role, age or social status. To what degree this changed the status quo in homes, especially those with adolescent slave boys, is hard to say. The ancient Greek and Roman codes are still in evidence in most contemporary Mediterranean societies, despite Christian and Muslim condemnation of homosexual activity. Monastic writings indicate that boys were considered a real temptation to monks, and the *Secret History* of Procopius in the sixth century suggests the Empress Theodora was used 'as a kind of male prostitute' before she was developed enough to have vaginal intercourse with a man (9.15). Still, the home was no longer a space for licit homosexual activity. Female homosexual activity, at least in the context of the home, is barely mentioned outside the poetry of Sappho. Both Greek and Latin sources generally associate this with prostitutes and brothels.

One set of household slaves was technically exempt from suspicion of sexual misconduct but also deeply distrusted. Eunuch slaves were a common feature of elite and imperial Roman households. They were uncommon in Classical Greece, but known through the Hellenistic period. Alexander the Great famously added the eunuch slave Bagoas, formerly the property of the Persian king, to his retinue as a favoured bedfellow. Eunuchs were often used as personal slaves and attendants for freeborn wives and daughters because, presumably, they were incapable of active sexual relations. Several satirists, including Christians such as Tertullian and Jerome, claim that highborn women have affairs with their eunuch slaves as a contraceptive measure. They may be observing social realities or drawing on previous satire. Juvenal, for example, reserves special animosity for women who, he says, have male slaves emasculated when their genitals are full grown but their beards have not yet come in.

> Some women like feeble eunuchs, their ever soft kisses, their desperation of growing a beard, and the lack of the need for abortion. Their pleasure reaches a peak when their groins are handed over to the doctors already mature with the warmth of youth, with their comb already black. Once the balls have dropped, the only loss is the barber's. The man castrated by his mistress is conspicuous from afar and noticed by all he enters the bath: he challenges Priapus, the guardian of the garden. Let him sleep with his mistress, but don't let him near your boyfriend once he comes of age.
> —Juvenal, *Satires* 6.366–78; trans. Andrew Wallace-Hadrill

As fictive boys, eunuchs could be sexual partners for free men long past the usual age, but they are mostly recorded as personal slaves and guards for the chastity of wealthy freeborn women. Free eunuchs were uncommon and little is known of their domestic arrangements. Voluntary castration was practised by some devotees of Attis and Cybele and a small number of Christian ascetics. Valuable imperial eunuchs, often bureaucrats or military functionaries, were sometimes manumitted as a reward for extraordinary service. They cannot have established a true male-line household, but may have adopted heirs.

GENDERED DIVISION OF LABOUR WITHIN THE HOME

The principal difference between the ancient home, or any premodern home, and the contemporary home in capitalist society, is the role of productive labour. With industrialization the home became the refuge *from* masculine productive labour outside the home. Feminine labour was recategorized as non-productive, natural, caring and nurturing. Since feminine labour did not earn a wage, it could not be understood as work. In Greek and Roman antiquity, the home was the space of productive labour par excellence. There were strongly gendered and classed divisions in labour, but most productive work took place within the bounds of the *oikos* or *domus* and their associated agricultural lands. Work that took place within the walls of the home included food preparation, preservation and storage, the unending labour of cleaning and laundering, spinning and weaving, artisan labour performed by either poor citizens in their homes or skilled slaves in the homes of the wealthy, financial transactions and recordkeeping, maintenance of patronage relationships, child-rearing and education, nursing, musical and other entertainment work, visual arts including painting and mosaic work, courtyard gardening, personal attendance on freeborn men, women and children, which could include hairdressing, bathing, dressing, makeup, perfuming, etc., carrying of messages, midwifery (in the homes of clients), doctoring and spell-making. While masculine business could take place elsewhere and agriculture might be on lands not attached to the main place of residence, there was little productive labour that did not take place in the home, whether that home was a large rural estate or a tiny living space with workshop attached. Although men's work could take place outside the home, it would be inaccurate to draw a strict line between women's work in the home and men's work in the *agora* or *forum*. Freeborn men did a great deal of their work either within the home or in spaces directly attached to the home. Freeborn women, however, were expected to do their work within the walls of the home, but often in public spaces of the home.

Weaving, especially, was closely associated with feminine virtue. Penelope displayed her fidelity to Odysseus by both staying at home and being seen to produce cloth. The association between the freeborn woman's chastity and her domestic textile labour lasted from the Homeric age well into the Roman Christian era. When the church historian Sozomen praises Empress Pulcheria and the other imperial princesses who are devoted to a religious life he comments on their weaving and associates their exemplary virtue with the wellbeing of the state, a common theme going back at least to the early Empire:

> They all pursue the same mode of life; they are sedulous about the priests and the houses of prayer, and are munificent to needy strangers and the poor. These sisters generally take their meals and walks together, and pass their days and their nights in company, singing the praises of God. As is the custom with exemplary women, they employ themselves in weaving and in similar occupations. Although princesses, born and educated in palaces, they avoid levity and idleness, which they think unworthy of any who profess

virginity, so they put such indolence far from their own life. For this reason the mercy of God is manifested and is conquering in behalf of their house; for He increases the emperor in years and government; every conspiracy and war concocted against him has been overthrown of itself.
—*Ecclesiastic History* 9.3; trans. Hartranft

Although cloth was a commodity in Rome as it had not been in Greek antiquity, most cloth continued to be produced in the home. Freeborn women were encouraged to weave themselves and to oversee workshops of slave girls. Cloth not used by the household was sold for profit. Spinning seems to have been a strictly feminine task. In Rome, at least, servile men also wove cloth. Both male and female slaves are recorded as expert weavers, and it was one of the forms of labour for which slaves could receive individual compensation. A Greek letter from a woman in Egypt in the third century BCE exhorts a man, perhaps a male relative, to appropriately compensate a slave girl for irreproachable textile production (*SB* 22.15276, in Bagnall and Cribiore 2006). John Chrysostom indicates the association between weaving and both servility and effeminacy in his condemnation of ascetic men who cohabited with dedicated Christian virgins. He lampoons the monk who says he requires a woman in the house on account of the labour she performs:

> For what, tell me, do they say these household matters are for which they deem it necessary to utilize the virgin's managerial skills? Do you have a crowd of recently purchased foreign maids who need to be trained in wool-working and in other duties? Do you have a storeroom for your tremendous treasures and expensive garments?
> —*Adversus eos* 9; trans. Clark

> To tell the truth, if a man lives with women in such intimacy and is reared in their company, he is at a loss to escape being some kind of vagabond, the dregs of the earth, one of the rabble. If he says anything, his talk will entirely concern weaving and wool; his language will be tainted with the characteristics of women's speech. And anything he may do, he will carry out with great servility (the freedom appropriate to a Christian is like a far-distant colony to him); he becomes unfit for any of the splendid deeds of virtue.
> —*Adversus eos* 11; trans. Clark

Despite the shame attached to a man who did textile work, Kyle Harper (2011) estimates the commodity value of cloth as second only to that of foodstuffs in the late Roman era. Women's funerary markers often bore a spindle as a stand-in for the deceased virtuous femininity and *lanifica* or 'wool-working' was a common funerary inscription for women. Its relative invisibility in economic histories of antiquity is due first to its place as a feminine and servile form of labour, and second to the ephemeral nature of both product and tools – the archaeological record is biased towards goods that do not decay.

As the selections from Chrysostom indicate, wool-working was only one, highly idealized, part of a freeborn woman's domestic labour. While poorer women doubtless did all work on their own or joined a small number of slaves in daily tasks, wealthier women were expected to take on the role of chief supervisor. The ideal household in Xenophon's *Oeconomicus* describes the role of the household manager to his fifteen-year-old bride in the following terms:

> 'You must receive the produce that is brought in from the outside and distribute as much of it as needs dispensing; but as for the proportion of it which needs putting on one side, you must look ahead and make sure that the outgoings assigned for the year are not dispensed in a month. When wool is brought into you, you must try to make certain that those who need clothes get them. And you must try to ensure that the grain is made into edible provisions. One of your responsibilities, however,' I added, 'will probably seem rather unpleasant: when any servant is ill, you must make sure he is thoroughly looked after.'
>
> 'Anyway,' I said, 'some of your specific responsibilities will be gratifying, such as getting a servant who is ignorant of spinning, teaching it to her and doubling her value to you; or getting one who is ignorant of housekeeping and service, teaching her to be a reliable servant, and ending up with her being of inestimable value; or having the right to reward those in your household who are disciplined and helpful, and to punish anyone who is bad . . .'
>
> —7.36–7; trans. Tredennick and Waterfield

Xenophon's householder also instructs his wife on the fastidious organization and care of household implements. For wealthier citizen women, planning entertainments such as lavish dinner parties was part of the expected work. While a senior female slave could be appointed as a housekeeper, the free woman was often severely condemned if she shirked her duties as chief overseer. The upper classes assumed that slaves would fall into laziness and uproar if not closely supervised and regularly punished for wrongdoing. This role seems to have been attractive to some women, who often had little real power among their equals, but limitless power over inferiors. The abusive mistress is a stock character in comedy, mime and satire, and was picked up by Chrysostom in his preaching. His interlocutors beg to know how they should manage slaves without violence, and Chrysostom agrees that slaves are 'an evil tribe' but urges some restraint. 'What is most disgraceful of all, some mistresses are so ruthless and harsh that when they lash their slaves, the stripes don't dissipate within the day' (*On Ephesians* 15.3–4; trans. Harper). The work of the free woman was economically productive and closely linked to the work of household slaves.

The work performed by female slaves ranged from the hard, unskilled labour of milling grain, which was considered both feminine and demeaning, to highly specialized occupations such as tutor, midwife, scribe, musician or perfumer. Female slaves served as personal attendants for the owning family, did innumerable household tasks of cleaning and food preparation, made up textile-production workshops and cared for the young.

Many wealthy and even moderately well-off households employed slave or freed women as wet nurses. The nurse was also a stock character in drama and comedy and is mentioned with affection in letters and other documents (Figure 6.2). Aelius Aristides claims that the god Asclepius saved his old nurse, Philumene, 'than whom nothing was dearer to me' countless times through the intervention of dreams (*Orations* 2.47–78). A nurse might be a lifelong companion for a freeborn woman, especially, and make up a part of her trousseau on marriage. Although nursing one's own child was praised by moralists, most upper-class ancients looked on nursing as servile. The vigorous, rustic women of ancient times may have virtuously nursed their own children, but this was a memory of a purer, simpler time. Juvenal, in his satire 'Against Women', claims the last era that produced chaste wives was also the era when people lived in caves rather than cities and women 'had udders for big babies to drink from' (6.9, Trans. Wallace-Hadrill). Soranus, a Greek physician of the Methodist school writing in the early second century CE, admits that maternal milk is the best, if possible, but recommends against the mother being the first nurse for the child and gives lengthy instructions for selection of the best nurse. In addition to various physical characteristics associated with good health, and thus good milk, the nurse should be sober, abstain from sex and speak a good quality of Greek. He disparages Roman nurses, who, he claims, know little about good child-rearing practices. He gives a comprehensive food and exercise regime for the wet nurse, or rather nurses, since he warns against habituating the infant to only one nurse since she might fall ill or die before weaning:

> she should go out for a walk, and following this she should also take exercise in a carriage drawn by animals. She should also work her body hard at such exercises as are apt to shake all parts, but particularly those of the hands and shoulders, so that the nourishment may be carried more to these parts. Such exercises are: playing with a ball, especially a hollow one, and throwing light weights; for those who are too poor, however, rowing or drawing up water in a vessel, winnowing and grinding grain, preparing bread, making beds and whatever is done with a certain bending of the body.
> —*Gynaecology* 2.14.24, trans. Temkin

FIGURE 6.2: Statuette of a nurse with child. Credit: The British Museum.

Childcare went beyond nursing, of course. Women, both slave and free, spent great energy on child-rearing and education, particularly that of young children and girls. Freeborn boys, especially the wealthy, would pass to the care of male tutors or pedagogues.

The labour of slaves, both male and female, ran the gamut from exceptionally useful to utterly frivolous. Imperial and elite Roman households are recorded as keeping dwarf slaves who performed comic routines, decorative young boys and girls as non-functional attendants, slaves whose only role was to carry about sweet-smelling flowers. Male slaves, however, had a wider range of possible employments than did female slaves and could rise to positions of exceptional trust and power over lesser slaves. Unlike American slave owners who banned literacy among slaves, Greek and Roman owners could purchase educated men who had been captured in war or fallen into slavery through financial mishap. They also regularly invested in the education of slaves who could then be employed in secretarial and business or educational positions. The best-known educated slave is Epictetus, the Stoic philosopher and tutor of Emperor Marcus Aurelius. Wealthy households, however, almost always employed a male slave or freedman as the tutor and guardian-companion of freeborn boys, the pedagogue. The slave pedagogue existed in a precarious situation. He exercised considerable control over his charge and could be viciously punished for neglecting his duties, but as the boy grew older, the pedagogue (even if freed) could fall victim to cruel abuse by spirited teens, with little recourse. Libanius describes boys placing pedagogues on carpets, stretching out the four corners and tossing them up into the air (*Oration* 58.7.20). Despite strong stereotypes of the native stupidity of slaves, both Greeks and Romans exploited the intellectual labour of slaves, especially male slaves. Non-literary training of male slaves in skilled craftsmanship was also common, and, like business and education, these tasks tended to be carried out in domestic space, although workshop or factory-like conditions were not unknown.

One aspect of slave labour in the ancient home that affected both male and female slaves was the ability of owners to rent out their slaves to other households and the ability of some slaves to hire themselves out for pay in other households. In the early second century CE a woman writes to her daughter and complains that her slave girls are seeking better wages in other households. 'I at last got the material from the dyer... I am working with your slave girls as far as possible. I cannot find girls who can work with me, for they are all working for their own mistresses. Our workers marched through all the city eager for more money' (*P. Brem.* 63; trans. Bagnall and Cribiore). Male slaves had many more opportunities than women for earning extra wages to put towards personal belongings or the purchase of freedom. Male slaves in imperial and elite households could invest on their own behalf, sometimes with their owners as silent partners in more unsavoury schemes such as taverns or brothels, and even own slaves of their own.

The gendered division of labour was evident for all classes of men and women in the ancient world. Men tended to do work both in and outside the home, women predominantly inside the home. Both, however, did productive labour and the home was a key site of production. Besides the obvious economic value of domestic work, the division of labour, along both gender and status lines, served to mark hierarchies within the home. A virtuous free woman's work could make a man effeminate. Dignified free men's work would make a woman ridiculous. Male slaves were punished by being worked in the mill, the domain of female slaves. Especially servile work like personal attendance was avoided by even the poorest free persons. Again, with the exception of sex work, there is little evidence that the rise of Christianity had much effect on the ideals or realities of gendered divisions of labour within the ancient household, other than transferring some matronly ideals to the consecrated virgin.

GENDER AND CULTURAL PRODUCTION WITHIN THE HOME

The ancient world provided freeborn men with a number of public spaces conducive to intellectual conversation, literary composition and competitive display of cultural competence. The Greek *agora* and the Roman forum, the gymnasium, theatre, schools, courtrooms, senates, town councils and games provided these opportunities. Much intellectual conversation, composition and display, however, took place in domestic settings. The Platonic dialogues are set in a number of locations, but the *Symposium*, one of the best-known in antiquity as it is now, took place in a domestic setting. The Greek dinner party was an intensely homosocial affair. Respectable Greek women did not attend. Slave girls as servers, entertainers and sex partners might be present, but young men might also perform these roles. While simple relaxation or drunken revelry were both possibilities, the cultural ideal included high-minded conversation and display of literary and rhetorical skills. The Greek style of dinner party was adopted by the Romans from the second century BCE and was an exceptionally elaborate affair by imperial times. Roman matrons, unlike Greek freeborn women, could attend dinner parties in their own homes or with their husbands in friends' homes. Dinner parties remained appropriate settings for learned conversation, the display of rhetorical skill and the composition of verse. Slaves or hired performers added to the salon-like atmosphere and the entrance of the home served as art gallery and display of the host's fine lineage, with busts of ancestors, and fine artistic taste, with costly paintings, mosaic, sculpture and vessels. The first-century CE Roman satire *Satyricon* lampoons the pretentions of the wealthy freedman Trimalchio at length. Two poor but well-educated young freeborn men attend the dinner as hangers-on of a rhetorician. Trimalchio displays his lack of education and poor taste throughout by garbling Greek mythology, inventing inappropriate verse and interrupting the better-educated with crass business stories. His wife behaves lewdly and attacks him for kissing an especially pretty slave boy. The dinner party is a disaster, but indicates the relevant cultural expectations. As with every other aspect of domestic life in the ancient world, social hierarchy determined as much as gender hierarchy at a dinner party. Seating followed a strict social hierarchy: there were the servers and the served. Freeborn men dominated, especially in Greek contexts. There are suggestions that freeborn women could also partake in the intellectual conversation. Juvenal satirizes elite Roman women who study literature and hold forth at dinner parties:

> Even worse is the woman who sits down at table and begins to praise Virgil, pardons Dido on the point of death, and sets the poets up for comparison, with Virgil in one scale and Homer in the other. The grammarians surrender, professors of rhetoric concede defeat, the whole crowd falls silent, not so much as a word from the lawyer or the auctioneer.
> —6.434–8; trans. Andrew Wallace-Hadrill

Juvenal and others suggest that intellectual activity masculinizes women and makes them ridiculous, or insufferable, but other authors praise educated women. Educated women, whether Greek or Roman, would have received their education at home, with tutors, rather than in schools for the most part, and would have had little other opportunity for display. Records remain of singing and lyric poetry competition for girls in Greek games or choirs in ancient Sparta and Lesbos, but most female literary production must have been domestic. Sappho, the most famous female writer of Greek antiquity, may have composed and performed in public settings, but it is more likely that the aristocratic woman was educated at home by tutors and gathered female students in a domestic educational setting. Although very little female literary composition remains, one should not assume that only a little ever existed. Female homosocial gatherings certainly produced song, storytelling and other verbal arts that are entirely lost to us. This is especially true of servile women's cultural production – and men's. For these groups, entertainment and cultural production must often have accompanied work. We have faint echoes of this in the casual mentions of things like 'the songs of the weaving women' (Harper 2011: 135). Learned men often rail against the 'nonsense' and 'superstitious tales' that older female servants, and especially wet nurses, told children. Contemporary ethnographies tell us what rich artistry and compositional skill often go into such all-female, unwritten narrative traditions.

The dinner party was not the only domestic space where intellectual production flourished in antiquity. The inner chamber, or *cubiculum*, of the Roman house was a space not only for sleep, eroticism and reproduction, but also for quiet reflection and intellectual labour. Authors such as Cicero, Quintillian, Livy and Tacitus designate the small inner chamber as the ideal space for composition, especially of verse, and private recitation. The results of intellectual labour in this most 'secret' space of the home would eventually reach a public audience. Intimates might share intellectual conversation or private rehearsals in this space as well. This sort of intellectual activity was almost always presented as masculine, but as Christianity took up the theme of literary activity in the *cubiculum* pious women entered the scene. The *cubiculum* was an idealized space for prayer, recitation of scripture and religious reading. Here, early Christian authors conflated the literary and sexual resonances of the space. Jerome, in his famous letter to the virgin Eustochium, describes the consecrated virgin's intercourse with the Word, via the medium of scriptural reading and recitation, with explicitly sexual language:

> Ever let the privacy of your chamber guard you; ever let the Bridegroom sport with you within. Do you pray? You speak to the Bridegroom. Do you read? He speaks to you. When sleep overtakes you He will come behind and put His hand through the hole of the door, and your heart shall be moved for Him; and you will awake and rise up and say: 'I am sick from love.' Then He will reply: 'A garden enclosed is my sister, my spouse; a spring shut up, a fountain sealed'.
> —*Epistles* 22.25; trans. Fremantle

Likewise, Jerome's contemporary, Pelagius, encourages the consecrated virgin Demetrias to spend time in study and prayer in her inner chamber and later to display the divine nourishment she has received through memorization and recitation of scripture to her family and household in a more public area of the home. Here, the echo is of men's moral self-improvement through philosophical study in the *cubiculum*. Before the Christian era, there was little in the way of literary activity in this domestic space attributed to women, although this cannot be taken as evidence that none existed. Some women did study philosophy or write verse, and they may have used similar domestic spaces for these activities.

The inner chamber was a space for intellectual production and improvement in city homes, but the entire country estate was associated with intellectual activity. The Roman ideal of *otium*, leisure for intellectual and artistic development, was closely associated with elite country estates. Again, the retreat to a country estate for study and composition was understood as a masculine and upper-class pursuit. Pliny the Younger often expresses a longing for the intellectual leisure of the countryside in his letters. In two, he gives lengthy descriptions of his idyllic country estates, one near Rome and one in Tuscany. He remarks on their natural light, good air, harmonious architecture, picturesque views and suitability for both private study and the reception of like-minded guests. His seaside estate, less than twenty miles from Rome, boasts a little four-room detached apartment in the garden, with sun rooms on either side, receiving room and bedroom. The *cubiculum* is soundproofed by means of a double wall with air cushion. Pliny rejoices in this home-within-a-home, which safeguards both his intellectual labours and the harmonious functioning of a large household:

> When I retire to this garden-apartment, I fancy myself a hundred miles from my own house, and take particular pleasure in it at the feast of the Saturnalia, when, by the license of that season of joy, every other part of my villa resounds with the mirth of my domestics: thus I neither interrupt their diversions, nor they my studies.
> —*Letters* 2.17; trans. Melmoth

This sort of intellectual retreat is not associated with soft living or effeminacy. The philosophical gentleman who prefers his country home to the luxuries of the city is an old-fashioned, frugal, hearty type, who exhibits the masculine self-control made difficult by the temptations of the city. Pliny describes the ideal of retirement in his friend Spurinna, who spends his days reading, conversing, taking the air in a carriage, exercising, writing, taking an invigorating bath, listening to poetry or other literature and dining on good but simple fare with friends (*Letters* 3.1). Pliny praises his manly speech and vigorous old age. The intellectual retreat is the most appropriate retirement for a man's man who has fulfilled his civic duties. This sort of retreat is taken up by early Christian authors, especially those who understand the Christian life as an ascetic, philosophical and inherently masculinizing discipline. Women do appear in descriptions of ascetic life as philosophical retreat, but they are often stylized and rely on the Diotima tradition from Plato's *Symposium*, in which a more or less mythical woman imparts semi-divine knowledge to the male gathering. Good examples are Augustine's mother Monnica at the retreat in Cassiciacum as described in *Confessions* or Gregory of Nyssa's sister Macrina in *Life of Macrina* and *On the Soul and the Resurrection*. Macrina and other ascetic Christian women did manage country estates, sometimes as proto-monastic institutions. Teaching and study may well have been a part of their daily routine. Most evidence of Christian women's intellectual activity, however, comes from more urban domestic settings. Since women were generally under guardianship, they were not able to make their own decisions on where to reside in the same way that men were. Additionally, upper-class women on country estates did not leave behind the labours of civic life; they simply changed the location of their continuing domestic responsibilities.

One form of domestic cultural production was almost entirely associated with women, both in Greek and Roman antiquity. The composition and performance of mourning verse was women's speciality. While men gave eulogies, often in non-domestic spaces, women sang mourning verse in the home during the laying-in-state of the corpse. This continued in the procession and at the grave site, but the initial mourning took place in the home. Despite Christian attempts to curb what theologians saw as excessive displays of grief, the practice continued, especially in Greek-speaking areas. Twentieth century ethnographies give witness to an unbroken, though certainly not unchanging, tradition of feminine funerary composition that is only now beginning to disappear in the Mediterranean, both Christian and Muslim. Although Gregory of Nyssa's record of Macrina's philosophizing may be largely invented, his record of the mourning verses sung by her surviving female companions after her death are more likely to be authentic feminine composition.

HOME, GENDER AND DEITIES

Ancient men and women shared their homes with ancestors, deities and a host of spiritual forces, nearly all of which were gendered. While temples and gravesites, groves and arenas all hosted religious activity, a great deal of ancient religion happened in domestic space (see below ch. 8). Like the businesses of production and reproduction, this was work closely tied to the gender and social standing of the practitioner. Domestic religion left far less to the archaeological and literary record than public religiosity, but we have echoes and tantalizing fragments that suggest a rich life of worship within the ancient home.

Protection of the home was a key focus of domestic religion in antiquity. Greeks worshipped several domestic forms of Zeus, who guarded boundaries and increased wealth. The father of the home was the chief officiant in the worship of these protector deities. Hermes was also associated with protection of boundaries. The Roman home, especially the country home, was protected by gods of doorways, latches and hinges, and the garden was protected by the ever-erect Priapus. Violation of the home was imagined in explicitly sexual terms and placards accompanying Priapus statues threatened explicitly sexual punishment to the would-be intruder. In one example, women will be vaginally raped, boys anally raped and grown men orally raped (Williams 2010: 27). In addition to protecting the household boundaries from intruders, the inhabitants of the ancient home had to worry about spiritual attacks, especially in the form of the evil eye. Many of the apotropaic images and objects were sexual in nature. Phalluses, often winged, were common decorative motifs for oil lamps. Couples in the act of lovemaking were also regularly displayed. The *kai su* mosaics in Hellenistic homes featured phallic imagery and sharp objects attacking the evil eye, dwarves and hunchbacks sporting enormous erections, and other fantastical images intended to turn back the malicious influence of the eye (Figure 6.3). The

FIGURE 6.3: Mosaic of lucky hunchback (a *kai su* mosaic). Credit: Tolga TEZCAN via Getty Images.

inscription *kai su*, 'and you', in Greek, might best be translated 'back at you!' with an accompanying rude hand gesture. In this protective religious imagery, we see a divinization both of male sexual aggression and of fertility.

In Greek homes, the goddess Hestia presided over the hearth. New members of the household, freeborn and slave, were welcomed with rituals at the hearth. The male head of the household performed most hearth rituals. Women were responsible for lifecycle religious activity such as birth rituals, wedding songs (often obscene) and, as mentioned above, death rituals, especially mourning. Although the gender of both practitioners and deities was important, there was no strict correlation between the gender of the worshipper and that of the deity. Roman women, like Greek women, were involved in many lifecycle rituals, but unlike Greek women they had an important role at the hearth, overseen by the goddess Vesta. Household gods, *lares* and *penates*, and the *genius* of the male line, were installed in cupboard shines and attended daily by both sexes. The domestic cult of Vesta had a civic analogue in the Vestal virgins. The chastity of Roman matrons, and especially women of the imperial household, was closely associated with piety and protection of the home/state. A freeborn woman's sexual decorum, especially if she was *univira*, only ever married to one man, gained her special religious status and privileges.

One form of ancient religious practice that often took place in the domestic sphere is difficult to name without bringing in pejorative associations. 'Magic' was ubiquitous. As many have noted, 'magic' is often simply the religion of the out group. A curse, love-spell, protection amulet, healing charm or homing beacon for lost property is only 'magic' if someone else is doing it. While both Greeks and Romans complain about superstition and magic, archaeological evidence shows consistent use of spells at all levels of society. Women are sometimes accused of having a leaning towards magic or 'foreign' superstitions, but extant spells and practical handbooks for magicians do not indicate a preponderance of feminine magical practice. Certainly, domestic matters including sexual and conjugal conflict were common themes, but so were illness, loss of money, gambling and a host of other mundane problems.

Like Greek and Roman polytheism, ancient Christianity existed in both public and private spaces. The earliest Christian worship took place in domestic gatherings and over meals in homes, then moved into more public church buildings and funerary sites. It never left the domestic sphere, however. While the central rituals of baptism and Eucharist moved more and more to public spaces, domestic prayer, especially in the 'inner chamber', remained normative. This was equally true for men and women in a household. Religious reading, for the literate, was often domestic, as was theological composition and conversation. Large elite homes were sometimes converted to semi-monastic estates and included their own church structures or rooms converted into worship spaces. These could function as single-sex communities or as double monasteries.

Gregory of Nyssa's sister Macrina presided over a large country estate that she ran as monastery with a male and female side. Most ancient Christians, however, did not lead ascetic lifestyles. Christian prayer, reading and imagery were integrated into the daily routine of the household. Clothing and household goods began, rather slowly, to lose their phallic and sexual themes and add the cross or other Christian imagery. While changing sexual mores may be partly responsible, the increasing apotropaic power of the cross is a more likely cause. Likewise, magical practice continued, with the name of Jesus added to those of Egyptian gods, Greek and Roman gods and Jewish angels in spells and amulets.

Whether Christianity significantly changed gender roles in the ancient household is a vexing question. The development of monastic life as a single-sex alternative to domestic life is most notable. Many early ascetics continued to live in their own homes or gather in small group homes in urban areas. Yet New Testament authors and most Christian theologians describe the ideal Christian marriage in almost precisely the same terms used by their Greek and Roman predecessors. A harmonious home was one in which hierarchy, including gender hierarchy, was maintained. The best wife was subservient, modest and chaste. The best husband has mastery over himself and his entire household. In theory, at least, the slaves of the household might expect less sexual exploitation. Christian freeborn wives, however, are admonished to suffer drunken, violent and unfaithful husbands with patience. Christian authors still presume the female slave is a likely mistress. Rebukes against use of boys for sex are stronger, but Christian sources still presume that attractive slave boys are a temptation and that male prostitutes are available. The gendered division of labour did not change at all. Despite profound changes in religious and sexual ideology, the gendered functioning of the ancient home did not undergo much change with the coming of Christianity. Changes that mark the beginning of the Middle Ages are far more closely attached to changes in the ethnic makeup of the Mediterranean world.

CHAPTER SEVEN

Hospitality and Home

MARIE-ADELINE LE GUENNEC

Hospitality was a crucial concept in the ancient Mediterranean world. Its importance is attested around the Mediterranean basin throughout antiquity, from archaic times to the transition between late antiquity and the Middle Ages. In this context, hospitality, which can be defined, in the most basic terms, as the practice of the free reception of external individuals or groups, indeed played a vital role in facilitating human circulation on a local and interregional scale, and hence contributed to the connectivity of the ancient Mediterranean basin.[1] Nevertheless, this function was never limited to the host's mere welcoming and entertaining of a guest, but had varied purposes, ranging from social and political support between hosts and guests to juridical, religious and/ or social integration of the outsider. In this chapter, we shall discuss more precisely the complex relationship between home and hospitality in the ancient Mediterranean.

Domestic hospitality may be one of the phenomena mentioned in this book for which the ideas of regional diversity and chronological evolution, though justified on the practical level, nevertheless seem not totally pertinent. In fact, in a Mediterranean basin dominated for centuries by Greco-Etrusco-Roman and Judeo-Christian cultures, the concepts and values related to hospitality appear reasonably stable from Classical times to late antiquity (Avon-Soletti 2005). Inherited traditions and models, which sometimes date back to legendary times, notably affect the conception of hospitality throughout antiquity. From this perspective, two models in particular appear to be decisive: on one hand, Homeric hospitality, as depicted in the hospitality type-scenes of the *Iliad* and *Odyssey* (Kakridis 1960; Lacore 1991; Reece 1993; Hiltbrunner 2005: 26–33), and on the other hand, hospitality as shown in the Old Testament, especially in the areas east of the Mediterranean (Gorce 1925; Hiltbrunner 2005). We should not be surprised, then, that in the sixth century CE, a member of the Apamea elite in Syria still chose to decorate one of his house's guestrooms in the 'House of the Deer' (Morvillez 2002) with two verses from the *Odyssey* in mosaic, fourteen centuries after the redaction of the poem: 'Hail, stranger; in our house thou shalt find entertainment, and then, when thou hast tasted food, thou shalt tell of what thou hast need' (*Odyssey* 1.123–4, Loeb Trans.). Throughout antiquity, elites, to whom most available evidence pertains, would continue to receive and entertain each other, from the Homeric kings to the Christian aristocrats of late antiquity. In the latter context, the major source of innovation would then be the appearance, together with the spread of the Christian faith, of a justification of hospitality in the need for universal charity preached by the Gospel.

The observation of this structural persistence explains why this chapter will not, for the most part, be organized chronologically. Rather, common definitions, customs and types of interactions between hospitality and home shall be explored, which otherwise might have become repetitive from one historical section to another. In this chapter, I will mainly focus on Classical antiquity, from Greek cities to the pagan and Christian Roman Empires, from the fifth century BCE to the sixth century CE. However, for the reasons cited above, evidence pertaining to more remote time periods will necessarily be brought into the discussion.

WHAT IS ANCIENT MEDITERRANEAN HOSPITALITY?

Hospitality comes from the will or obligation of a community – whether reduced to the basic cell of the more or less extended family or forming a more complex society – to negotiate its relationship to strangers they happen to come into contact with. Traditionally, this encounter can evolve in two divergent directions: *philoxenia*, love of the stranger, which comes from seeing – in the stranger, in the other, in the unknown – a powerful being, a representative of humankind and/or another self, with whom one can develop peaceful and friendly relations; or *xenophobia*, fear of the stranger, which expresses a reaction of fear and rejection of an entity that is considered alien to the group and, thus, a factor of risk and danger (Hiltbrunner 2005: 9). Beyond the ancient world, this duality has been notably highlighted and studied by anthropologists in various contemporary societies, as for instance in A. Van Gennep's fundamental work on 'rites of passage' (Van Gennep (1909) 2011).

Hospitality can find its justification within the framework of both of these cultural patterns. In a philoxenic environment, hospitality, whether restricted to one-to-one private relationships or understood as a more universal and altruistic practice of reception (see below), is the most obvious way to display the individual's and the group's openness towards newcomers. On the contrary, in a xenophobic context, hospitality can be considered a regime of exception, aiming to avoid the exclusion or even elimination imposed on the stranger, while nevertheless regulating his/her access to the group, so as to propitiate the mysterious and hazardous forces that he/she might represent.[2]

In fact, in ancient Mediterranean cultures, both of these attitudes seem to be linked to a much deeper belief: the idea that gods, both propitious and inauspicious, could be hiding in the outsider, in the stranger. This assumption justifies hospitality and even demands it, for fear that divine forces might turn against the individual or the community that mistook and rejected the sacred arrivals. Take for instance Antinous, one of Penelope's most prominent suitors, who mocks and insults Odysseus, who, returning home after years away and dressed as a beggar, is received as a stranger in his own palace in Ithaca. Those witnessing the altercation rebuke Antinous for his behaviour towards the unknown guest, considering it both risky and sacrilege:

> Then Antinous, son of Eupeithes, answered him: 'Sit still, and eat, stranger, or go elsewhere; lest the young men drag thee by hand or foot through the house for words like these, and strip off all thy skin.' So he spoke, but they all were filled with exceeding indignation, and thus would one of the proud youths speak: 'Antinous, thou didst not well to strike the wretched wanderer. Doomed man that thou art, what if haply he be some god come down from heaven! Aye, and the gods in the guise of strangers from afar put on all manner of shapes, and visit the cities, beholding the violence and the righteousness of men'.
> —*Odyssey* 17.477–87; Loeb trans.

The motif of *theoxenia*, that is, hospitality shown to divine incomers wandering around the human realm, is attested in most ancient European mythologies and cultural references. For the Greco-Roman context, a very famous example of this *theoxenia* can be found in the story of Philemon and Baucis, known to us exclusively in Ovid's *Metamorphoses*. Rather than a proper myth, this story should be thought of as a symbolic illustration of the concept of divine hospitality. It involves a couple of old and poor Phrygians who open their humble house to Jupiter and Mercury, disguised as mortal travellers, after the two gods had been turned away by other inhabitants of the locality. The couple spare the gods nothing, despite their scarce resources; after a simple but pleasant meal, the divine guests identify themselves, punish the other inhabitants, change the house of Philemon and Baucis into a temple, of which the poor couple are made guardians, and then reward them with the promise of a common death, when the last hour would come for one of them (Ovid, *Metamorphoses* 8.624–724). Similar motifs can be found all around the ancient Mediterranean.

Theoxenia is particularly present in the Old Testament, where the reception of God or his various representatives among men is a privileged way to express the encounter between the divine and humankind. We shall refer, of course, to Abraham's hospitality, in Genesis 18, and to its counterpart, the story of Abraham's nephew Lot in Sodom (Genesis 19). Ultimately, in the New Testament, the requirement for hospitality is reiterated by Jesus, but *theoxenia* is replaced by the exigency of universal philanthropic reception, with the idea that in every human being, even the humblest, it is Christ who is received (see especially Matthew 25.34–46). The opening of one's house motivated by hospitality is then justified by the respect due to the divine and by the fear of leaving it outside.

Most likely following this concept of *theoxenia*, ancient hospitality, especially when practised at home, was placed under the protection of various divinities. In Classical antiquity, it was entrusted to the tutelage of the most eminent god of the Olympian Pantheon, Zeus *Xenios* for the Greeks and Jupiter *Hospitalis* for the Romans. The two gods oversaw the respect of reciprocal duties between hosts and guests, as their *epikleseis*, specific qualifying adjectives, showed. This assignment already appears in the Homeric poems, for instance, when Odysseus reminds the Cyclops Polyphemus of the fact that 'Zeus is the avenger of suppliants and strangers – Zeus, the strangers' god (*xeinios*) – who ever attends upon reverend strangers' (*Odyssey* 9. 270–1, Loeb trans.). While Romans knew of a general category of *dii hospitales*, who were not identified further, the role of Jupiter in this domain remained evident, echoing back to Greek tradition directly, as Cicero explains to his brother Quintus: 'But I am not going so far as to offend him, for fear he implores the protection of Jupiter *Hospitalis*, and rouses a rally of all the Greeks, for it was through them that we became reconciled' (Cicero, *Letters to His Brother Quintus* 2.12.3, Loeb trans.).

The divine nature of hospitality thus enforced the mutual protection of host and guest. Conversely, any attempt on the host or guest's person was perceived as sacrilegious, as was the attitude of Herakles, received as a guest under Eurytos' roof, who kills his host's son, in spite of all the sacred rights of hospitality, 'in his own house, ruthlessly, and had regard neither for the wrath of the gods nor for the table which he had set before him' (*Odyssey* 21.26–8, Loeb trans; though it is true that in the classical version of the myth, Eurytos offended Herakles first and chased him out of his house, as Sophocles relates in his *Trachiniae*). In the same way, when a young Capuan plans to assassinate Hannibal during a banquet in 216 BCE, his father tries to divert him from his goal, asking him: 'from the hospitable board, to which you were invited by Hannibal with but two other Campanians, do you rise with the intention of staining that very board with the blood of a guest?' (Livy 23.9.4, Loeb trans.). In both examples, violence inflicted on a host in his own house by his guest is condemned; but the guest's person was protected as well, such that, as Tacitus puts it in *Annals* 15.52, 'Piso refused [murdering Nero] if they stained with the blood of an emperor, however contemptible, the sanctities of the guest-table and the gods of hospitality', Loeb trans. As these different examples distinctly show, the sacred dimension of hospitality in ancient Mediterranean cultures was essentially linked to the sacredness of domestic space in its materiality: respecting one implied honouring the other. Infringements on the hospitality relationship were thus both an impious rupture of the oaths sworn between host and guest and a stain inflicted on the house where the crime occurred.

Hospitality was a sacred value shared by most ancient Mediterranean cultures. Nevertheless, this notion was far from being consistent in its definition: with the same words pertaining to free reception, various phenomena can be covered, even within one single culture. In this context, the existence of ritualized and fixed hosting conventions between individuals and/or groups, forming proper hospitality networks, is especially notable. Such conventions have been mostly studied in the Archaic and Classical Greek and Roman worlds, where they are indeed particularly well attested (see for instance Hellegouarc'h 1963; Gauthier 1972; Badian 1972; Bolchazy 1977; Herman 1987; Mitchell 1997; Peachin and Caldelli 2001; Hiltbrunner 2005). From this perspective, hospitality pacts between private individuals are frequently distinguished from pacts where at least one of the sides is or represents a public entity, such as a state, city, magistrate or priest. We can rely here on the ancient terminology itself, namely on the Greek designations of *xenia* (private hospitality) and *proxenia* (public hospitality) and, even more obviously, on the equivalent Latin expressions *hospitium priuatum* and *hospitium publicum*. In practice, however, these different types of relationships could overlap, a phenomenon that contributed to reinforcing the relationship between individuals, homes and communities concomitantly united by private and public reception pacts. While the formality of private conventions of *xenia*/*hospitium* etc. incontestably weakened with time, public hospitality as a formal pact remained active for longer, at least until the unification of the Mediterranean basin under Roman control had eliminated the need for such international conventions. In its broadest sense, hospitality as practice of free reception could then be based on the most diverse solidarities: civic, religious, professional, familial or even purely philanthropic.

Of course, in the ancient Mediterranean, hospitality networks were not the only resources available to travellers and foreigners in need of accommodation and orientation in a new environment. With the expansion of mobility, other infrastructures dedicated to reception progressively appeared or increased throughout the Mediterranean basin. We mainly consider two systems of accommodation, for the most part known for the Roman period: commercial accommodation provided by establishments comparable to our modern inns (Kleberg 1957); and public stations dedicated to the reception of soldiers and officials on missions (Crogiez-Pétrequin 1993; Black 1995; Eck 1999; Corsi

2000; Kolb 2000 etc.). In late antiquity, then, a network of places devoted to the accommodation and care of pilgrims and travelling clerics, as well as the poor, sick and elderly, gradually appeared under the sponsorship of the Christian Church (Gorce 1925; Hunt 1984). However, despite this complex galaxy of reception structures, hospitality, and especially hospitality at home, remained a central value that survived the ancient Mediterranean basin's geopolitical and cultural evolutions, most likely because of its antiquity and its sacredness.

Hospitality in the ancient Mediterranean was obviously aimed at the accommodation and entertainment of the outsider. Hosts were supposed to provide for their guests. Ancient hospitality was significantly symbolized by four items: fire, water, information and shelter, all services that could be found at the domestic hearth (Hiltbrunner 2005: 16, with further evidence). But its role was never limited to these basic functions, vital in themselves to the traveller and the stranger. In the ancient Mediterranean, hospitality was also understood as a socio-political and juridical regime of reception granted to the hosted stranger, aimed at his integration into the community. The terminology reveals this aspect quite explicitly, since, for example, in ancient Greek (*xenos*) and in Hebrew (*ger*) the word denoting guest could also be used to mean stranger (Benveniste 1969: 87–101). In this perspective, the importance of hospitality was particularly essential for the rudimentary development of 'international law', a shared legal setting that could be codified from the above interactions between communities and foreigners. For instance, in Rome, Theodor Mommsen originally considered hospitality an exception to the general *Rechtlosigkeit* (lack of rights) of the outsider in Archaic Rome ([1892] 1984–5: 590). Once again, vocabulary conveys different patterns: some languages would have a single word to designate both partners in the hospitality relationship, such as the Greek *xenos*, a sign of a rather philoxenic and open atmosphere. Others would differentiate between host and guest in this respect, in a perspective that appears mostly preferential to the former. This is the case in Archaic Latin, where the host is notably called *hospes*, *hosti-pet, master of the guest (*hostis*), showing a hierarchical conception of hospitality. With the progressive increase in contact between the Roman community and outsiders and the development of a *ius gentium*, this aspect of hospitality became less crucial and the terminology evolved towards an indistinguishable *hospes*, whereas *hostis* came to designate a public enemy of Rome (Benveniste 1969: 87–101). More generally, during Classical times, hospitality seems to lose its position as a juridical tool, but not its sacredness or its logistical importance for newcomers.

On the other hand, we should not forget that, in addition to its decisive role in the reception and integration of strangers, hospitality, especially table hospitality, involved practices of reception between equals or towards inferiors of the same community. These practices were designed to display the host's social status and to earn the support and gratitude of his guests: we shall especially think of the domestic banquet, which will be explored in further detail in the last section of this chapter. Therefore, in the historical context of the ancient Mediterranean, hospitality must be considered a complex social phenomenon, a total social fact, whose significance exceeded its material functions of accommodating and entertaining guests, known or unknown, and which contributed to the opening of the ancient house and household towards the outside.

ENTERING THE HOUSE

In this context, home and its material counterpart, house, were essential to the practice and significance of ancient hospitality: in Greek, it was even a verb originating from the domestic hearth, the functional and symbolic centre of the Mediterranean house, *hestiân*, which was commonly used for the reception of guests at home (Gherchanoc 2012: 94, with references to ancient texts). In ancient Mediterranean civilizations, at least early on when state structures were not yet strengthened, private households would indeed be responsible for filtering newcomers, granting or denying them domestic hospitality, a choice that would lead either to the stranger's integration into the group or to his expulsion from the limits of the community. The house was thus the place par excellence where hospitality was supposed to be performed, whether the outsider received full accommodation there, was welcomed at the common table or just got basic help and information before resuming his journey. In addition, it was fundamentally in the home, especially among the elite, that numerous guests would be entertained, and hosts would compete in splendour and ostentation. Moreover, the importance of house and home was never limited to private hospitality, insofar as public guests would also be received, more or less willingly, by private individuals of the local elite into their own dwellings (see for instance the various case studies pertaining to the accommodation of the Roman emperor by private citizens in Halfmann 1986; Hostein and Lalanne 2012). Hospitality contributed to the social structuring of the ancient home and house, from the inside and in the relationship with the outside (Wallace-Hadrill 1988, 1994: 1–61).

The complexity of the association between hospitality and home can be clearly seen in the importance given, in ancient cultures, to various customs and rites aimed at controlling guests' access to the host's house, which simultaneously contributed to showing the solemnity of the relationship existing between partners. According to the anthropologist A. Van Gennep ([1909] 2011), hospitality, just like birth, adolescence, marriage, death and so on, should be considered a rite of passage in itself, supposed to manage the material and symbolic crossing of a community limit, the first manifestation of which seems to be the threshold of a host's house. This passage was marked by a succession of codified stages that Van Gennep identifies as *preliminary rites*, rites of the outsider's separation from his previous environment, *liminary rites* performed in the marginal phase before the future guest's actual access to the home/community, and finally *postliminary rites*, rites of aggregation into the new world, whether the guest should merely pass through it on his journey or decide to remain there as a new member of the receiving community.

Ancient evidence is particularly abundant on the issue of *liminary* rites, notably through the elicitation of identification and approval of guests wishing to enter a house where they have, or even more where they have not, been invited. Unknown newcomers were therefore urged to reveal their identity by answering a series of systematic questions, before being accepted under someone's roof, or at least, in a rather philoxenic attitude, just after receiving initial assistance and refreshment. We can refer, for instance, to an important hospitality scene in Homer's Odyssey, where Odysseus' son Telemachos and his companion Peisistratos, in search of information about Odysseus' fate, arrive at the palace of Menelaus, King of Lacedaemon. After offering to share the common meal with the strangers, Menelaus, who has tried in vain to guess who they are, asks them to identify themselves formally, a necessity that is ultimately spared them, since Helen recognizes Odysseus' son (Odyssey 4.1–304). Mutual recognition, based on one's account of personal identity and lineage, could even occur by accident. Homer's Iliad includes a famous episode between the Achaean Diomedes and Glaukos, ally of Troy. Meeting each other, not at home but on the battlefield, they suddenly realize that their respective ancestors were host and guest, and decide to keep the old alliance by exchanging weapons and refusing to fight: another sign that both to them and to Homer's audience, in the long run, hospitality meant much more than mere logistical support (Iliad 6.212–36).

The identification of hosts and guests was not always left to the honesty and trust of the parties. When they had formed an alliance of reciprocal accommodation, partners would exchange specific objects, called *symbola* in Greek and *tesserae* in Latin, either identical or shared in two matching halves, many examples of which have been brought to light, mostly in the Etruscan and Roman worlds (Figure 7.1); in public contexts, such conventions were remembered more formally, with commemorative inscriptions such as tables, decrees (Figure 7.2) and so on (Étienne, Le Roux and Tranoy 1987; Ariño 2012; Beltran Lloris 2016). Partners would identify themselves by displaying these tokens, reviving the existing relationship to gain access to the other's house, with this token as a key. They could be passed on to a third party, to allow someone else to benefit from a host's hospitality. This is why Jason, sending Medea away from Corinth, offers his rejected companion *symbola* that would guarantee her the help of Jason's *xenoi* abroad (Euripides, *Medea* 610–13). The role of these symbolic reminders is even more important when we

HOSPITALITY AND HOME 149

FIGURE 7.1: *Tessera hospitalis* in the form of a hand from Contrebia Belaisca inscription in Celtiberian, meaning 'Lubos from the Alisokum, son of Avalos, with the city of Contrebia Belaisca'. Credit: Bibliothèque Nationale de France.

FIGURE 7.2: Proxeny Decree (Attic, fourth century BCE). Credit: Musée Calvet, Avignon.

think that conventions of hospitality were hereditary, passed down through the male line. They could thus put individuals completely unknown to each other in contact and created the need of an undisputed way of recognition: just like the situation of Diomedes and Glaukos alluded to above. Tokens were a secure and efficient way of ensuring this intergenerational identification between hosts and guests. This aspect is particularly well illustrated by a famous passage in the *Poenulus* of Plautus, where Hanno, a Carthaginian wandering around the Mediterranean basin in search of his two daughters, succeeds in identifying Agorastocles as the adopted son of his host, previously the host of his father, thanks to their respective *tesserae hospitales*, and is consequently accommodated in his home:

> **Hanno** Ye gods and goddesses who cherish this city, I reverently entreat you that, having come here, the object of my coming may be happily attained, and may ye permit me, I implore you, here to find my daughters and my brother's son. Well, this is where Antidamas was a family friend of mine in former days. And now they tell me he has paid his debt to nature. I'm informed that his son, Agorastocles, is here, however: and it's to him this token of our family hospitality goes. [. . .]
>
> **Agorastocles** I am a native of Carthage myself, sir, I may inform you.
>
> **Hanno** Well, well, compatriot! Greetings!
>
> **Agorastocles** Gad, sir, and to you, whoever you are! And if you have need of anything, I beg you speak, command me, in the name of our common country.
>
> **Hanno** I thank you, sir. But do you know a young man here named Agorastocles?
>
> **Agorastocles** Why sir, if it's the adopted son of Antidama you look for, I am your man myself.
>
> **Hanno** Eh? What's that you say?
>
> **Agorastocles** That I am the son of Antidama.
>
> **Hanno** In that case, if you wish to compare the tokens of our family friendship, look, here is mine.
>
> **Agorastocles** Come, sir, come, show it to me. Yes, it exactly matches the one I have at home.
>
> **Hanno** Well, well, my friend! Hearty greetings! Why, your father Antidama, you know, was an old family host of mine. I shared this token of that hospitality with him.

> **Agorastocles**   Then as my friend you're to be my guest here. The hospitality of a friend and the Carthage that gave me birth are things I don't disclaim.
> —Plautus, *Poenulus* 950–8, 1038–55; Loeb trans.

Between better-acquainted hosts and guests and in the context of more familiar relationships, of course, such formalities would have been less important. Nevertheless, hospitality under one's roof or at one's table remained a controlled social event, especially among the elite, at least as the evidence available allows us to account for this practice. Romans, for instance, resorted to invitation or recommendation letters, such as the one that the young Lucius presents to his future host in Hypata, Milo, on behalf of a family friend, in the *Metamorphoses* of Apuleius:

> I responded to this with a laugh, 'My friend Demeas was certainly kind and thoughtful sending me off with a letter of introduction to a man like that, at least there'll be no smoking fires or cooking fumes to fear.' And with that I walked to the house and found the entrance. The door was stoutly bolted, so I banged and shouted. At long last the girl appeared: 'Well you've certainly given the door a drubbing! Where's your pledge for the loan? Or are you the only man who doesn't know we only take gold and silver?' 'No, no,' I replied, 'just say if your master's home.' 'Well why do you want him then?' 'I've a letter for him, from Demeas of Corinth.' 'Wait right here', she said, 'while I announce you.' And with that she bolted the door again and vanished into the house. Soon she returned; flung open the door, and proclaimed: 'He says to come in'.
> —Apuleius, *Metamorphoses* 1. 21–2; Loeb trans.

In this case, the hospitality granted by the intercession of a common friend remains nevertheless rather miserly because of old Milo's greediness. These letters seem to be a less formalized version of the *symbola/tesserae* alluded to above. They were essential, from the host's point of view, in order to prepare for the arrival of invited guests and to ascertain the identity of unknown newcomers. Also from the guest's point of view, they were necessary in order to avoid the suspicion of being a parasite, an accusation commonly found in Greek and Roman satiric literature about guests who ignored the necessity of such introductions, so as to be certain of a reception at the host's house, especially when on a journey. A significant part of ancient daily correspondence, of which we have a few famous examples published in antiquity, was thus dedicated to the sending, asking and answering of such invitations and letters of recommendation.[3] In the finest houses, the slave personnel included servants specifically in charge of checking guests' accreditations, such as doorkeepers, of which Petronius, *Satyricon* 28, for example, gives us a pleasant illustration for

Roman Italy. In short, this body of evidence shows how entering a host's house in the ancient world was a serious and codified process, which perfectly illustrates the original function of hospitality as a way for outsiders to access homes and communities.

ORDO HOSPITALITATIS

After the critical step of the guests' admission, interaction between hosts and guests continued to follow precise rites and customs, still with the goal of regulating the presence of others in one's home. From Archaic times throughout antiquity, the practice of hospitality involved two phases, often marking the beginning and the end of the guest's stay at the host's house: the sharing of a common meal, most often including sacrificed meat and wine, and the mutual exchange of gifts. This succession is attested in evidence from the Homeric poems onwards, as essential to the creation and strengthening of the relationship between *xenoi*.

Commensality was central to the definition and practice of ancient hospitality: so central, in fact, that the Greek word *xenia* often meant the hospitality meal itself. An invitation to stay at one's house would necessarily include a festive meal, or even be specifically devoted to it. Banquets were important social occasions that helped, through the game of mutual invitations, to reinforce relationships between individuals – relatives, friends, allies or inferiors – as well as homes and communities. Among the elite, domestic banquets took on a socio-political purpose, as a way to demonstrate one's personal network and social status in order to gain influence in the public sphere. Referring to the Mycenaean period, but with an observation that could be valid for all of antiquity, P. Schmitt-Pantel mentions the dual function of ancient banquets, 'à la fois facteur d'unité par la création d'une identité commune et facteur de division comme marqueur de l'inégalité sociale' (2012: 74). Of course, it would be illusory to presume to explore all the countless realities associated with such a complex phenomenon as the ancient Mediterranean banquet. The focus will thus be placed on two examples, taking into account only domestic banquets and excluding civic and religious public celebrations: the Greek *symposion* and Roman *conuiuium*. This will be a chance to discuss the material structures associated with the practice of hospitality in ancient houses.

The ancient Greek banquet, which is particularly known through the cases of Sparta, Crete, Corinth and of course Athens, was set up in two phases: the first, called *deipnon*, was dedicated to the consumption of food, whereas the second, called *symposion*, was based, as the Greek word indicates, on the sharing of drinks, especially wine (Figure 7.3).[4] Historians remain divided as to whether this distinction dates back to Homeric society, or only to Archaic aristocracies (Schmitt-Pantel 2012: 75). The essential socializing occurred during the drinking

FIGURE 7.3: Representation of a Greek *symposion* ("Diver's tomb", Paestum, sixth century BCE). Credit: Angelafoto / Getty Images.

party, which is widely considered a strictly male event, except for the presence of *hetairai*, courtesans, and female entertainers. This idea of gender distribution has however been brought into discussion in the last decades (see for instance Nevett 1999; Gherchanoc 2012: 102–5, with further literature on this issue). This male orientation represented a distinction between Greek and Roman habits, which would explain why a first-century BCE Greek had to tell a Roman official that 'it is not the custom of the Greeks to allow their women to recline at a *conuiuium* of men' (Cicero, *Verrines* 2.1.26.66, Loeb trans.). The evidence, which again pertains mostly to the habits of the elite, seems to attest some direct continuities in the nature of the banquet from Archaic to Hellenistic times, even though banquets of the Hellenistic kings aimed more directly at increasing the distance between the monarch and his guests/subjects through the exhibition of abundance and luxury (Vössing 2004). Greek banquets were, again, subject to religious rituals: a blood sacrifice, if meat was to be eaten, and wine libations, opening the symposium itself. Greek wine was not consumed pure, a custom that would have been considered barbarian, but was mixed with cold, hot or salty water and spices, following rules strictly codified and expressed by a guest chosen to be the head of the banquet. Characterized by festive habits with respect for moderation and self-control, the banquet is depicted in ancient sources as an important setting for intellectual exchange, the education of youths and civic cohesion (see of course, for Classical Athens, Plato's *Symposium*). A specialized room, the *andrôn*, a word showing the masculine aspect of the social event, was dedicated to the banquet's organization, isolating it from the spaces of everyday domestic life and allowing some privacy to the guests, especially when it was joined to an independent part of the house (which was the case for double-courtyard houses). Noted from at least the eighth century BCE on, probably taking after Near Eastern habits, the *andrônes* had standard, square-shaped dimensions and a specific layout suited to dining couches (*klinai*) distributed around three sides of the room on a raised platform, which made them particularly identifiable in Greek houses: two standard types are particularly well known, one with seven couches, the other eleven. This structure created something like an open circle, which perfectly symbolized the Greek conception of the banquet as a time of communication and conviviality between hosts and guests.

Many of these characteristics can be found in Roman dining habits as well, as they borrowed Greek features passed down through the Etruscan as well as Hellenistic civilizations during the first centuries of Rome's existence, although the exact chronology of these cultural transfers remains uncertain.[5] Just like the Greeks, Romans organized their day around a main meal, the *cena*, beginning in the afternoon ; the festive version of this *cena* was called *convivium*. The main differences from the Greek *deipnon/symposion* were the presence of women for the entire meal (even if, at least initially, women were not supposed to consume wine or recline like men, see below) and most of all the absence of a temporal distinction between eating and drinking. At a Roman *convivium*, food and wine would be consumed simultaneously throughout the banquet, with a complex succession of courses, with various intermittent amusements. Some hosts would organize *commissationes*, drinking parties occurring after the meal, but this practice, present from the late Republic on, was stigmatized as a quest for inebriation and a sign of depravity (see Badel 2006). On the other hand, though wine was still consumed diluted with water, the mixing proportions no longer obeyed common rules but were based on individual choice, according to one's preferences. Gastronomy was an important matter during the banquets of the Roman elite, at least from the second century BCE, with the arrival of cooks from the conquered Hellenistic East in Rome (see Livy 39.6). The cookbook of Apicius accounts for the advanced skills achieved by Roman cooks in the art of cuisine, of which Petronius gives us a rather caricatured vision in the famous *Cena Trimalchionis* (*Satyricon* 28–78).

More so than its Greek forerunner, the material organization of the Roman banquet was highly hierarchical. Theoretically, being allowed to recline was a sign of status in itself. It was forbidden to children, slaves, freedmen or women (Roller 2006), although depictions of banquets found in Pompeii and elsewhere nevertheless encourage a reconsideration of this last exclusion (Dunbabin 2003). Guests would then recline on *triclinia*, couches supporting from one to three individuals (Figure 7.4). These couches were then organized in three-couch sets around a table (*mensa*), since, according to Varro, the number of guests should be between the number of Graces and the number of Muses, that

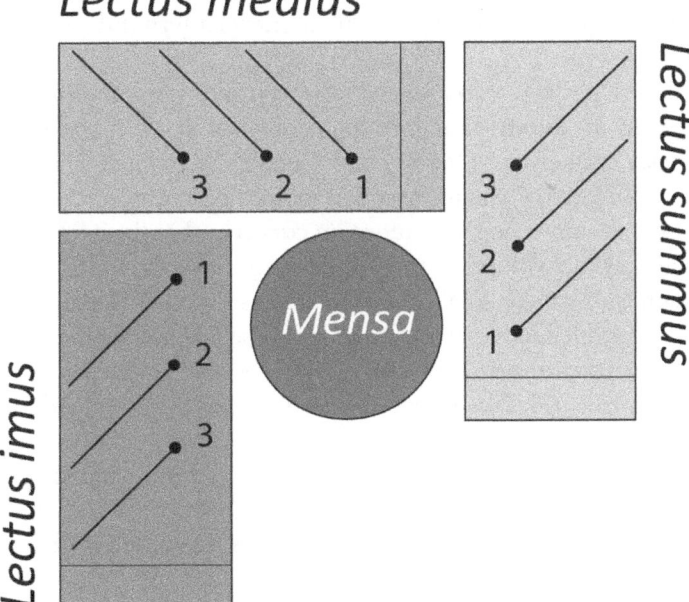

FIGURE 7.4: Organization of the Roman *triclinium*. Credit: Marie-Adeline Le Guennec.

is, between three and nine (after Macrobius, *Saturnalia* 1.7). Opulent houses and public spaces would nevertheless disregard this canonical norm by using multiple couch sets. The division of guests on these couches followed their social hierarchy: the place of honour, called *consularis locus* (place of the consul) was the first one to the left of the central bed, while the host would recline, face to face with the guest he wanted to honour, on the right side of the bottom bed (*imus lectus*) This organization led to more intimate and direct communication compared to the *andrôn*; however, the respect for hierarchy was more visible, and the symbolic aspects of *conuiuium* as a vector of power and prestige were clearer. This *triclinium*, evidenced from at least the second century BCE, lent its name to the reception hall of the Roman house, made easily identifiable by couch bases in masonry and/or matching floor mosaics. The *domus* and *villae* of the elite could have several *triclinia*, this time intended as rooms, positioned and furnished according to the seasons, so as to allow hosts and guests to enjoy the pleasures of commensality all year long. Smaller *oeci* (dining rooms) allowed more intimate dinner parties (see Vitruvius, *De Architectura* 6.3.10–4). This material organization saw a major development in the introduction, from the second century CE, of the *stibadium* (also known as *sigma*), a semi-circular single couch installed on a raised platform at the bottom of the room, which allowed more space for service and amusements. This however did not lead to the disappearance of the hierarchical distribution of guests, which simply followed from then on a new pattern (Ellis 1997; Dunbabin 2003: 141–74).

These different types of reception rooms could be connected to sleeping rooms reserved for guests, thus forming proper domestic reception sections in ancient houses, called *hospitalia* by the architect Vitruvius. This architectural practice contributed to the autonomy and privacy of guests in relation to the rest of the household, indicating an interesting concern: that the guest should feel at home when staying with his host. Once more, this practice is accounted for amongst high-status milieux. Vitruvius attributes the recourse to *hospitalia* to a Greek, or rather, Hellenistic context, where these *hospitalia* are perceived as an extension of the *andrôn* (6.7.4). But similar phenomena emerge from sources from the Roman world. For instance, Trimalchio, in the *Satyricon* of Petronius, among the various amenities of his *domus*, mentions a *hospitium*, a guestroom 'to take a hundred guests' (*Satyricon* 77; see also Sidonius Apollinarius, *Letters* 2.2.13, who describes the *deuersorium*, lodging, made available by his host in his *villa*). Archaeology gives us some material on these guestrooms/*hospitalia*. Identifiable cases are nevertheless few, since rooms dedicated to the accommodation of guests do not really differ from those used by regular household members. Regarding late antiquity, a rather solid case has been revealed at the site of Apamea, the capital of the late Roman province Syria Secunda, in the so-called 'House of the Deer' urban *domus* (Figure 7.5), where, as mentioned above, the insertion of Homeric verses into a floor mosaic allows us to identify a guest area (Morvillez 2002; see also Guizani 2013 for an attempt to identify such guest rooms in African *domus* during the second and third centuries CE).

In addition to being fed and accommodated, guests would be entertained at home with the widest variety of amusements. In a famous letter (*Letters* 2. 9), Sidonius Apollinaris describes the *ordo hospitalitatis* (scheme of entertainment) that an aristocrat from the fifth century CE would enjoy at a host's villa: outdoor meals, physical and intellectual games, hunts, public readings, all kinds of pleasures are put together by this rural house for the delight of the guests. The offering of hospitality gifts, known as *xenia*, was an essential step of this *ordo*. This practice helped put the hospitality relationship in a gift/counter-gift economy, which implied, just like the act of reception itself, immediate or future reciprocity (after the fundamental work of Mauss 2002, see for example Scheid-Tissinier 1994). This way, the link between individuals and homes appeared even stronger and open to the future (Gherchanoc 2012: 95).

For example, it was a habit in the Roman world for the hosts to precede, accompany or follow an invitation to a banquet or to stay at one's house with the delivery of delicate foods or drinks, if possible produced at home (or rather, at one's villa). At the end of the first century CE, the Roman poet Martial dedicates an entire book of his *Epigrams* to those *xenia*, maliciously proposing

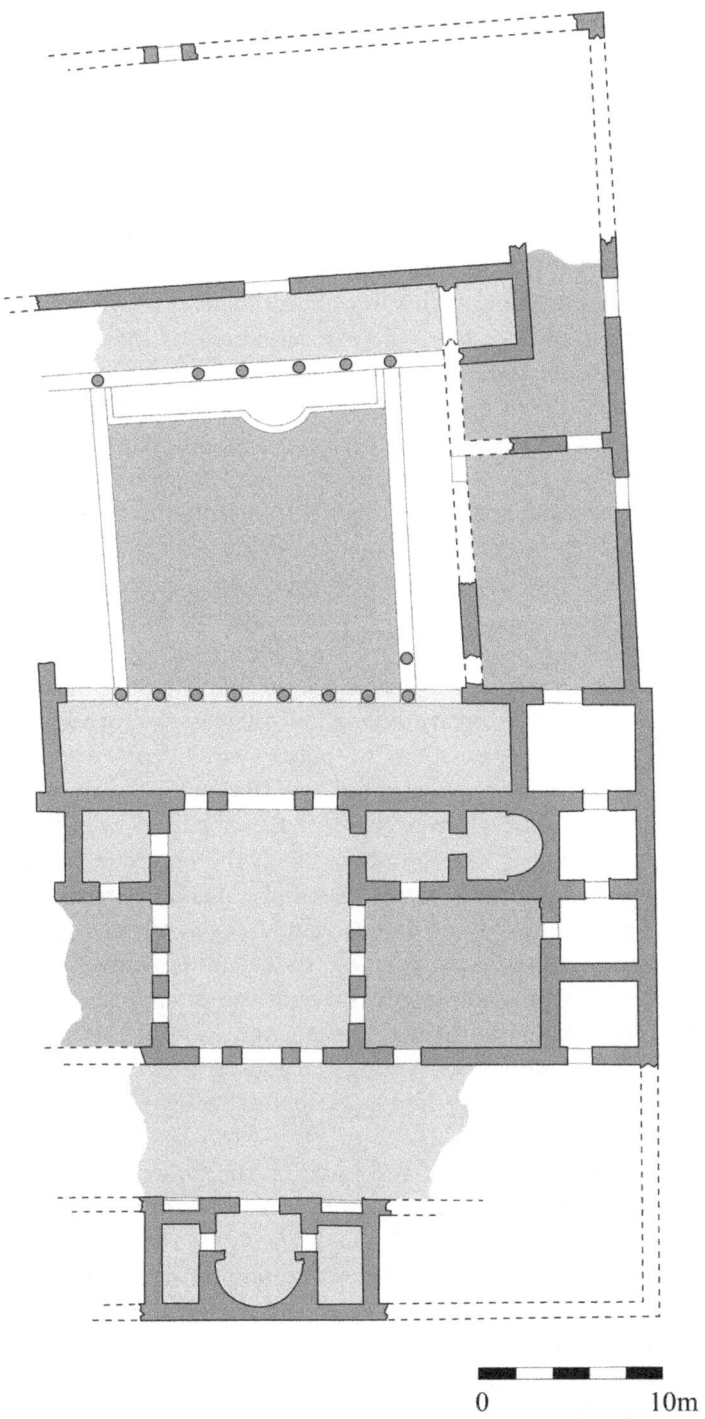

FIGURE 7.5: Plan of the House of the Deer (Apamea, Syria, sixth century CE). Credit: Sophie Hay after J. Balty.

to his readers to replace the costly and refined gifts with poetic descriptions of them, so that one can 'send these couplets to your guests (*hospitibus*) instead of a gift, if sesterces are as scarce with you as they are with me' (Martial, *Epigrams* 13.3.5–6, Loeb trans; see Leary 2001); a collection of short charming pieces then follows, where the properties and various uses of these alimentary *xenia* are detailed, ranging from incense (13.4) to beans (13.7), asparagus (13.21), wine from Setia (13.112) and even turtledoves (13.53) or sucking pigs (13.41). Following Vitruvius, *De Architectura* 6.7.4, floor mosaics or pictures of Hellenistic origin including similar motifs of foodstuffs are interpreted as a graphic version of these *xenia*. These forerunners of modern still lifes are particularly witnessed, during the Roman period, in the African provinces, where they decorate the reception rooms (*triclinia* and *oeci*) of luxurious houses. These graphic *xenia* are thus a way to display the gifts symbolizing hospitality for eternity, in the spaces of the house that were specifically dedicated to its celebration (for an examination of the historiography on this issue and some case studies based on the African corpus, see Balmelle et al. 1990).

CONCLUSIONS

Home is thus a key notion to the analysis of ancient Mediterranean hospitality, since the Greek *oikos*, the Roman *domus* and so on were the spaces par excellence where hospitality was supposed to be performed. By practising or denying domestic hospitality, not only homes but also communities demonstrated their openness or autarky, especially in Archaic times, when there were few alternative ways to receive strangers. On the other hand, the entertaining of numerous guests at home was a chance to show the social status of hosts and guests, since reciprocal hospitality was one of the complex relationships that structured ancient Mediterranean societies, from the inside and in contact with others. In this perspective, its significance seems especially important among the elite. This aspect was clearly exhibited through the phenomenon of the banquet, whose importance as an occasion of socializing and conspicuous consumption remains constant throughout antiquity and contributes decisively to the stability of ancient Mediterranean hospitality.

But by giving access to house and home to the Other, whether known or, more so, unknown, hospitality can represent a factor of risk for the domestic cell and for the community as well. It would in any case lead to a reconstruction of the home structure, at least for the duration of the guest's stay. Hence, ancient hospitality followed precise rules and norms aimed at regulating the access and presence of the guest in the domestic space, as well as the behaviour of the host towards him. But, once the threshold of the host's door was crossed, thanks to hospitality and the link of *philia*, or friendship, that it created, the guest would be included in the household. This inclusion remained nevertheless limited in time, since, as a young Athenian ironically says to an old aristocrat of Ephesius in the *Braggart Warrior* of Plautus, 'no guest can accept the hospitality of a friend like this without becoming an affliction after a three days' stay; but after a ten days' stay he becomes a whole *Iliad* of afflictions' (740-3, Loeb trans.). A time would necessarily come for the guest to leave his host's house and to decide whether to leave behind or join the community to which domestic hospitality gave him essential, but temporary, access.

ACKNOWLEDGMENTS

I am most grateful to Andrew Wallace-Hadrill and Joanne Berry for their invitation to contribute to this stimulating volume.

NOTES

1. On the issue of ancient Mediterranean connectivity, based on the seminal works of Braudel on the Mediterranean in the early modern period (Braudel 1976), see especially Horden and Purcell (2000: 342–400) on the mobility of goods and people.
2. In the documentation available, most hospitality scenes pertain to male guests; this situation changes at the end of the period considered in this chapter with the diffusion of the practice of feminine Christian pilgrimages and, consequently, the apparition of evidence relating directly to hospitality towards women (see the cases of Egeria in the fourth century CE and of Melania the Younger in the fifth century CE).
3. See, for instance, for the Roman world, Cicero, *Letters to Atticus* 13.50; *Letters to Friends* 13.78; Horace, *Epistles* 1.5; Pliny the Younger, *Letters* 1.15, 3.12, 6.14; Martial, *Epigrams* 2.18, 2.79, 5.78; Sidonius Apollinaris, *Letters* 6. 5, 8. 11. Again, the assistance requested or provided in such letters in the name of hospitality, for the benefit of the partners or of third parties, was rarely limited to mere accommodation, but often included political, social, juridical or even financial support.
4. The literature on this issue is of course extensive and constantly growing. For generic approaches, see, among others, Dupont 1977; Lissarrague 1987; Murray 1990; Slater 1991; Murray and Tecusan 1995; Catoni 2010; Nadeau 2010; Schmitt-Pantel 1992, 2015; Gherchanoc 2012; and Corner 2015. A historiographical account with further reference is found in Schmitt-Pantel 2012.
5. Again, the literature on the Roman banquet is endless. In addition to the references mentioned above covering both the Greek and Roman worlds, see Nielsen and Sigismund Nielsen 1998; Gold and Donahue 2005; Dunbabin 2003; Donahue 2004; and Schnurbusch 2011.

CHAPTER EIGHT

Religion and Home

CARLOS MACHADO

Throughout antiquity, houses were intimately associated with religious cults and traditions. House-owners and their families were surrounded by objects and images that reminded them that daily life was immersed in what today we call religion (the ancients did not separate these categories as we do). The houses of rich and poor were important spaces for interacting with the gods and expressing one's religious affiliation. Domestic structures were the setting for different forms of worship, from prayers to sacrifices. Religious ideas were taught and debated, being transmitted from parent to child and from friend to friend. At the same time, religious feelings and practices helped to shape not only the ways in which people used their houses, but also how they conceived them. The young Greeks and Romans who grew up seeing members of the household displaying their piety for their preferred deities learned that religion was not confined to the temples, churches and festivals that marked the rhythm of public spaces and civic institutions. They learned, furthermore, that the house was a sacred space, guarded by the gods of the family and by the spirit of their ancestors.

In spite of their importance, houses and domestic spaces have played a limited role in studies of ancient religious life, more concerned with the public aspects of religious cult. Scholars have coined the term '*polis* religion' to refer to the close relationship between the religious institutions and the political and social structures of the ancient city-state (Sourvinou-Inwood 1990; Scheid 2016). According to this view, ancient religions were essentially different from those familiar to us: there is supposedly an unbridgeable gap between the public and ritualistic nature of Greek and Roman religions and the interior and private character of Christianity, for example – a distinction that is exaggerated on both counts. More recently, scholars have started to paint a more complex picture of this past, putting more emphasis on the diversity of religious traditions that coexisted in city-states. Many and varied religious groups and agents were involved in this process, importing their cults and ideas from other parts of the Mediterranean and beyond (Woolf 2009; Rüpke 2013). In this context, houses have attracted a renewed interest from ancient historians and archaeologists (Bodel and Olyan 2008; Bowes 2008). Located between the socio-cultural imperatives of the wider community and the idiosyncrasies of their residents, houses are now seen as of crucial importance for our understanding of ancient religions. At the same time, it is clear that houses were inhabited by an otherworldly population of deities and spirits, who helped ancient homeowners to see their dwellings as sacred spaces.

THE RELIGIOUS MEANING OF THE HOME

The religious meaning of the home was frequently taken for granted by the women and men of antiquity. In the fourth century BCE, Aristotle observed that a candidate for the archonship in Athens was asked by city authorities, 'first, "Who is your father and to what *deme* does he belong, and who is your father's father, and who your mother, and who her father and what his deme?" then whether he has a family Apollo (Apollo *Patroos*) and Zeus of the enclosure (Zeus *Herkeios*), and where these shrines are' (*Athenian Constitution* 55.3). Establishing one's identity, but also where his domicile was, were crucial elements in the definition of Athenian citizenship. The gods associated with the domestic spaces and the family that lived there were the proof that the family was established in that place, and that they possessed firm roots in the *polis*. To own a house meant to establish a close relationship with the divine. This was one of the main elements in the definition of a house, as suggested by Xenophon in his *Oeconomicus* (9.6), where the equipment used for sacrifices is listed as the first type of furnishing to be brought to a new home. Houses were conceived of as sacred spaces, where members of a specific social unit (the household) maintained an intimate relationship with gods and other supernatural beings, like ancestors.

The most eloquent illustration of the identity between a house, its owner and his or her religious convictions is provided by the debates surrounding the destruction of the *domus* of the politician and orator Cicero, on the Palatine hill in Rome (Papi 1995). On the occasion of his exile, in 58 BCE, the house that had cost him 3.5 million sesterces was razed to the ground, its building materials were spoliated and the site was burnt down. A temple dedicated to Freedom (Libertas) was erected in the area by the man behind Cicero's downfall, the tribune of the plebs Clodius. Cicero returned to Rome in the following year, and he presented the case for the restoration of his house before the college of pontiffs in a speech known to us as *On His House* (*De Domo Sua*). As he observed, '[w]hat is more sacred, what more inviolably hedged about by every kind of sanctity, than the home of every individual citizen? Within its circle are his altars, his hearths, his household gods, his religion, his observances, his ritual' (*On His House* 109).

If anything, the relationship between the religious dimension of the *domus* and the identity of its owners was more pronounced in the oligarchic Rome of Cicero than in the democratic Athens of Aristotle. Cicero's wealthier contemporaries, being in control of seemingly unlimited economic resources and having access to the cultural models of the Hellenistic East, openly incorporated decorative elements associated with temples and sanctuaries into the architecture of their houses (Coarelli 1996). Columns, statues of deities (frequently of Greek origin) and other forms of decoration were used to assert the special standing of homeowners at a time of political competition and cultural experimentation. The house of Julius Caesar, for example, was decorated with a pediment, like a temple, as a sign of distinction awarded by a vote in the senate (Plutarch, *Life of Caesar* 63.6; Suetonius, *Divus Julius* 81.3). The close association between the house, its gods and their shrines meant that one could stand for the other, as the practice of speaking of houses by referring to their

FIGURE 8.1: Domus della Fortuna Annonaria, Ostia. Credit: Carlos Machado.

religious associations gained currency. As Cicero himself observed, when referring to his own past actions during the disbanding of Catiline's conspiracy against the Republic, 'the man who had saved our shrines (*delubra*) was driven away from them' (*On the Laws* 2.42). Writing approximately four centuries after these developments, it would have been natural for the pagan senator Symmachus to refer to his house as his Lar, the tutelary deity of his family: *Letter* 7.19 (Figure 8.1).

GODS OF THE HOUSE, GODS OF THE CITY

Since the earliest documented periods of Mediterranean antiquity, members of households posited an intimate connection between their dwellings and specific gods. This was already the case during the Bronze Age, but it becomes particularly clear for Greek and Roman communities from the seventh century BCE onwards, as soon as written evidence becomes available. This has led scholars to speak of household gods and family religion, especially with respect to Greek *poleis*. As Aristotle observed in his *Athenian Constitution*, mentioned above, there were gods that were closely connected with domestic spaces and their inhabitants. Apollo *Patroos* and Zeus *Herkeios*, for example, were deities associated with the protection of the *oikos* and the family (Mikalson 2005: 133–60; Parker 2005: 9–36). In the Homeric saga, Odysseus is said to have had an altar to Zeus *Herkeios* in the courtyard of his palace at Ithaka: the lyre-player who used to entertain the banquets held in the hero's absence considered seeking refuge there, when Odysseus unleashed his wrath on the suitors who had taken over his house (*Odyssey* 22.333–7). The epithet *herkeios* refers specifically to the physical boundaries of the house, but the god seems to have been associated with the family itself (Sophocles, *Antigone* 487; Parker 2005: 17).

More directly concerned with the protection of the household and its material wellbeing was Zeus *Ktesios*, 'of the acquisitions' (Mikalson 1983: 70–2). This was represented by a jar filled with ambrosia (water, olive oil and fruits) and wrapped in wool (Athenaeus, *Deipnosophists* 11.433b–c). A speech of the Athenian orator Isaeus, in the fourth century BCE, presents the case of a man claiming to be the grandson of a certain Ciron, and therefore entitled to his property, arguing that the claimant always took part in the sacrifices performed by his grandfather to this specific god, noting that the celebration was restricted to members of the family (Isaeus 8.16). It is not clear whether Ciron was particularly selective in only allowing his family to take part in this cult, or whether this was Isaeus' rhetorical strategy to emphasize the familial bonds between the claimant and the property being claimed, but the fact that the argument could be used indicates that it was acceptable to contemporaries. Other house-owners had a more inclusive approach. This is indicated in the speech of another fourth-century Attic orator, Antiphon, this time arguing the case of a citizen who accused his stepmother of murdering his father, Philoneos. Here, Philoneos is described inviting a friend and his own mistress to take part in the celebration of Zeus *Ktesios* and the banquet that followed it, when he was poisoned (*Antiphon*, 1.16–20). The gods of a household might have been closely associated with the family, but worshipping them could be a more or less open affair according to the wishes of the (male or female) house-owner.

Different deities were associated with a variety of aspects of the household and family life. This is the case of Apollo *Aguieus*, possibly represented by a pillar guarding the front of the house (Aristophanes, *Wasps* 875). The entrance of the house seems indeed to have been an important place for deities and monuments that represented them (Thucydides 6.27.1). Hecatea, representations of the goddess Hecate in the form of decorated pillars, were also placed there – a practice that seems to have been particularly common in Athens (Aristophanes, *Wasps* 799–804; Parker 2005: 18–19). A variety of gods could articulate different conceptions of house-owners and members of their households, emphasizing different types of association. This is pointed out by Socrates, in a passage of Plato's *Euthydemus*, where he explains the absence of altars of Zeus *Patroos* in Athenian houses: 'None of the Ionians, I replied, give him this title, neither we nor those who have left this city to settle abroad: they have an ancestral Apollo, because of Ion's parentage. Among us the name "ancestral" is not given to Zeus, but that of the enclosure (*Herkeios*) and of the tribe (*Phratrios*), and we have an Athena of the tribe (*Phratria*)' (302D). The close connection of specific deities with the family and the household is not questioned, but we are reminded that it could be manifested in many different ways.

The most important deity in a domestic context was Hestia, a goddess who was identified with the hearth (her name means, in fact, 'hearth', in Greek), and therefore the centre of family and domestic life (Burkert 1985, 170; Vernant 2006; see Figure 8.2). According to the *Homeric Hymn to Aphrodite* (24–32), she was a maiden who refused to marry Poseidon and Apollo; as a reward, Zeus assigned her a central position among mortals and immortals, as well as the right to keep the noblest part of sacrifices, the fat (*Homeric Hymn to Hestia*, 1–6). From the Archaic period, authors placed Hestia at the centre of the Greek conception of home, making her involved in some of the most important ceremonies that marked the life of the *oikos*. These included the presentation of a new baby, marking her/his official acceptance by the family; the introduction of the bride into the groom's family during the celebrations of a wedding; and also the incorporation of slaves into the household. In other words, the goddess who was most closely connected with the house also oversaw the expansion and reproduction of the social group that lived there.

Hestia's centrality – both conceptual and ritual – suggests a fixed space in the Greek house, a stone hearth, for example. Unfortunately, however, stone hearths are only rarely attested in the archaeological record, and it seems that the centre

FIGURE 8.2: Athenian *pyxis*, showing Hestia holding a sceptre and fruit in a wedding procession, *c*. 470 BCE. Credit: The British Museum.

of the house was moved from room to room in portable braziers, according to the convenience of the family (Jameson 1990b: 193). Even in well-excavated cities like Halieis and Olynthos, where the study of domestic structures has unearthed rich information about different aspects of daily life, the evidence available is poor and mostly related to portable altars (Cahill 2002; Ault 2005; Nevett 1999). As Robert Parker put it, 'the fixed centre of the turning world turns out to have been portable' (2005: 14). This preference for a moveable hearth might be due to the fact that, being associated with the preservation of the family, Hestia had to be moved whenever the family moved to a new house. Or perhaps it is because Greek religious systems were flexible enough to adapt to the uses and needs of daily life. In any case, household religion and the ideas about the gods seem to have been more flexible than our texts imply.

The case of Hestia is also instructive because, although profoundly identified with the home, she could also be found in prominent public spaces. The goddess of the hearth was worshipped at an altar in the temple of Zeus at Olympia, for example (Pausanias 5.14.4). More importantly, she was present in the civic hearth, located in Prytaneia in different cities: structures used for public functions such as banquets and cults, as well as archives (Miller 1978). Just as with Hecate,

Apollo and Zeus in their different guises, the worship of Hestia suggests that Greeks were able to conceptualize the differences between family and household on one side and the city and civic institutions on the other, while at the same time crossing these boundaries whenever necessary.

Rather than a separate religious space, isolated from the 'public' aspects of city life, the house was fully integrated into the religious life of the *polis*. In fact, participation in the great civic festivals – such as the Dionysia at Athens, for example – also involved celebrations at home, which served not only as setting for gatherings and libations but also as a starting point for processions (Isaeus 8.15–16; Aristophanes, *Acharnanians* 247–52). The cultic activities performed at home could complement public religious life, but they could also go beyond that. This is suggested by Plutarch, writing in the second century CE, when he discusses a traditional sacrifice performed by the city's archon at the public hearth (probably in the Prytaneion) and by the other citizens at home, directed at expelling ravenous hunger (*boulimía*) from the house and the city (*Convivial Questions* 6.8 [693F–694]). The ritual took place at home, where a servant was ritually struck and driven away, as well as in public. There was a structural homology between the domestic and the public spheres, not only in the way the actions took place, but also in the purpose of the ritual – a private and public concern. The house was not subordinated to the temples and civic spaces of the city: it was a religious space in its own right, fully integrated into the religious life of the community.

WORSHIPPING AT HOME

Deities of different nature remained a constant presence in Mediterranean houses, for all of Antiquity (Bodel and Olyan 2008). We are particularly well informed about Roman culture, as a variety of texts and material remains attest to this belief. As with Hestia among the Greeks, Romans associated the goddess Vesta with the hearth. In this case, however, we are less well informed about her private worship than about her public, official cult (Orr 1978: 1560–1). Janus, a god associated with passageways, was celebrated near the entrance of houses, as suggested in a passage in Ovid's *Fasti* (1.134–6). Of all the gods in the Roman pantheon, Roman domestic religion was more closely identified with a particular group of deities, the *penates*, the *lares* and the *genius* of the house-owner (Orr 1978: 1562–75). It is worth considering them briefly, before we turn to the more complicated issue of how (and where) they were venerated at home.

The *penates* were connected with the protection of the household, sometimes more specifically with domestic storerooms. They were closely associated with Vesta, and it was thought that the *penates* of Rome were kept in her round temple by the forum. There were different types of *lares* (tutelary deities), associated with domains as diverse as public games (*lares ludentes*), roads (*viales*) and the imperial household (*Augusti*). The household or family *lares* played an important role in the Roman conception of domestic life, being closely identified with the family across generations (Plautus, *Aulularia* 1). The more abstract *genius*, in its turn, represented the religious dimension of the house-owner, the *paterfamilias* (Sofroniew 2015: 33–42).

As in the case of Greece, the boundaries between these deities were ill defined, and new gods were frequently introduced into the domestic realm. Visual representations found in houses could focus on one or more household gods instead of the others, but our picture might be affected by the different media employed to depict them: it is often the case that paintings survived, but not statuettes, for example. The *penates* could be associated with the *lares* (Cicero, *On the Republic* 5.7), and could be identified with different deities. At home, Cicero venerated a statue of the goddess Minerva as his Lar, associating her with the protection of the whole city (*On the Laws* 2.42; Bodel 2008: 252). Accordingly, when leaving for his exile, he took it to the most prestigious temple in Rome, the Capitol, and dedicated it there – an act that not only advertised his piety but also brought prestige to him and his goddess. We should not dismiss Cicero's actions as mere political posturing. Members of a household were expected to show special reverence for their deities, irrespective of their social and economic condition. The Lar in Plautus' *Aulularia*, guardian of a household in financial difficulty, complains that the owner of the house himself never showed him any respect, but notes that his daughter did it frequently (24–5). Wealthy Romans visiting their rural properties were advised to pay a visit to the *lares familiares* first, before inspecting their domains (Cato, *On Agriculture* 2.1).

Romans worshipped their preferred gods and goddesses in different spaces of the house. All they needed was a representation of the deity and a portable altar, brazier or lamp. Ritual practice and the choice of gods must have varied from house to house, and we must be careful not to allow our preconceived notions of what was 'Roman' (or not) distort our picture. Roman cities were marked by great religious, cultural and architectural diversity, defying generalized statements about any aspect of their history. It is with this caution that we should approach the rich archaeological evidence from Pompeii, a well-preserved city whose domestic architecture has been thoroughly studied. Pompeian houses do not offer a fixed model of domestic religion, but they do illustrate the range of possible behaviours and conceptions available to members of households across the empire.

The *domus* of Pompeii reveal a significant variety of forms of celebrating one's piety, with three main types of *lararia*, domestic shrines, being attested. These include wall-paintings depicting household gods, niches (curved or rectangular) on walls and *aediculae*, small shrines resembling temples, sometimes decorated with columns, pediments, paintings and statuettes (Boyce 1937: 10–17; Sofroniew 2015: 31). These different types of structure could be located in different parts of the house, from grand reception spaces like the *atrium* to more reserved areas (Van Andringa 2009: 218–44). A good example is found in the house of Balbus (I.8.18), where a small niche with statuettes was found in the kitchen. The structure was framed by a painting depicting an altar, snakes and the *lares*, indicating the participation of servants in a cult associated with the family and especially the *paterfamilias* (Foss 1997: 199–201). Grander *domus* could house more than one such structure, with a more elaborate shrine in the *atrium* and others in different rooms.

The so-called House of the Menander (I.10.4), a large residence that was in the process of renovation at the time of the eruption of Vesuvius, is a good example of how different *lararia* could be combined. An *aedicula*-like shrine was installed in the *atrium*, by the entrance, on top of a small podium and decorated with columns and a pediment (Ling 1997: 265). A painted *lararium* (now gone) was seen in the kitchen, near the hearth (Ling 1997: 278). The most important of these structures seems to have been the one located in one of the exedras on the southern end of the peristyle. It consisted of an altar on top of a raised podium, with a semi-circular niche containing five wooden statuettes (Ling 1997: 275). It is possible that the spatial distribution of these shrines corresponded to their degree of openness or accessibility, or to the type of social group that would have had access to each. The social composition of the religious community that frequented the house could be defined according to the nature of the occasion being celebrated.

The house-owner naturally had pride of place in the rituals that took place in his home, be it through the choice of deities that were worshipped – including his ancestors, celebrated in wax images displayed in the *atrium* – or through the actual performance of rituals. At the same time, houses and domestic life offered countless opportunities for religious transactions and expressions of piety by different members of the household. So it is that Felix, probably a slave, scratched a graffito with a vow to the *lares* in a kitchen (*CIL* IV, 9887: house II.1.1). In the so-called house of Polybius (IX.13.1–3), a certain Publius Cornelius Felix and a slave, Vitalis, made a vow for the safe return of the house-owner, Caius Iulius Philippus, also in the area of the kitchen (*AE* 1977, 219). Not far from it, a painting depicts a scene of sacrifice with a round altar being attended by a woman (Figure 8.3). She is accompanied by a male figure holding a cornucopia, probably representing the *genius* of the house-owner, and flanked by the household *lares*. Writing in the second century BCE, Cato (*On Agriculture* 143.2) had observed about the wives of the slaves responsible for running rural properties: 'On the Kalends, Ides and Nones, and whenever a holy day comes, she must hang a garland over the hearth, and on those days pray to the household gods as opportunity offers.' The participation of slaves and dependants was a crucial element in the religious life of the family.

Shrines in domestic spaces were not officially considered sacred, as this required consecration by public magistrates and priests acting on behalf of the

FIGURE 8.3: Painted *lararium* from the *domus* of Julius Polybius, Pompeii. Credit: DEA/Archivo J. Lange/Getty Images.

people (*Digest* 1.8.6.3; Gaius, *Institutes* 2.5). Therefore the management of a house as a space for religious worship was largely its owner's business. This might explain why niches could be blocked from view whenever new residents moved into a house, choosing new rooms as spaces for worship (Van Andringa 2009: 230). Next to the House of the Menander and in the same city block, a painted *lararium* located next to the entrance of house I.10.1 was blocked from view by the construction of a staircase leading to the upper floor (Ling 1997: 23). As time passed and the ownership of a house changed hands, new arrangements had to be made to accommodate the needs of the household, and this included the deities too.

Beyond the performance of rituals, houses and domestic spaces were venues for a variety of forms of interaction with the supernatural and the divine. Petronius' *Satyricon* narrates a visit to the house of the millionaire freedman Trimalchio on the occasion of a banquet, providing a number of insights into these interactions. The guests encounter religious representations from the moment they enter the house, from paintings depicting their host accompanied by deities on different episodes of his life to a small *lararium* with statues of the *lares* in silver and a marble statue of Venus (*Satyricon* 29). The *atrium* of the house was decorated with paintings of the *Iliad*, the *Odyssey* and the games offered by one Laenas, probably a local magistrate (*Satyricon* 30). This is certainly a jab at Trimalchio's lack of discernment, equating the Homeric epics to a small local spectacle. The criticism is more effective, however, because it also refers to the frescoed mythological scenes that decorated the houses of wealthy Romans in different parts of the empire. At the entrance to the *triclinium*, an inscription commemorated the house-owner as one of the Augustales, a group of disputed function but which had some connection with the cult of emperors (*Satyricon* 30). During the meal, the diners were presented with a plate decorated with the zodiacal signs and a choice of food to match them (*Satyricon* 35). This gave Trimalchio the opportunity to expound his very personal interpretation of the sky and of the zodiac (*Satyricon* 39).

By the time when Petronius was writing, wealthy Romans had for centuries been importing and copying a great variety of works of art, especially of Greek origin. House-owners had access to a sophisticated visual culture that was quickly incorporated into the decoration of public and private buildings. Statues, paintings and mosaics helped to expand the repertoire of images of gods and religious concepts that gave meaning to Roman houses (Zanker 1998). Scholars tend to emphasize the artistic meaning of these objects to the detriment of their religious significance, but we should remember that these works of art were open to numerous alternative readings and interpretations, in terms both of their iconography and of the myths and cosmologies to which they referred. The house of Trimalchio, imagined as it is, is a good example of how religiously inspired decoration – including the *lararium* – could serve different functions in a variety of domestic settings. It helped to frame the residents' identity, communicating their religious sympathies to the visitors. It celebrated their social standing and participation in the community's cultic life, through the medium of inscriptions and honorific monuments. It offered the opportunity for engaging in religious discussions, stimulating the interpretation of images and the exposition of religious concepts in a context in which the house-owner was frequently the teacher – or the teacher's patron (Figure 8.4). Houses could therefore fulfill a dynamic role in ancient religious life, and this is what we must consider now.

HOUSES AND RELIGIOUS CHANGE

The historian Livy narrates the persecution moved by the senate and Roman authorities against the cult of Bacchus, in 186 BCE (Livy 39.8–19; Beard, North, and Price 1998: 91–6). In his account, the cult is treated as a pestilential evil that entered Rome from Greece through Etruria as a contagious disease, corrupting morals and causing violence – it was a threat to the Roman Republic. According to Livy's highly elaborate account, the cult spread from friend to friend, from family to family, from parents to sons, through a series of domestic networks. In spite of its dubious reliability, the narrative illustrates the role

FIGURE 8.4: Mosaic with scene of Venus, House of Amphitrite, Bulla Regia. Credit: Sophie Hay.

played by houses in ancient religious life – a role that could sometimes be seen as clearly subversive. Houses were sheltered spaces that could to some extent be closed to the outside world, providing an ideal setting for encounters and discussions protected from the gaze (and surveillance) of the wider community. It is not surprising, therefore, that ancient writers were often concerned with the potential use of domestic spaces for the dissemination of dangerous ideas.

Plato proposed, in the *Laws*, that no one should possess a domestic shrine, and that all sacrifices should be carried out by official priests in public. This would prevent well-meaning mistakes, as well as impious developments that might threaten the state (*Laws* 909E–910D). This same argument appeared in mitigated form in Cicero's *On the Laws* (2.19), which stated that 'No one shall have gods to himself, either new gods or alien gods, unless recognized by the State. Privately they shall worship those gods whose worship they have duly received from their ancestors.' Private shrines were acceptable as long as they honoured gods inherited from the ancestors and acknowledged by the community. The introduction of new or alien deities, he observed, might cause confusion and give origin to rites unknown to priests (*On the Laws* 2.25–6).

Houses were a dynamic element in ancient religious life. Being subject to the religious choices of their owners and other members of the household, they were more open to the influence of relatives, friends, clients and guests enjoying the benefit of hospitality. At the same time, the social and cultural hierarchies that gave shape to the household played an important part in the spread of new religious ideas, as friends and clients were exposed to the religious choices of their patrons and associates. This is best illustrated by a series of references in the earliest Christian texts, most notably the Acts of the Apostles and the Pauline epistles. These describe a diverse religious community going through an accelerated process of self-definition and expansion, as it encountered different religious and social groups across the eastern Mediterranean (Meeks 1983). Houses played a fundamental part in this process, serving as a shelter against persecutors, as a venue for meetings and finally as a space for worship (Blue 1994; Gehring 2004).

It was probably to a house in Jerusalem, to a 'room upstairs' according to Acts (1.12–15), that the apostles returned after Christ ascended to heaven; there they stayed and prayed together, in a founding moment in the history of the community. Domestic spaces continued to play a prominent part among the Christians of Jerusalem, for the simple virtue of being private: after being freed from prison by an angel, the apostle Peter went to the house of Mary (mother of John), where the others were gathered and praying. A servant named Rhoda answered the door, and Peter was allowed in after she warned his friends of his arrival. There he told them of his adventures, and asked them to repeat them to their fellow believers (Acts 12.12–17). Christians were able to make use of these specific spaces, owned by specific members of the community, which provided them with a shelter at times of persecution – but also allowed them to expand the circle of believers by passing on stories about what they learned and lived through.

Houses continued to play an important part during the apostle Paul's missionary travels around the eastern Mediterranean. The narrative of the Pauline mission in the Acts of the Apostles accompanies his itinerary from city to city, following a well-defined pattern that identifies three main types of spaces and social interactions: a visit to the Jewish community, usually in a synagogue; an address to the local population (or part of it), in a public space; and a stay in the house of a local acquaintance or a sympathizer (Meeks 1983:

25–32). At Philippi, a gentile worshipper of the Jewish god, Lydia, listened to Paul's preaching and, after converting her entire household, urged the apostle and his companions to stay in her house (Acts 16.1–15). Here we see a woman who was the head of a household, who probably enjoyed a prosperous economic situation (she was a dealer in purple cloth) and who could both offer protection to the apostle and use her social capital to expand the number of believers. Her house continued being used as a meeting space by members of the nascent community after Paul left the city (16.40). In Corinth, Paul stayed with the Jewish traders Aquila and Priscilla, recently arrived from Italy (18.1–3). He frequented the synagogue, until deciding to preach to the gentiles: 'Then he left the synagogue and went to the house of a man named Titius Justus, a worshipper of the God: his house was next to the synagogue. Crispus, the official of the synagogue, became a believer in the Lord, together with all his household; and many of the Corinthians who heard Paul became believers and were baptized' (18.6–8).

As with any account of the origins of a successful religious group, it would be naive to accept the narrative of Acts at face value. We can accept it, however, as indicative of what early Christians thought of as plausible occurrences in their social life. Houses articulated social hierarchies and religious bonds, providing followers of different religious groups with a powerful tool for refining and spreading their ideas. They were not religiously exclusive spaces either, and members of different groups could visit them and debate their beliefs. In Rome, leaders of the Jewish community are said to have come to Paul's lodgings, where '[f]rom morning until evening he explained the matter to them, testifying to the kingdom of God and trying to convince them about Jesus both from the law of Moses and from the prophets. Some were convinced by what he had said, while others refused to believe' (28.23–4).

Once the Christian community was established in a new city, houses continued being used as places of assembly by its members. The epistles of Paul mention a number of houses in different places, referring to the community that gathered in that space. In his letter to the nascent community in Rome, Paul sends greetings to Phoebe, who had been his benefactor (possibly his host) in Cenchreae, the port town of Corinth, as well as to Aquila and Priscilla, and also the church 'in their house' (Romans 16.1–5). 'Nympha and the church in her house' are mentioned in Paul's letter to the Colossians (4.15), and another missive is addressed to Philemon, two of his associates and the church in his house (Philemon 1–2). Christians were not innovating, in this sense. The introduction of a foreign cult associated with a house is well illustrated by the much older but particularly revealing case of the temple of the Egyptian god Serapis at Delos, some time in the third or second century BCE. We are informed about this by an inscription set up by the priest Apollonius II (*IG* XI.4, 1299; Danker 1982: 186–91). The cult arrived in Delos with Apollonius' grandfather, who brought the cult statue and founded a community in a rented house. Apollonius II inherited the statue and the office of priest, and following an instruction received in a dream built a Serapeum on 'defiled ground' (literally, 'a plot full of dung'), which he bought with his own funds. However, as archaeological work carried out in the area of the temple revealed, the structure was actually built in a residential area, and it incorporated a group of previously existing domestic structures (White 1990: 35–6). The cult of Serapis went from being associated with a domestic space used for religious functions to being located in a religious structure built at the expense of a residential area. Religious communities were thus closely identified with the benefactors who sheltered them, and a similar type of dynamic seems to have taken place in the case of early Christianity.

It is difficult to determine the extent to which the houses mentioned in Paul's letters were still used for residential and domestic purposes, or whether their function as a venue for religious assembly took over. These were flexible spaces that could be adapted and put to different forms of use without major construction work, and previous attempts at identifying a specific architectural model as a house-church have now been largely discredited (White 1990). A good example of this is the house identified as having belonged to the apostle Peter in Capernaeum, in Galilee. According to a tradition preserved in the Gospels, Jesus used Peter's house as a base for a large part of his missionary work (Gehring 2004: 35–42). A fourth-century CE text, the *Itinerary of Egeria*, mentions the existence of a church built on the site of the house, and excavations carried out in the city revealed a late antique church built on top of an earlier residence – quickly identified as that where Christ sojourned (Blue 1994: 138–40; Gehring 2004: 32–4). There is no evidence to confirm this association with the apostle, however. What these discoveries suggest, instead, is that there was a local tradition connecting a church (possibly the one excavated) with the site believed to have been the house of Peter. Memory and tradition confirmed the importance of domestic spaces in the history of early Christianity, contributing to the expansion and organization of the community. The memory of the house of Peter, together with the traditions associated with the late antique church, reminds us of the important role that houses, even after their destruction, could continue to play in the way Christians and other religious communities defined their own history and identity.

THE HOUSEHOLD AS A RELIGIOUS COMMUNITY

The spread of Christianity was part of a broader process of religious change that involved the whole of the Mediterranean world – and beyond. This included the development of more interiorized forms of religion, a greater concern with the definition of religious truth and the appearance of new forms of religious authority, based on charismatic qualities rather than on civic institutions like the pagan priesthoods of old (Stroumsa 2009). Houses played an important role in these transformations, occupying a more prominent place in religious life than in previous centuries, as the already ill-defined frontiers between domestic and civic religion became fainter. The houses of late antiquity came under closer scrutiny of public and ecclesiastical authorities, at the same time that the hierarchies that shaped the household helped to define the way religion was experienced in the public sphere. These developments can be observed in different parts of the ancient world, but nowhere as clearly as in the city of Rome, the (by now) former capital of the empire.

To a very large extent, houses continued being used for religious purposes in the same ways as they were in Classical Athens, or in early imperial Pompeii. Houses served, for example, as meeting spaces where religious ideas could be discussed, and knowledge about the gods could be exchanged. We find a wonderful (fictional) example in the *Saturnalia*, a poem on the festival celebrating the god Saturn written by Macrobius in the first decades of the fifth century CE. The poem describes a series of meetings held at the house of the senator Praetextatus, in which a group of pagan friends discusses issues such as the origins and nature of the festival, the origins and meaning of different religious institutions, and a number of mythological, historical and grammatical questions (Cameron 2011). Arcane information and obscure literary references are shared among the guests, who instruct and correct each other while banqueting. As Praetextatus and his friends debate the rites and institutions of traditional Roman religion, they try to establish what is correct – or true – about them. The fact that Macrobius was probably a Christian, and that much of the discussion he presents is more indicative of late antique culture than of the origins of the Saturnalia, does not reduce the interest of this example for us.

Christians used their houses for similar purposes, just as they had done at the time of the apostles. Discussing issues of the faith, aspects of worship and even the political life of the church seems to have been a common occurrence in the houses of members of the Christian community, but in this case the consequences could be more troubling. To a degree that was unknown among pagans, late antique Christians were involved in a series of fierce debates concerning the definition of religious orthodoxy, a debate that involved not only members of the ecclesiastical hierarchy and the imperial government (as emperors converted to the new religion), but also the women and men on the street. The preacher Jerome warned his friend, the Christian lady Julia Eustochium, against those who frequented houses of the Roman elite, pretending to live a sainted life, and offered not only bad advice but also a wrong instruction. It was better to live in ignorance about details of the Scripture than to seek advice from the worthless, he observed (*Epistle* 22.29).

Christian house-owners were exposed to the danger of misguided teachers, heretics and men of sainted appearance who sought to take advantage of their listeners. At a time when complex issues such as the nature of Christ and the definition of the Trinity were hotly discussed and theological consensus was the subject of political confrontation, house-owners could suddenly find themselves on the wrong side of doctrinal debate. By offering a protected, secluded space where only those invited were allowed to be present, the houses (and households) of powerful patrons – men and women who could support and promote the teachings of their preferred clerics – became important arenas in the theological debates that took place in the fourth and fifth centuries (Maier 1995). It is not surprising, then, that bishops and their clergy kept a close eye on domestic spaces. Persecuted by the bishop Damasus (366–84), the presbyter Macarius used a network of houses to meet and pray with his supporters. His luck was short-lived, however, and when the house in which he was assembled with his followers was stormed by representatives of the bishop and imperial officials, he was dragged through the streets of Rome and thrown into prison (*Libellus Precum* 79–80).

Just as Paul did in the early decades of the Christian community (but in a very different context), Romans continued to use their domestic spaces to discuss and spread religious ideas and interpretations. It was in a villa near Milan that Augustine experienced his definitive conversion to Christianity: there, surrounded by tranquillity and in the company of his friends, he found the time to read, listen and learn about the faith with the intellectual rigour and the emotional intensity that he needed (*Confessions* 8; Brown 1967: 151–81). Imperial authorities were aware of the role played by *domus* in the spread of religious ideas, and their potential for allowing dangerous developments. This is illustrated by a law addressed by the emperors Valentinian I and Valens to the prefect of Rome in 372, which determined that '[w]herever an assembly of the Manichaeans or such a throng is found, their teachers shall be punished with a heavy penalty. Those who assemble shall also be segregated from the company of men as infamous and ignominious, and the houses and habitations in which the profane doctrine is taught shall undoubtedly be appropriated to the resources of the fisc' (*Theodosian Code* 16.5.3).

The importance of houses as a space for disseminating religious ideas (and subversive interpretations) was enhanced by their use as spaces for worship. As Jerome reminded the aristocratic Laeta about the education of her daughter, the young Christian should wake up at night to pray and recite the psalms; to sing hymns in the morning; and to light the evening lamp, a traditional practice that he described as an 'evening sacrifice' (*Letter* 107.9). Kim Bowes showed, in an insightful study of religious change in late antiquity, that the use of houses for Christian worship was an empire-wide phenomenon, and Rome provides us with some of its most remarkable examples (Bowes 2008). On the summit of the Caelian hill, not far from the Colosseum and the temple of the deified emperor Claudius, an early imperial apartment block (*insula*) was converted into a private house in the course of the third century. The house was decorated with fresco paintings imitating marble decoration and religious motifs, in the same way as the earlier houses of Pompeii. At some point during the fourth century, however, a shrine (the so-called *confessio*) was adapted at mezzanine level, equipped with a small opening that almost certainly served as a private reliquary. This is indicated by the paintings on the walls, depicting scenes of prayer and of a group of Christians being martyred (Brenk 1995: 188). The idea that Christian house-owners could install private shrines and spaces for worship in their houses is also indicated by a reference in the biography of the Christian lady Melania, who spent the eve of the feast of St Laurence holding vigil in the chapel at her family's house (*Life of Melania* 5). Having a specific space for worship at home gave members of the household the opportunity to celebrate their religious beliefs on their own terms, independently from the official religious authorities – in this case, the bishop and his clerics. This was potentially troubling in the case of Christian Rome. Visits by members of the clergy gain a new significance, in this context, as they effectively confirmed the religious authority of the house-owner and his household. Romans were thus able to create their own domestic communities, disseminating their own ideas and favouring specific saints and martyrs, instead of simply following the priorities of their ecclesiastical leaders.

On the Esquiline hill, the excavation of a fourth-century house on Via Giovanni Lanza suggests that interesting developments were also taking place in pagan households (Guidobaldi 1986: 194–8; see Figure 8.5). Here, a domestic shrine was decorated with an eclectic mix of approximately twenty statues, statuettes and busts, all produced in earlier periods. Placed at the back of the structure, a statue of Isis-Fortuna confirmed the syncretistic sympathies of the house-owner. Next to the shrine, an opening on the wall gave access to a staircase leading to a mithraic cave, a room designed for the worship of the god Mithras, in which members of the household could gather to worship together. Pagan worship had traditionally been marked by a high degree of flexibility, but this is a remarkable indication of the extent to which many different cults and traditions – including the initiation in the cult of Mithras – could be combined under the authority of one *paterfamilias*. It is difficult to know on what occasions cults taking place in the houses of pagans and Christians were open to people outside the inner circle of the household, but it seems safe to assume that friends and clients were a frequent presence in domestic cults.

Houses played a defining role in the religious transformations that we associated with the end of antiquity. Their decoration gave an incentive to discussions of religious ideas, while their gates and doorways provided the privacy (and freedom) necessary for them. Domestic shrines allowed household worshippers to express and experience their own preferences, while celebrating their participation in the community during the larger festivals that took place in temples or churches. Houses were, furthermore, spaces where pious women

FIGURE 8.5: *Lararium* and *Mithraeum* of *domus* on Via Giovanni Lanza, Rome. Drawing from Bullettino Comunale. Credit: Public Domain.

and men could adopt a more sainted way of life, embracing religious values acknowledged by an external audience as a genuine source of leadership. The admonitory letters of Jerome and the popularity of biographies of ascetic saints are a good indication of how these values could gain currency – the *Life* of the Egyptian monk Antony had a profound impact on Augustine and his friends, for example. Pagans were also involved in these developments, and they could also be turned into social models, as the inscriptions celebrating their involvement in different cults, their piety and sainted behaviour attest to (Kahlos 2002).

It was among the most devoted Christian circles, however, that houses reached their full potential as religious spaces, as members of the community converted their dwellings into religious retreats (Ferrari 1957). It was Jerome who observed, in a letter datable to 412, that Rome had by that stage been converted into a new Jerusalem, occupied by male and female monasteries (*Letter* 127.8). Jerome was, as usual, advocating on behalf of his own interests: his observation was made in a letter praising Marcella, a member of a wealthy family who, after becoming widow at a young age, adopted a life of chastity, humility and mortification (*Letter* 127.2–4). Praising his disciple was a form of self-promotion, but Jerome's letter offers important insights nevertheless. Marcella lived in her house on the Aventine, surrounded by her friends (to whom she was a mother), inspired by the examples provided by the biographies of Eastern saints that had started to reach Western readers a few decades earlier (*Letter* 127.5–7). Marcella and her household prayed and studied, continuing to be instructed by Jerome even after he left the city. Their house served as a place of learning (Jerome advises another correspondent to look for books there: *Letter* 47.3) and as a stronghold against heresy, when Marcella abandoned her secluded life to get involved in the theological controversies that threatened Rome's orthodoxy (*Letter* 127.9–10).

By the end of the period with which we are concerned, houses played a crucial role in the way the cities of the former Roman empire were transformed. Foundations like that of Marcella became religious centres in their own right, representing both the denial of civic and urban values, as nuns and monks sought spiritual and social isolation from their fellow citizens, and a space where the Christian community as a whole hoped to find salvation through the prayers and example of these religious leaders. During the centuries that followed, similar structures were founded in different parts of Rome and elsewhere, sometimes by bishops and members of the clergy, sometimes by lay benefactors – more often than not occupying a previously existing domestic space (Machado 2012: 124–30). Here, more than at any time since the beginning of antiquity, home and religion were completely identified.

BIBLIOGRAPHY

Adams, E. ([2013] 2016), *The Earliest Christian Meeting Places: Almost Exclusively Houses?* London: Bloomsbury.
Allison, P. (2004), *Pompeian Households: An Analysis of the Material Culture.* Los Angeles: Cotsen Institute of Archaeology.
Ames, K. L. (1981), 'Meaning in Artifacts: Hall Furnishings in Victorian America', in T. J. Schlereth (ed.), *Material Culture Studies in America*, 206–21. Nashville, TN: American Association for State and Local History.
Andrianou, D. (2006a), 'Chairs, Beds and Tables: Evidence for Furnished Interiors in Hellenistic Greece', *Hesperia* 75:2, 219–66.
Andrianou, D. (2006b), 'Late Classical and Hellenistic Furniture and Furnishings in the Epigraphical Record', *Hesperia* 75:4, 561–84.
Andrianou, D. (2007), 'A World in Miniature: Hellenistic Miniature Furniture in Context', *BABesch* 82:1, 41–50.
Andrianou, D. (2009), *The Furniture and Furnishings of Ancient Greek Houses and Tombs.* Cambridge: Cambridge University Press.
Ariño, B. D. (2012), 'Las tábulas de hospitalidad y patronato del Norte de África', *Mélanges de l'École française de Rome – Antiquité* 124:1, 205–29.
Arjava, A. (1996), *Women and Law in Late Antiquity.* Oxford: Clarendon Press.
Ault, B. A. (2005), *The Excavations at Ancient Halieis, volume 2: The Houses.* Bloomington: Indiana University Press.
Ault, B., and L. Nevett, eds (2005), *Ancient Greek Houses and Households: Chronological, Regional and Social Diversity.* Philadelphia: University of Pennsylvania Press.
Avon-Soletti, M.-T. (2005), 'La pérennité des principes régissant les lois de l'hospitalité', in D. Nourrisson and Y. Perrin (eds), *Le barbare, l'étranger: images de l'autre: actes du colloque, Saint-Étienne, 14 et 15 mai 2004*, 403–419. Saint-Étienne: Publications de l'Université de Saint-Étienne.
Badel, C. (2006), 'Ivresse et ivrognerie à Rome (IIe s. av. J.-C.–IIIe s. ap. J.-C.)', *Food & History* 4:2, 75–89.
Badian, E. (1972), *Foreign* Clientelae: *264–70 BC.* Oxford: Clarendon Press.

Bagnall, R. S., and R. Cribiore with E. Ahtaridis (2006), *Women's Letters from Ancient Egypt, 300 BC–AD 800*. Ann Arbor: University of Michigan Press.

Baker, H. S. (1966), *Furniture in the Ancient World: Origins and Evolution, 3100–475 BC*. London: Macmillan.

Balch, D. L., and C. Osiek, eds (2003), *Early Christian Families in Context: An Interdisciplinary Dialogue*. Grand Rapids, MI: Eerdmans.

Balmelle, C., A. Ben Abed-Ben Khader, W. Ben Osman, J.-P. Darmon, M. Ennaïfer, S. Gozlan and R. Hanoune (1990), *Recherches franco-tunisiennes sur la mosaïque de l'Afrique antique. I, Xenia*. Rome: École française de Rome.

Barrett, C. (2017), 'Recontextualizing Nilotic Scenes: Interactive Landscapes in the Garden of the Casa dell'Efebo, Pompeii', *American Journal of Archaeology* 121:2, 293–332.

Barton, S. C. (1997), 'The Relativisation of Family Ties in the Jewish and Greco-Roman Traditions', in H. Moxnes (ed.), *Constructing Early Christian Families: Family as Social Reality and Metaphor*, 81–100. London and New York: Routledge.

Beard, M., J. North and S. Price (1998), *Religions of Rome, volume 1: A History*. Cambridge: Cambridge University Press.

Beltran Lloris, F. (2016), '*Honos clientium instituit sic colere patronos*: A Public/Private Epigraphic Type: *Tabulae* of Hospitality and Patronage', in R. Benefiel and P. Keegan (eds), *Inscriptions in the Private Sphere in the Greco-Roman World*, 131–45. Leiden and Boston: Brill.

Benveniste, É. (1969), *Le vocabulaire des institutions indo-européennes. 1, Économie, parenté, société*. Paris: Éditions de Minuit.

Berry, J. (1997a), 'The Conditions of Domestic Life in AD 79: A Case-study of Houses 11 and 12, Insula 9, Region I', *Papers of the British School at Rome* 65, 103–25.

Berry, J. (1997b), 'Household Artefacts: Towards a Reinterpretation of Roman Domestic Space', in R. Laurence and A. Wallace-Hadrill (eds), *Domestic Space in the Roman world: Pompeii and Beyond. Journal of Roman Archaeology* Supplement 22, 183–95.

Black, E. W. (1995), Cursus publicus: *The Infrastructure of Government in Roman Britain*. Oxford: Tempus Reparatum.

Blue, B. (1994), 'Acts and the House Church', in D. Gill and C. Gempf (eds), *The Book of Acts in its First Century Setting, volume 2: The Book of Acts in Its Graeco-Roman Setting*, 119–222. Grand Rapids, MI: Eerdmans.

Bodel, J. (2008), 'Cicero's Minerva, *Penates*, and the Mother of the Lares: An Outline of Roman Domestic Religion', in J. Bodel and S. Olyan (eds), *Household and Family Religion in Antiquity*, 248–75. Malden, MA: Blackwell.

Bodel, J., and S. Olyan, eds (2008), *Household and Family Religion in Antiquity*. Malden, MA: Blackwell.

Bolchazy, L. J. (1977), *Hospitality in Early Rome: Livy's Concept of its Humanizing Force*. Chicago: Ares.

Bonini, P. (2006), *La casa nella Grecia romana: Forme e funzioni dello spazio privato fra I e VI secolo*. Rome: Quasar.

Bowes, K. (2008), *Private Worship, Public Values, and Religious Change in Late Antiquity*. Cambridge: Cambridge University Press.

Boyce, G. K. (1937), *Corpus of the Lararia of Pompeii* (Memoirs of the American Academy in Rome 14). Ann Arbor: University of Michigan Press.

Bradley, K. R. (1991), *Discovering the Roman Family: Studies in Roman Social History*. Oxford: Oxford University Press.

Braudel, F. (1972), *The Mediterranean and the Mediterranean World in the Age of Philip II*, trans. S. Reynolds. London: Fontana/Collins.
Bray, J. (2013). 'The Family in Medieval Islamic Societies', in L. Brubaker and S. Tougher (eds), *Approaches to the Byzantine Family*, 109–30. Farnham: Ashgate.
Brenk B. (1995), 'Microstoria sotto la Chiesa dei SS. Giovanni e Paolo: la cristianizzazione di una casa privata', *Rivista dell'Istituto di Archeologia e Storia dell'Arte*, s. 3, 18, 169–206.
Brown, P. (1967), *Augustine of Hippo*. Berkeley: University of California Press.
Brown, P. (1988), *The Body and Society: Men, Women, and Sexual Renunciation in Early Christianity*. New York: Columbia University Press.
Brubaker, L., and S. Tougher, eds (2013), *Approaches to the Byzantine Family*. Farnham: Ashgate.
Brun, J.-P. (2000), 'The Production of Perfumes in Antiquity: The Cases of Delos and Paestum', *American Journal of Archaeology*, 104:2, 277–308.
Brun, J.-P., and N. Monteix (2009), 'Les parfumeries en Campanie antique', in J.-P. Brun (ed.), *Artisanats antiques d'Italie et de Gaule: Mélanges offerts à Maria Francesca Bonaiuto*, 115–33. Naples: Centre Jean-Bérard.
Brunet, M. (1998), 'L'artisanat dans la Délos hellénistique: essai de bilan archéologique', *Topoi* 8:2, 681–91.
Budetta, T., and M. Pagano (1988), *Ercolano: legni e piccoli bronzi. Testimonianze dell'arredo e delle suppellettini della casa romana*. Rome: CETSS.
Buonocore, M. (1984), *Schiavi e liberti dei Volusi Saturnini: Le iscrizioni del colombario sulla via Appia antica*. Rome: L'Erma di Bretschneider.
Burkert, W. (1985), *Greek Religion*. Malden, MA: Blackwell.
Burr, D. (1933), 'A Geometric House and a Proto-attic Votive Deposit', *Hesperia* 2, 542–640.
Cahill, N. (2002), *Household and City Organization at Olynthus*. New Haven and London: Yale University Press.
Cahill, N. (2005), 'Household Industry in Greece and Anatolia', in B. A. Ault and L. C. Nevett (eds), *Ancient Greek Houses and Households: Chronological, Regional, and Social Diversity*, 54–66. Philadelphia: University of Pennsylvania Press.
Caldelli, M. L., and C. Ricci (1999), *Monumentum familiae Statiliorum: Un riesame*. Rome: Quasar.
Callow, C., and M. Harlow (2012), 'Left-over Romans: The Life Course in the Late Antique West', in M. Harlow and L. Larsson Loveń (eds), *Families in the Roman and Late Antique World*, 221–37. London: Continuum.
Cameron, A. (2011), *The Last Pagans of Rome*. Oxford: Oxford University Press.
Capanna, M. C., F. Cavallero and S. G. Malatesta (2012), 'Analisi ed edizione di un'insula a Pompei: Regio VI, insula 11', in *Florens 2012: Studi e ricerche*, 291–331. Florence: Bandecchi & Vivaldi.
Cartledge, P. (2001), *Spartan Reflections*. Berkeley: University of California Press.
Catoni, M. L. (2010), *Bere vino puro: immagini del simposio*. Milan: Feltrinelli.
Clark, E. A. (1979), *Jerome, Chrysostom, and Friends*. Lewiston, NY: Edwin Mellen Press.
Clark, G. (1993), *Women in Late Antiquity: Pagan and Christian Lifestyles*. Oxford: Clarendon Press.
Clarke, J. R. (1991), *The Houses of Roman Italy 100 BC–AD 250: Ritual, Space and Decoration*. Berkeley, Los Angeles and Oxford: University of California Press.
Coarelli, F. (1996), 'Architettura sacra e architettura private nella tarda repubblica', in F. Coarelli (ed.), *Revixit Ars*, 327–43. Rome: Quasar, 1996.

Cohon, R. (1984), *Greek and Roman Stone Table Supports with Decorative Reliefs*. Ann Arbor, MI: University Microfilms International.
Cooper, K. (1996), *The Virgin and the Bride: Idealized Womanhood in Late Antiquity*. Cambridge, MA: Harvard University Press.
Cooper, K. (2007), *The Fall of the Roman Household*. Cambridge: Cambridge University Press.
Corner, S. (2015), 'Symposium', in J. Wilkins and R. Nadeau (eds), *A Companion to Food in the Ancient World*, 234–42. Oxford: Wiley Blackwell.
Corsi, C. (2000), *Le strutture di servizio del* cursus publicus *in Italia: ricerche topografiche ed evidenze archeologiche*. Oxford: J. and E. Hedges.
Cova, E. (2013), 'Cupboards, Closets and Shelves: Storage in the Pompeian house', *Phoenix* 67:2–3, 373–91.
Cova, E. (2015), 'Stasis and Change in Roman Domestic Space: The *Alae* of Pompeii's Regio VI', *American Journal of Archaeology* 119:1, 69–102.
Cox, C. A. (1998), *Household Interests: Property, Marriage Strategies, and Family Dynamics in Ancient Athens*. Princeton: Princeton University Press.
Crogiez-Pétrequin, S. (1993), 'Les Stations du "*cursus publicus*" en Italie', unpublished doctoral thesis, Université Paris-Sorbonne, Paris.
Danker, F. W. (1982), *Benefactor: Epigraphic Study of a Graeco-Roman and New Testament Semantic Field*. St Louis, MO: Clayton.
De Wet, C. L. (2015), *Preaching Bondage: John Chrysostom and the Discourse of Slavery in Early Christianity*. Oakland: University of California Press.
Deetz, J. (1982), 'Households: A Structural Key to Archaeological Explanations', *The American Behavioural Scientist* 25:6, 717–24.
Dench, E. (2005), *Romulus' Asylum: Roman Identities from the Age of Alexander to the Age of Hadrian*. Oxford: Oxford University Press.
Dixon, S. (1992), *The Roman Family*. Baltimore: Johns Hopkins University Press.
Donahue, J. F. (2004), *The Roman Community at Table during the Principate*. Ann Arbor: University of Michigan Press.
Dunbabin, K. M. D. (1978), *The Mosaics of Roman North Africa: Studies in Iconography and Patronage*. Oxford: Clarendon Press.
Dunbabin, K. (1998), 'Ut Graeco more biberetur: Greeks and Romans on the dining couch', in I. Nielsen and H. S. Nielsen (eds), *Meals in a Social Context*, 81–101. Aarhus: Aarhus University Press.
Dunbabin, K. M. D. (2003), *The Roman Banquet: Images of Conviviality*. Cambridge: Cambridge University Press.
Dupont, F. (1977), *Le plaisir et la loi: du 'Banquet' de Platon au 'Satiricon'*. Paris: Maspero.
Dwyer, E. (1982), *Pompeian Domestic Sculpture: A Study of Five Pompeian Houses and their Contents*. Rome: Bretschneider.
Eck, W. (1999), *L'Italia nell'Impero romano: stato e amministrazione in epoca imperiale*. Bari: Edipuglia.
Ellis, S. P. (1997), 'Late-antique Dining: Architecture, Furnishings and Behavior', in R. Laurence and A. Wallace-Hadrill (eds), *Domestic Space in the Roman World: Pompeii and Beyond. Journal of Roman Archaeology* Supplement 22, 41–51.
Ellis, S. P. (2000), *Roman Housing*. London: Duckworth.
Étienne, R. (1960), *Le quartier nord-est de Volubilis*. Paris: De Boccard.
Étienne, R., P. Le Roux and A. Tranoy (1987), 'La *tessera hospitalis*, instrument de sociabilité et de romanisation dans la péninsule Ibérique', in F. Thélamon (ed.),

Sociabilité, pouvoirs et société: actes du colloque de Rouen, 24–26 novembre 1983, 323–36. Mont-Saint-Aignan: Publications de l'Université de Rouen.

Evans Grubbs, J. (1995), *Law and Family in Late Antiquity: The Emperor Constantine's Marriage Legislation*. Oxford: Oxford University Press.

Ferrari, G. (1957), *Early Roman Monasteries: Notes for the History of the Monasteries and Convents at Rome from the V through the X Century* (Studi di Antichità Cristiana 23). Vatican City: Pontificio Istituto di Archeologia Cristiana.

Finley, M. I. ([1956] 1977), *The World of Odysseus*. London: Chatto and Windus.

Flohr, M. (2007), '"*Nec quicquam ingenuum habere potest officina*"? Spatial Contexts of Urban Production at Pompeii, 79 CE', *BABesch* 82:1, 129–48.

Flohr, M. (2013), *The World of the Fullo: Work, Economy, and Society in Roman Italy*. Oxford: Oxford University Press.

Flueckiger, J. B. (2006), *In Amma's Healing Room: Gender and Vernacular Islam in South India*. Bloomington: Indiana University Press.

Foss, P. (1997), 'Watchful Lares: Roman Household Organization and the Rituals of Cooking and Dining', in R. Laurence and A. Wallace-Hadrill (eds), *Domestic Space in the Roman World: Pompeii and Beyond. Journal of Roman Archaeology* Supplement 22, 196–218.

Fowden, G. (2014), *Before and after Muḥammad: The First Millennium Refocused*. Princeton and Oxford: Princeton University Press.

Foxhall, L. (1989), 'Household, Gender and Property in Classical Athens', *Classical Quarterly* 39:1, 22–44.

Foxhall, L. (2000), 'The Running Sands of Time: Archaeology and the Short-term', *World Archaeology* 31:3, 484–98.

Foxhall, L. (2013), *Studying Gender in Classical Antiquity*. Cambridge: Cambridge University Press.

Frantz, A. (1988), *Excavations in the Athenian Agora Volume XXIV: Late Antiquity:* AD *267–700*. Princeton: American School of Classical Studies at Athens.

Gardner, J. (1986), *Women in Roman Law and Society*. London: Croom Helm.

Gardner, J. F., and T. Wiedemann (1991), *The Roman Household: A Sourcebook*. London and New York: Routledge.

Gauthier, P. (1972), Symbola*: les étrangers et la justice dans les cités grecques*. Nancy: Université de Nancy II.

Gehring, R. (2004), *House Church and Mission*. Peabody, MA: Hendrickson.

Gentili, G. (1987), 'Verucchio', in G. Bermond Montanari (ed.), *La Formazione della Città in Emilia Romagna*, 207–83. Bologna: Nuova Alfa.

Ghedini, F., and S. Bullo (2007), 'Late Antique Domus of Africa Proconsularis: Structural and Decorative Aspects', in L. Lavan, L. Ozgenel and A. Sarantis (eds), *Housing in Late Antiquity: From Palaces to Shops*, 337–66. Leiden and Boston: Brill.

Gherchanoc, F. (2012), *L'oikos en fête: célébrations familiales et sociabilité en Grèce ancienne*. Paris: Publications de la Sorbonne.

Girri, G. (1956), *La* taberna *nel quadro urbanistico e sociale di Ostia*. Rome: L'Erma di Bretschneider.

Glancy, J. A. (2002), *Slavery in Early Christianity*. Oxford: Oxford University Press.

Gold, B. K., and J. F. Donahue, eds (2005), *Roman Dining*. Baltimore: Johns Hopkins University Press.

Golden, M. (1988), 'Did the Ancients Care when their Children Died?', *Greece and Rome* 35, 152–63.

Goldhill, S. (1992), *Aeschylus: The Oresteia*. Cambridge: Cambridge University Press.

Gorce, J.D.B. (1925), *Les voyages, l'hospitalité et le port des lettres dans le monde chrétien des IVe et Ve siècles*. Wépion-sur-Meuse: Monastère du Mont-Vierge.

Gowers, E. (1993), *The Loaded Table: Representations of Food in Roman Literature*. Oxford: Clarendon Press.

Graham, J. W. (1974), 'Houses of Classical Athens', *Phoenix* 28, 45–54.

Gros, P. (2001), *L'architecture romaine du début du IIIe siècle av. J.-C. à la fin du Haut-Empire: 2, Maisons, palais, villas et tombeaux*. Paris: Picard.

Grubbs, J. E., and T. Parkin, eds (2013), *The Oxford Handbook of Childhood and Education in the Classical World*. Oxford: Oxford University Press.

Guidobaldi, F. (1986), 'L'edilizia abitativa unifamiliare nella Roma tardoantica', in A. Giardina (ed.), *Società romana e impero tardoantico, vol. 2: Roma. Politica, economia, paesaggio urbano*, 165–237. Rome: Laterza.

Guizani, S. (2013), 'Les *cubicula* au temps d'Apulée', *Africa* 23, 179–89.

Hales, S. (2003), *The Roman House and Social Identity*. Cambridge: Cambridge University Press.

Halfmann, H. (1986), *Itinera principum: Geschichte und Typologie der Kaiserreisen im Römischen Reich*. Stuttgart: Steiner.

Harlow, M., and L. Larsson Lovén, eds (2012), *Families in the Roman and Late Antique World*. London: Continuum.

Harlow, M., and R. Laurence (2010), *A Cultural History of Childhood and Family in Antiquity*. London and New York: Bloomsbury.

Harper, K. (2011), *Slavery in the Late Roman World AD 275–425*. Cambridge: Cambridge University Press.

Harvey, F. D. (1984), 'The Wicked Wife of Ischomachus', *Echos du Monde Classique* 3:1, 68–70.

Harvey, K. (2012), *The Little Republic: Masculinity and Domestic Authority in Eighteenth-Century Britain*. Oxford: Oxford University Press.

Hellegouarc'h, J. (1963), *Le vocabulaire latin des relations et des partis politiques sous la République*. Paris: Les Belles Lettres.

Hellmann, M.-Chr. (1992), *Recherches sur le vocabulaire de l'architecture grecque, d'après les inscriptions de Délos*. Paris: École française d'Athènes.

Hellmann, M.-Chr. (2010), *L'architecture grecque: 3. Habitat, urbanisme et fortifications*. Paris: Picard.

Herman, G. (1987), *Ritualised Friendship and the Greek City*. Cambridge: Cambridge University Press.

Hersch, K. (2010), *The Roman Wedding: Ritual and Meaning in Antiquity*. Cambridge: Cambridge University Press.

Hiltbrunner, O. (2005), *Gastfreundschaft in der Antike und im frühen Christentum*. Darmstadt: Wissenschaftliche Buchgesellschaft.

Hoepfner, W., and E. L. Schwandner (1994, 2nd ed.), *Haus und Stadt im klassischen Griechenland: Wohnen in der klassischen Polis* 1. Munich: Deutscher Kunstverlag.

Hopkins, K. (1980), 'Brother–Sister Marriage in Roman Egypt', *Comparative Studies in Society and History* 22:3, 303–54.

Horden, P., and N. Purcell (2000), *The Corrupting Sea: A Study of Mediterranean History*. Oxford: Blackwell.

Hostein, A., and S. Lalanne, eds (2013), *Les voyages des empereurs dans l'Orient romain: époques antonine et sévérienne*. Arles: Errance.

Huebner, S. R. (2007), 'Brother–Sister Marriage in Roman Egypt: A Curiosity of Humankind or a Widespread Family Strategy?', *Journal of Roman Studies* 97, 21–49.

Hunt, E. D. (1984), *Holy Land Pilgrimage in the Later Roman Empire: AD 312–460*. Oxford: Clarendon Press.
Hylen, S. E. (2015), *A Modest Apostle: Thecla and the History of Women in the Early Church*. Oxford: Oxford University Press.
Jameson, M. (1990a), 'Domestic Space in the Greek City-State', in S. Kent (ed.), *Domestic Architecture and the Use of Space*, 92–113. Cambridge: Cambridge University Press.
Jameson, M. (1990b), 'Private Space and the Greek City', in O. Murray and S. Price (eds), *The Greek City: From Homer to Alexander*, 171–98. Oxford: Clarendon Press.
Johnston, S. I. (2007), 'Magic', in S. I. Johnston (ed.), *Ancient Religions*, 139–52. Cambridge, MA: The Belknap Press of Harvard University Press.
Just, Roger, (1989), *Women in Athenian Law and Life*. London: Routledge.
Kahlos, M. (2002), *Vettius Agorius Praetextatus: A Senatorial Life in Between*. Rome: Institutum Romanum Finlandiae.
Kakridis, H. J. (1960), 'La Notion de l'amitié et de l'hospitalité chez Homère', unpublished doctoral thesis, École pratique des hautes études, Paris.
Kastenmeier, P. (2007), *I Luoghi del Lavoro Domestico nella Casa Pompeiana*. Rome: L'Erma di Bretchneider.
Kent, S. (1984), *Analysing Activity Areas: An Ethnoarchaeological Study of the Use of Space*. Albuquerque: University of New Mexico Press.
Kent, S., ed. (1990), *Domestic Architecture and the Use of Space: An Interdisciplinary Cross-Cultural Study*. Cambridge: Cambridge University Press.
Kerr, R. (1871, 3rd ed.), *The Gentleman's House: or, How to Plan English Residences from the Parsonage to the Palace. With Tables of Accommodation and Cost and a Series of Selected Plans*. London: John Murray.
Kertzer, D., and R. Saller, eds (1991), *The Family in Italy From Antiquity to the Present*. New Haven: Yale University Press.
Kleberg, T. (1957), *Hôtels, restaurants et cabarets dans l'antiquité romaine. Études historiques et philologiques*. Uppsala: Almqvist & Wiksells.
Kolb, A. (2000), *Transport und Nachrichtentransfer im Römischen Reich*. Berlin: Akademie Verlag.
Kuefler, M. (2001), *The Manly Eunuch: Masculinity, Gender Ambiguity, and Christian Ideology in Late Antiquity*. Chicago: University of Chicago Press.
Kyrieleis, H. (1993), 'The Heraion at Samos', in N. Marinatos and R. Hägg (eds), *Greek Sanctuaries: New Approaches*, 125–53. London and New York: Routledge.
Lacey, W.K. (1980) [1968], *The Family in Classical Greece*. Auckland: University of Auckland.
Lacore, M. (1991), *Le rôle de l'hospitalité dans la poésie grecque d'Homère aux tragiques (du symbole au prétexte)*. Villeneuve d'Ascq: Presses universitaires du Septentrion.
Laes, C. (2011), *Children in the Roman Empire*. Cambridge: Cambridge University Press.
Laidlaw, A. (2007), 'Mining the Early Published Sources: Problems and Pitfalls', in J. Dobbins and P. Foss (eds), *The World of Pompeii*, 620–36. London: Routledge.
Lapatin, K. (2015), *Luxus: The Sumptuous Arts of Greece and Rome*. Los Angeles: Getty Publications.
Laser, S. (1968), *Hausrat. Archaeologia Homerica* 2 P. Göttingen: Vandenhoeck und Ruprecht.

Lattimore, R. (1962), *Themes in Greek and Latin Epitaphs*. Urbana: University of Illinois Press.
Lavan, L., L. Ozgenel and A. Sarantis, eds (2007), *Housing in Late Antiquity: From Palaces to Shops*. Leiden and Boston: Brill.
Lawton, C. (2006), *Marbleworkers in the Athenian Agora*. Princeton: American School of Classical Studies at Athens.
Lazer, E. (2009), *Resurrecting Pompeii*. London: Routledge.
Leary, T. J., ed. (2001), *Martial Book XIII: The Xenia*. London: Duckworth.
Lefebvre, H. (1991), *The Production of Space*, trans. D. Nicholson-Smith. Oxford: Blackwell.
Leyerle, B. (2001), *Theatrical Shows and Ascetic Lives: John Chrysostom's Attack on Spiritual Marriage*. Berkeley: University of California Press.
Ling, R. (1997), *The Insula of the Menander at Pompeii, volume 1: The Structures*. Oxford: Oxford University Press.
Lissarrague, F. (1987), *Un flot d'images: une esthétique du banquet grec*. Paris: A. Biro.
Lucie-Smith, E. (1994), *Furniture: A Concise History*. London: Thames and Hudson.
Lynch, K. M. (2011), *The Symposium in Context: Pottery from a Late Archaic House near the Athenian Agora*. Princeton: American School of Classical Studies at Athens.
MacDowell, D. M. (1989), 'The Oikos in Athenian Law', *Classical Quarterly* 39, 10–21.
Machado, C. (2012), 'Between Memory and Oblivion: The End of the Roman *domus*', in C. Witschel and R. Behrwald (eds), *Historische Erinnerung im städtischen Raum: Rom in der Spätantike*, 111–38. Stuttgart: Franz Steiner.
Maier, H. (1995) 'The Topography of Heresy and Dissent in Fourth-Century Rome', *Historia* 44:2, 232–49.
Maiuri, A. (1925), 'La Raffigurazione del "Placentatius" in Quattro Bronzetti Pompeiani', *Bollettino d'Arte* (2nd series) 5:5, 268–75.
Maiuri, A. (1932), *La Casa del Menandro e il suo tesoro di argenteria*, 2 vols. Rome: La libreria dello stato.
Maiuri, A. (1942), *L'ultima fase edilizia di Pompei*. Rome: Istituto di studi romani.
Martin, D. B. (1997), 'Paul without Passion: On Paul's Rejection of Desire and Sex and Marriage', in H. Moxnes (ed.), *Constructing Early Christian Families: Family as Social Reality and Metaphor*, 201–15. London and New York: Routledge.
Mastroroberto, M. (1992), 'Gli Arredi', in R. Capelli (ed.), *Bellezza e Lusso: Immagini e documenti di piaceri della vita*, 145–8. Rome: Leonardo-De Luca.
Mauss, M. (2002), *The Gift: The Form and Reason for Exchange in Archaic Societies*, trans. W. D. Halls. London and New York: Routledge.
Mazarakis Ainian, A. (1992), 'Nichoria in the Southwestern Peloponnese: Units IV-1 and IV-5 Reconsidered', *Opuscula Atheniensia* 19:7, 75–84.
McHugh, M. (2017), *The Ancient Greek Farmstead*. Oxford: Oxbow.
Meeks, W. (1983), *The First Urban Christians: The Social World of the Apostle Paul*. New Haven: Yale University Press.
Mikalson, J.D. (1983), *Athenian Popular Religion*. Chapel Hill: University of North Carolina Press.
Mikalson, J. D. (2005), *Ancient Greek Religion*. Oxford: Blackwell.
Miller, S. (1978), *The Prytaneion: Its Function and Architectural Form*. Berkeley: University of California Press.
Mitchell, L. E. (2007), *Family Life in the Middle Ages*. London : Greenwood Press.
Mitchell, L. G. (1997), *Greeks Bearing Gifts: The Public Use of Private Relationships in the Greek World, 435–323 BC*. Cambridge: Cambridge University Press.

Mols, S. T. A. M. (1993), 'Osservazioni sulla Forma e sulla Tecnica del Mobilio Ligneo di Ercolano', in L. Franchi dell'Orto (ed.), *Ercolano 1738–1988, 250 Anni di Ricerca Archeologica*, 489–98. Rome: L'Arma di Bretschneider.

Mols, S. T. A. M. (1994), *Houten Meubels in Herculaneum: Vorm, Techniek en Functie*. Indagationes Noviomagenses 10. Nijmegen: STAM.

Mols, S. T. A. M. (1999), *Wooden Furniture in Herculaneum: Form, Technique, and Function*. Amsterdam: Gieben.

Mommsen, T. ([1892] 1984–5), *Le droit public romain*, trans. P. F. Girard. Paris: De Boccard.

Monteix, N. (2010), *Les lieux de metier: Boutiques et ateliers d'Herculanum*. Rome and Naples: École Française de Rome/Centre Jean-Bérard.

Morgan, J. E. (2011), 'Families and Religion in Classical Greece', in B. Rawson (ed.), *A Companion to Families in the Greek and Roman Worlds*, 447–64. Oxford: Wiley-Blackwell.

Morris, I. (2005), 'Archaeology, Standards of Living, and Greek Economic History', in J. G. Manning and I. Morris (eds), *The Ancient Economy: Evidence and Models*, 91–126. Stanford, CA: Stanford University Press.

Morris, S., and J. Papadopoulos (2005), 'Greek Towers and Slaves', *American Journal of Archaeology* 109:2, 155–225.

Morvillez, E. (2002), 'Les appartements d'hôtes dans les demeures de l'Antiquité tardive: mode occidentale et mode orientale', *Pallas* 60, 231–45.

Moss, C. F. (1988), *Roman Marble Tables*. Ann Arbor, MI: University Microfilms International.

Moxnes, H., ed. (1997), *Constructing Early Christian Families: Family as Social Reality and Metaphor*. London and New York: Routledge.

Murray, O., ed. (1990), Sympotica: *A Symposium on the* 'Symposion'. Oxford: Clarendon Press.

Murray, O., and M. Tecusan, eds (1995), *In Vino Veritas*. London: British School.

Mylonas, G. E. (1946), 'Excursus II: The Oecus Unit of the Olynthian House', in D. M. Robinson (ed.), *Excavations at Olynthus Part XII: Domestic and Public Architecture*, 369–98, Baltimore: Johns Hopkins University Press.

Nadeau, R. (2010), *Les manières de table dans le monde gréco-romain*. Rennes and Tours : Presses Universitaires de Rennes and Presses Universitaires François Rabelais.

Nathan, G. (2000), *The Family in Late Antiquity. The Rise of Christianity and the Endurance of Tradition*. London and New York: Routledge.

Nevett, L. C. (1994), 'Separation or Seclusion? Towards an Archaeological Approach to Investigating Women in the Greek House in the Fifth to Third Centuries BC', in M. Parker-Pearson and C. Richards (eds), *Architecture and Order: Approaches to Social Space*, 98–112. London: Routledge.

Nevett, L. C. (1999), *House and Society in the Ancient Greek World*. Cambridge: Cambridge University Press.

Nevett, L.C. (2005), 'Between Urban and Rural: House-form and Social Relations in Attic Villages and Deme Centres', in B. A. Ault and L.C. Nevett (eds), *Ancient Greek Houses and Greek Households: Geographical, Regional and Social Diversity*, 83–98. Philadelphia: University of Pennsylvania Press.

Nevett, L.C. (2009), 'Domestic Facades: A Feature of the Greek "Urban" Landscape?', in S. Owen and L. Preston (eds), *Inside the City in the Greek World*, 118–30. Oxford: Oxbow.

Nevett, L. C. (2010), *Domestic Space in Classical Antiquity*. Cambridge: Cambridge University Press.
Nielsen, I., and H. Sigismund Nielsen, eds (1998), *Meals in a Social Context: Aspects of the Communal Meal in the Hellenistic and Roman World*. Aarhus: Aarhus University Press.
Nissin, L. (2009), '*Cubicula diurna, nocturna*: Revisiting Roman *cubicula* and Sleeping Arrangements', *Arctos* 43, 85–107.
Nissin, L. (2015), 'Sleeping Arrangements in the Houses of Herculaneum', in K. Tuori and L. Nissin (eds), *Public and Private in the Roman House and Society. Journal of Roman Archaeology* Supplement 102, 101–18.
Nissin, L. (2016), *Roman Sleep*. Helsinki: University of Helsinki.
Orlandos, A. K. (1991), 'Ἡ Οἰκία τῶν κλασικῶν Χρόνων', *Ἐνημερωτικό Δελτίο τῆς Ἀρχαιολογικῆς Ἑταιρείας* 18, 170–6.
Orr, D. (1978), 'Roman Domestic Religion: The Evidence of the Household Shrines', in W. Haase (ed.), *Aufstieg und Niedergang der römischen Welt*, II.16.2, 1557–91. Berlin: De Gruyter.
Osiek, C. (2011), 'What We Do and Don't Know about Early Christian Families', in B. Rawson (ed.), *A Companion to Families in the Greek and Roman Worlds*, 198–213. Oxford: Wiley-Blackwell.
Osiek, C., and D. L. Balch (1997), *Families in the New Testament World: Households and House Churches*. Louisville, KY: Westminster John Knox.
Papaioannou, M. (2007), 'The Roman *domus* in the Greek World', in R. Westgate, N. Fisher and J. Whitley (eds), *Building Communities: House, Settlement and Society in the Aegean and Beyond*, 351–61. London: British School at Athens.
Papi, E. (1995), 'Domus: M. Tullius Cicero (1)', in E. M. Steinby (ed.), *Lexicon Topographicum Urbis Romae, volume 2*, 202–4. Rome: Quasar.
Parker, R. (2005), *Polytheism and Society at Athens*. Oxford: Oxford University Press.
Parker-Pearson, M., and C. Richards, eds (1994), *Architecture and Order: Approaches to Social Space*. London: Routledge.
Parkin, T. (2003), *Old Age in the Roman World*. Baltimore: Johns Hopkins University Press.
Pasqui, A. (1897), 'La Villa Pompeiana della Pisanella presso Boscoreale', *Monumenti Antichi dell'Accademia dei Lincei* 7, 398–554.
Patterson, C. B. (1998), *The Family in Greek History*. Cambridge, MA: Harvard University Press.
Peachin, M., and M. L. Caldelli, eds (2001), *Aspects of Friendship in the Graeco-Roman World: Proceedings of a Conference Held at the Seminar für Alte Geschichte, Heidelberg, on 10–11 June, 2000*. Portsmouth, RI: Journal of Roman Archaeology.
Pernice, E. (1932), *Hellenistische Tische, Zisternenmündungen, Beckenuntersätze, Altäre und Truhen*. Berlin: De Gruyter.
Pirson, F. (1997), 'Rented Accommodation at Pompeii: the Evidence of the *Insula Arriana Polliana* VI.6', in R. Laurence and A. Wallace-Hadrill (eds), *Domestic Space in the Roman World: Pompeii and Beyond. Journal of Roman Archaeology* Supplement 22, 165–81.
Pirson, F. (1999), *Mietwohnungen in Pompeji und Herkulaneum: Untersuchungen zur Architektur, zum Wohnen und zur Sozial- und Wirtschaftsgeschichte der Vesuvstädte*. Munich: F. Pfeil.
Pomeroy, S. B. (1975, 1995), *Goddesses, Whores, Wives, and Slaves: Women in Classical Antiquity*. New York: Schocken.

Pomeroy, S. B. (1994), *Xenophon Oeconomicus: A Social and Historical Commentary*. New York: Oxford University Press.
Pomeroy, S. B. (1997), *Families in Classical and Hellenistic Greece*. New York: Oxford University Press.
Pomeroy, S. (2002), *Spartan Women*. New York: Oxford University Press.
Pomeroy, S. B., ed. (1999), *Plutarch's 'Advice to the Bride and Groom' and 'A Consolation to His Wife': English Translations, Commentary, Interpretive Essays, and Bibliography*. New York: Oxford University Press.
PPM: Pompei Pitture e Mosaici. Rome: Istituto della Enciclopedia Italiana, 1990–.
Pritchett, W. K. (1956), 'The Attic Stelai, Part II', *Hesperia* 25, 178–317.
Ransom, C. (1905), *Studies in Ancient Furniture: Couches and Beds of the Greeks, Etruscans and Romans*. Chicago: University of Chicago Press.
Rapoport, A. (1990), *The Meaning of the Built Environment: A Nonverbal Communication Approach*. Tucson: University of Arizona Press.
Rauh, N. K. (1993), *The Sacred Bonds of Commerce*. Amsterdam: Gieben.
Rawson, B., and P. Weaver, eds (1997), *The Roman Family in Italy: Status, Sentiment, Space*. Oxford: Oxford University Press.
Rawson, B. (2003), *Children and Childhood in Roman Italy*. Oxford: Oxford University Press.
Rawson, B., ed. (2011), *A Companion to Families in the Greek and Roman Worlds*. Oxford: Wiley-Blackwell.
Rawson, B., ed. (1986), *The Family in Ancient Rome*. London: Routledge.
Rawson, B., ed. (1991), *Marriage, Divorce and Children in Ancient Rome*. Oxford: Oxford University Press.
Reece, S. (1993), *The Stranger's Welcome: Oral Theory and the Aesthetics of the Homeric Hospitality Scene*. Ann Arbor: University of Michigan Press.
Rees, B. R. (1998), *Pelagius: Life and Letters*. Woodbridge: Boydell Press.
Reincke, G. (1935), 'Möbel', in G. Wissowa, W. Kroll and K. Ziegler, *Paulys Realencyclopädie der classischen Altertumswissenschaft*, supplement 6, 497–508. Stuttgart: J.B. Metzlersche Buchhandlung.
Reinders, H. R., and W. Prummel, eds (2003), *Housing in New Halos: A Hellenistic Town in Thessaly, Greece*. Lisse: Balkema.
Remijsen, S., and W. Clarysse (2008), 'Incest or Adoption? Brother–Sister Marriage in Roman Egypt Revisited', *Journal of Roman Studies* 98, 53–61.
Rice, E. E. (1983), *The Grand Procession of Ptolemy Philadelphus*. Oxford: Oxford University Press.
Richlin, A. (1992, rev. ed.), *The Garden of Priapus: Sexuality and Aggression in Roman Humor*. Oxford: Oxford University Press.
Richter, G. M. A. (1966), *The Furniture of the Greeks, Etruscans, and Romans*. London: Phaidon.
Rodriguez-Almeida, E. (1981), *Forma Urbis Marmorea: aggiornamento generale 1980*. Rome: Quasar.
Roller, M. B. (2006), *Dining Posture in Ancient Rome: Bodies, Values, and Status*. Princeton: Princeton University Press.
Rossiter, J. J. (2007), 'Domus and Villa: Late Antique Housing in Carthage and its Territory', in L. Lavan, L. Ozgenel and A. Sarantis (eds), *Housing in Late Antiquity: From Palaces to Shops*, 367–92. Leiden and Boston: Brill.
Rowlandson, J., and R. Takahashi, (2009), 'Brother–Sister Marriage and Inheritance Strategies in Greco-Roman Egypt', *Journal of Roman Studies* 99, 104–39.

Ruggiero, M. (1885), *Storia degli Scavi di Ercolano Recomposta su' Documenti Superstiti*. Naples: Accademia Reale delle Scienze.

Rüpke, J., ed. (2013), *The Individual in the Religions of the Ancient Mediterranean*. Oxford: Oxford University Press.

Saller, R. P. (1984), 'Familia, Domus, and the Roman Conception of Family', *Phoenix* 38, 336–55.

Saller, R. (1987), 'Men's Age at Marriage and Its Consequences in the Roman Family', *Classical Philology* 82, 21–34.

Saller, R. (1994, repr. 1996), *Patriarchy, Property and Death in the Roman Family*. Cambridge: Cambridge University Press.

Sarti, R. (2002), *Europe at Home: Family and Material Culture 1500–1800*, trans. A. Cameron. New Haven and London: Yale University Press.

Schäfer, T. (1989), *Imperii insignia: Sella curulis und Fasces zur Repraesentation Roemischer Magistrate*. Mainz: Philipp von Zabern.

Scheid, J. (2016), *The Gods, the State, and the Individual: Reflections on Civic Religion in Rome*. Philadelphia: University of Pennsylvania Press.

Scheid-Tissinier, É. (1994), *Les usages du don chez Homère: vocabulaire et pratiques*. Nancy: Presses universitaires de Nancy.

Schmitt-Pantel, P. (1992), *La cité au banquet: histoire des repas publics dans les cités grecques*. Rome: École française de Rome.

Schmitt-Pantel, P. (2012), 'Les banquets dans les cités grecques: bilan historiographique', *Dialogues d'Histoire Ancienne*, supplement 7, 73–93.

Schmitt-Pantel, P. (2015), 'Dining in Ancient Greece', in J. Wilkins and R. Nadeau (eds), *A Companion to Food in the Ancient World*, 224–33. Oxford: Wiley Blackwell.

Schnurbusch, D. (2011), *Convivium: Form und Bedeutung aristokratischer Geselligkeit in der römischen Antike*. Stuttgart: Steiner.

Schoevaert, J. (2018), *Les boutiques d'Ostie: l'économie urbaine au quotidien: Ier s. av. J.-C.–Ve s. ap. J.-C.* Rome: École française de Rome.

Sessa, K. (2007), 'Christianity and the *cubiculum*: Spiritual Politics and Domestic Space in Late Antique Rome', *Journal of Early Christianity* 15:1, 171–204.

Shaw, B. (1987), 'The Age of Roman Girls at Marriage: Some Reconsiderations' *Journal of Roman Studies* 77, 30–46.

Shaw, B., and R. P. Saller (1984), 'Close-Kin Marriage in Roman Society?', *Man* n.s. 19:3, 432–44.

Shaya, J. (2005), 'The Greek Temple as Museum: The Case of the Legendary Treasure of Athena from Lindos', *American Journal of Archaeology* 109:3, 423–42.

Slater, W. J., ed. (1991), *Dining in a Classical Context*. Ann Arbor: University of Michigan Press.

Sofroniew, A. (2015), *Household Gods: Private Devotion in Ancient Greece and Rome*. Los Angeles: Getty Museum.

Sogliano, A. (1908), 'Relazione degli scavi eseguiti dal dicembre 1902 a tutto marzo 1905', *Notizie degli Scavi di Antichità* series V, 5, 180–92.

Sourvinou-Inwood, C. (1990), 'What is Polis Religion?', in O. Murray and S. Price (eds), *The Greek City: From Homer to Alexander*, 295–322. Oxford: Clarendon Press.

Southon, E., 'Fatherhood in Late Antique Gaul', in M. Harlow and L. Larsson Loveń (eds), *Families in the Roman and Late Antique World*, 238–53. London: Continuum.

Southon, E., M. Harlow and C. Callow (2013), 'The Family in the Late Antique West (AD 400–700): A Historiographical Review', in L. Brubaker and S. Tougher (eds), *Approaches to the Byzantine Family*, 109–30. Farnham: Ashgate.

Sparkes, B., and L. Talcott (1970), *Excavations in the Athenian Agora Volume XII: Black and Plain Pottery*. Princeton: American School of Classical Studies at Athens.
Steingräber, S. (1979), *Etruskische Möbel*. Rome: Bretschneider.
Stroumsa, G. (2009), *The End of Sacrifice: Religious Transformations in Late Antiquity*. Chicago: University of Chicago Press.
Tadmor, N. (2001), *Family and Friends in Eighteenth-Century England: Household, Kinship, and Patronage*. Cambridge: Cambridge University Press.
Thompson, H. A., and R. E. Wycherley (1972), *Excavations in the Athenian Agora Volume XIV: The History, Shape and Uses of an Ancient City Centre*. Princeton: American School of Classical Studies at Athens.
Tran, N. (2011), 'Les gens de métier romains: savoirs professionnels et supériorités plébéiennes', in N. Monteix and N. Tran (eds), *Les savoirs professionnels des gens de métier: Études sur le monde du travail dans les sociétés urbaines de l'empire romain*, 119–33. Naples: Centre Jean-Bérard.
Tran, N. (2013), *Dominus tabernae: Le statut de travail des artisans et des commerçants de l'Occident romain*. Rome: École française de Rome.
Treggiari, S. (1975), 'Jobs in the Household of Livia', *Papers of the British School at Rome* 43, 48–77.
Treggiari, S. (1991), *Roman Marriage: Iusti Coniuges from the Time of Cicero to the Time of Ulpian*. Oxford: Clarendon Press.
Trümper, M. (1998), *Wohnen in Delos: Eine baugeschichtliche Untersuchung zum Wandel der Wohnkultur in hellenistischer Zeit*. Rahden: Leidorf.
Trümper, M. (2003), 'Wohnen und Arbeiten im hellenistischen Handelshafen Delos: Kontexte und Verteilung der *tabernae*', in M. Droste and A. Hoffmann (eds), *Wohnformen und Lebenswelten im interkulturellen Vergleich*, 125–59. Frankfurt and New York: Peter Lang.
Trümper, M. (2005), 'Modest Housing in Late Hellenistic Delos', in B. A. Ault and L. C. Nevett (eds), *Ancient Greek Houses and Households: Chronological, Regional, and Social Diversity*, 119–39. Philadelphia: University of Pennsylvania Press.
Trümper, M. (2011), 'Space and Social Relationships in the Greek *Oikos* of the Classical and Hellenistic Periods', in B. Rawson (ed.), *A Companion to Families in the Greek and Roman Worlds*, 32–52. Oxford: Wiley-Blackwell.
Tsakirgis, B. (2005), 'Living and Working Around the Athenian Agora', in B. A. Ault and L. C. Nevett (eds), *Ancient Greek Houses and Households: Chronological, Regional, and Social Diversity*, 67–82. Philadelphia: University of Pennsylvania Press.
Tsakirgis, B. (2009), 'Living near the Agora: Houses and Households in Central Athens', in J. Camp and C. Mauzy (eds), *The Athenian Agora: New Perspectives on an Ancient Site*, 47–54. Mainz: Philipp von Zabern.
Tulloch, J. H., ed. (2013), *A Cultural History of Women in Antiquity*. London and New York: Bloomsbury.
Tuori, K., and L. Nissin, eds., (2015), *Public and Private in the Roman House and Society*, Journal of Roman Archaeology, supplement 102.
Van Andringa, W. (2009), *Quotidien des dieux et des hommes: La vie religieuse dans les cités du Vésuve à l'époque romaine*. Rome: École française de Rome.
Van Gennep, A. ([1909] 2011), *Les rites de passage: étude systématique des rites de la porte et du seuil, de l'hospitalité, de l'adoption, de la grossesse et de l'accouchement, de la naissance, de l'enfance . . . .* Paris: Picard.
Vanesse, S. (2016), 'Between Street Vendors, Singing Slaves, and Envy', *Chronika* 6, 15–25.

Vernant, J.-P. (2006), 'Hestia-Hermes: The Religious Expression of Space and Movement in Ancient Greece', in J.-P. Vernant, *Myth and Thought among the Greeks*, 157–96. New York: Zone.

Vössing, K. (2004), Mensa regia: *Das Bankett beim hellenistischen König und beim römischen Kaiser*. Munich and Leipzig: K. G. Saur.

Walker, S. (1983), 'Women and Housing in Classical Greece', in A. Cameron and A. Kuhrt (eds), *Images of Women in Antiquity*, 81–91. London: Routledge.

Wall, Diana diZerega (1994), *The Archaeology of Gender: Separating the Spheres in Urban America*. New York and London: Plenum Press.

Wallace-Hadrill, A. (1988), 'The Social Structure of the Roman House', *Papers of the British School at Rome* 56, 43–97.

Wallace-Hadrill, A. (1994), *Houses and Society in Pompeii and Herculaneum*. Princeton: Princeton University Press.

Wallace-Hadrill, A. (2011), *Herculaneum, Past and Future*. London: Frances Lincoln.

Walter-Karydi, E. (1998), *The Greek House: The Rise of Noble Houses in Late Classical Times*. Athens: Athens Archaeological Society.

Watson, A., trans. (1998), *The Digest of Justinian*, volumes I–IV. Philadelphia: University of Pennsylvannia Press.

White, L. M. (1990), *The Social Origins of Christian Architecture, vol. 1: Building God's House in the Roman World* (Harvard Theological Studies 42). Valley Forge, PA: Trinity Press International.

Wilkinson, K. (2015), *Women and Modesty in Late Antiquity*. Cambridge: Cambridge University Press.

Williams, C. A. (2010), *Roman Homosexuality*. Oxford: Oxford University Press.

Wood, I.N. (2003), 'Deconstructing the Merovingian Family', in R. Corradini, M. Diesenberger and H. Reimitz (eds), *The Construction of Communities in the Early Middle Ages*, 149–71. Leiden: Brill.

Woolf, G. (2009), 'World Religion and World Empire in the Ancient Mediterranean', in H. Cancik and J. Rüpke (eds), *Die Religion des Imperium Romanum*, 19–35. Tübingen: Mohr Siebeck.

Zanker, P. (1998), *Pompeii: Public and Private Life*. Cambridge, MA: Harvard University Press.

Zarmakoupi, M. (2015), 'Les maisons des négociants italiens à Délos: structuration de l'espace domestique dans une société en mouvement', *Cahiers Mondes Anciens* 7. Available online: http://mondesanciens.revues.org/1588.

Zevi, F. (1964), *La casa Reg. IX.5.18-21 a Pompei e le sue pitture*. Rome: Bretschneider.

BIBLIOGRAPHY OF SOURCES

Collections of sources:

Gardner, J. F., and T. Wiedemann (1991), *The Roman Household: A Sourcebook*. London and New York: Routledge trans for this and several other authors

Pomeroy, S. B. (1994), *Xenophon Oeconomicus: A Social and Historical Commentary*. New York: Oxford University Press. As in Bibliog.

Pomeroy, S. B., ed. (1999), *Plutarch's 'Advice to the Bride and Groom' and 'A Consolation to His Wife': English Translations, Commentary, Interpretive Essays, and Bibliography*. New York: Oxford University Press.

Sources

Aeschines, *Speeches*. Translated by C. D. Adams (Loeb Classical Library 106: 1919)

Apuleius, *Metamorphoses (The Golden Ass)*, Vol. I, Books 1–6. Edited and translated by J. Arthur Hanson (Loeb Classical Library 44: 1996)

Aristotle Volume XXI, *Politics*. Translated by H. Rackham (Loeb Classical Library 264: 1932)

Cicero Vol. VII, *The Verrine Orations,* Volume I. Translated by L. H. G. Greenwood (Loeb Classical Library 221: 1928)

Demosthenes, *Orations,* Vol. VI *Orations 50–59: Private Cases. In Neaeram.* Translated by A. T. Murray (Loeb Classical Library 351: 1939)

Digest of Justinian, translated by Alan Watson, volumes I–IV. Philadelphia: University of Pennsylvannia Press: 1998.

Isaeus. Translated by E. S. Forster (Loeb Classical Library 202: 1927)

Jerome, *Letters and select works*, translated by W. H. Fremantle (New York : Christian Literature Company ; Oxford : Parker & Company, 1893).

Livy *History of Rome*, Vol. VI, Books 23–25, translated by Frank Gardner Moore (Loeb Classical Library 355: 1940)

Livy *History of Rome*, Vol. XI, Books 38–40, edited and translated by J. C. Yardley (Loeb Classical Library 313: 2018)

Plautus Vol. III *The Merchant. The Braggart Soldier. The Ghost. The Persian.* Edited and translated by Wolfgang de Melo (Loeb Classical Library 163: 2011)

Plautus Vol. IV, *The Little Carthaginian. Pseudolus. The Rope.* Edited and translated by Wolfgang de Melo (Loeb Classical Library 260: 2012)

Pliny, *Letters*, with an English translation by W. Melmoth (The Loeb classical library: London, 1915)

Plutarch, *Lives*, Vol. I. *Theseus and Romulus. Lycurgus and Numa. Solon and Publicola.* Translated by Bernadotte Perrin (Loeb Classical Library 46: 1914)

Soranus' *Gynecology*. Translated with an introduction by Owsei Temkin (Baltimore : Johns Hopkins, 1956)

Sozomen. *A Select Library of Nicene and post-Nicene fathers of the Christian church : second series Vol. II, Socrates, Sozomenus: Church histories.* Translated into English by Chester David Hartranft (Oxford and New York: Parker, The Christian Literature Company, 1891)

Varro, *On the Latin Language*. Translated by Roland G. Kent (Loeb Classical Library 333: 1938)

Xenophon, *Conversation of Socrates. Translated by* Hugh Tredennick and Robin Waterfield (Penguin Books, London: 1990)

CONTRIBUTORS

Joanne Berry is Associate Professor in the Department of Classics, Ancient History & Egyptology at Swansea University, UK. She holds a doctorate from the University of Reading, UK, on the domestic finds of Pompeian houses. Her publications include *The Complete Pompeii* (2013) and she co-edited (with Ray Laurence) a volume on cultural identity in the Roman world.

Michele George is Professor in the Faculty of Humanities at McMaster University, Canada, from which she holds a PhD. She has worked on domestic space in Roman houses and Roman slavery and material culture. Her publications include a monograph on *The Roman Domestic Architecture of Northern Italy* (1997) and she has edited books on *The Roman Family in the Empire: Rome, Italy and Beyond* (2005) and *Roman Slavery and Roman Material Culture* (2012).

Marie-Adeline Le Guennec is Professor of Ancient History at the University of Quebec in Montreal, Canada. She holds a doctorate from the University of Aix-Marseille, and is a former member of the École Française de Rome, Italy. Her publications include a major study of inns and hospitality in the Roman world, *Aubergistes et clients: l'accueil mercantile dans l'Occident romain (IIIe siècle av. J.-C. – IVe siècle apr. J.-C.)* (2019).

Carlos Machado is Senior Lecturer in Ancient History at the University of St Andrews, UK, where he is Director of the Centre for Late Antique Studies. He studied for a BA and an MSc in History in Brazil, and holds a doctorate from the University of Oxford, UK. He is a former scholar of the British School at Rome, and has held university lectureships in São Paulo in Brazil. His books include *Urban Space and Aristocratic Power in Late Antique Rome* (AD 270–535) (2019).

Lisa Nevett is Professor of Classical Archaeology at the University of Michigan, USA. She holds a doctorate from the University of Cambridge, UK. She currently co-directs a field project at Olynthos in northern Greece, and has published widely on Greek housing, including her books *Houses and Society in the Ancient Greek World* (1999) and *Domestic Space in Classical Antiquity* (2010).

Nicolas Tran is Professor of Ancient History at the University of Poitiers, France, a former member of the École Française de Rome, bronze medallist of the CNRS and Junior Member of the Institut Universitaire de France. His books include *Dominus tabernae: le statut de travail des artisans et des commerçants de l'Occident romain (Ier siècle av. J.-C. – IIIe siècle ap. J.-C.)* (2013).

Andrew Wallace-Hadrill is Emeritus Professor and Director of Studies in the Department of Classics of the University of Cambridge, UK. Formerly Director of the British School at Rome, he has directed projects in both Pompeii and Herculaneum. His publications on Roman domestic space include *Houses and Society in Pompeii and Herculaneum* (1994) and *Herculaneum, Past and Future* (2011).

Kate Wilkinson is Associate Professor of Women's and Gender Studies at Towson University, USA. She completed a doctorate in Religion at Emory University, USA, as well as the graduate certificate in Women's Studies. She received a master's degree in Theological Studies from Harvard Divinity School, USA, and her BA from Sarah Lawrence College, USA. She has published *Women and Modesty in Late Antiquity* (2015).

INDEX OF ARCHAEOLOGICAL SITES

Note: This index this includes places mentioned *as archaeological sites*. Athens for instance is frequently mentioned in non-archaeological contexts.

Apamea (Syria), house of the Deer: 142, 156, 157
Athens: 24, 61–79 *passim*, 85, 86, 105, 106, 117, 118, 121, 152
   Agora: 61, 62, 63–4, 67
   Akropolis: 61, 62
   Areopagus: 62, 64, 73, 74, 75, 76, 77, 78, 104, 105
   House of the Greek Mosaic: 67
   House of Mikion and Menon: 105
   House of the Parakeet Mosaic: 65, 66, 67, 74
   House of Simon: 105
   Omega House: 76
Attica
   Ano Voula: 70
   Atene: 71
   Piraeus: 105
   Thorikos: 69, 70

Boscoreale, Villa Pisanella: 96
Bulla Regia (Tunisia): 172

Capernaeum (Galilee): 175
Carthage (house of the Hill of Juno): 12–14
Contrebia Belaisca (Spain): 149
Corinth: 75

Delos: 10, 60, 71, 73, 74, 76, 87, 88, 106, 116, 117, 174, 175
   House of Dionysus: 72, 73
   House of the Seals: 116
   Quartier du Stade: 117

Halieis: 65, 66, 166
Halos (Thessaly): 106, 107
Herculaneum: 3, 4, 14, 83, 84, 92, 93, 94, 96, 98, 104, 111, 118
   Bottega con abitazione (V.10-11): 110
   House of the Bicentenary (V.1.5): 10, 11,12
   House of the Fullonica: 112, 115
   Insula Orientalis II, 9–10: 108

Karanis (Egypt): 83

Nichoria: 63, 78

Olympia, temple of Zeus: 166
Olynthos: 7–10, 12, 13, 14, 65, 66, 68, 69, 88, 105, 117, 118, 166
   House A vii 4: 8
   House A viii 7/9: 106
   House A 6: 106
   House B i 5: 106

Oplontis, Villa B (Lucius Crassius Tertius): 95
Ostia: 109, 163
    Domus della Fortuna Annonaria: 163

Paestum, Diver's tomb: 153
Pompeii: 3, 4, 77, 83, 93–101, 108, 109, 111, 117, 118, 154, 168, 176, 178
    Bakery (I.12.1/2): 116
    Caupona of Hermes (II.1.1): 169
    Fullery of Mustius (VI.15.3): 109
    Fullery of P. Veranius Hypsaeus (VI.8.20-1): 115
    House of Balbus: 169
    House of the Beautiful Impluvium (I.9.1): 95, 96
    House of Ceres (I.9.13): 97, 99–101
    House of the Chaste Lovers (IX.12.6): 82
    House of Cuspius Pansa (VI.6.22): 110
    House of the Ephebe (I.7,10-12): 94, 96, 97, 98
    House of Fabius Amandus (I.7.3): 96, 98
    House of Julius Polybius (IX.13.1-3): 169, 170
    House of the Labyrinth (VI.11.8-10): 111, 112
    House of the Menander (I.10.4): 88–9, 169–170
    House of M. Terentius Eudoxsus (VI.13,6/8/9): 117
    House of Paquius Proculus (I.7.1): 94, 96, 97
    House of Pinarius Cerealis (III.4.b): 116
    House of Polybius: 169
    House of the Vettii (VI.15.1/27): 95
    House of Vetutius Placidus (I.8.9): 97, 98
    Insula Arriana Polliana (VI.6): 110
    Insulae 7, 8, 9 of Regio I: 93–101
    Perfumery (VII.4.24-5): 115
    Tannery (I.5.2): 116
    Tomb of Navoleia Tyche: 88, 89
    Workshop (I.10.1): 170
    Writers' Workshop (I.7.15/16/17): 97
Priene: 106

Rome: 107, 108, 110
    Caelian Hill *insula*: 177, 178
    Esquiline Hill (via Giovanni Lanza): 178, 179
    Palatine hill: 162

Vindolanda: 83
Volubilis (Mauretania Tingitana): 109, 117, 118

INDEX OF ANCIENT SOURCES CITED

Aeschines, *Against Timarchus*: 105
Aeschylus, *Oresteia*: 18, 19
Anon., *Itinerary of Egeria*: 175
Antiphon, *Orations*: 164, 165
Apocryphal New Testament, *Life of Thecla*: 31
Apuleius, *Metamorphoses*: 103, 112, 113, 117, 151
Aristophanes, *Acharnians*: 167
Aristophanes, *Wasps*: 165
Aristotle, *Athenian Constitution*: 162, 163, 164
Aristotle, *Politics*: 20, 22, 23, 25, 34, 35, 36, 41, 46
Athenaeus, *Deipnosophists*: 87, 164
Augustine, *Confessions*: 32, 33, 137, 177
Augustine, *On the Goodness of Marriage*: 33, 125
Aulus Gellius, *Attic Nights*: 29

Cato, *On Agriculture*: 91, 92, 168, 169
Cicero, *de Domo Sua*: 25, 26, 114, 162, 163
Cicero, *de Finibus*: 25
Cicero, *de Officiis*: 25, 34
Cicero, *in Catilinam*: 108
Cicero, *Letters*: 56, 144, [181]
Cicero, *On the Laws*: 164, 173
Cicero, *On the Republic*: 168
Cicero, *Philippics*: 125, 126

Cicero, *Verrines*: 90, 153
CIL (*Corpus Inscriptionum Latinarum*): 52, 104, 108, 109, 117, 169
Codex Theodosianus: 32
Columella, *On Agriculture*: 28

Demosthenes, *Orations*: 38, 42
Digest of Justinian: 111, 170

Epictetus: 29, 30, 132
Euripides, *Medea*: 148

Gaius, *Institutes*: 49, 51, 52, 170
Gerontius, *Life of Melania the Younger*: 178
Gregory of Nyssa, *Life of Macrina*: 137, 140

Hesiod, *Works and Days*: 22
Homer, *Iliad*: 16, 17, 141, 148, 159, 170
Homer, *Odyssey*: 1, 4, 15–17, 26, 27, 84, 103, 141–4, 148, 164, 170
Homeric Hymns: 165
Horace, *Epistles*: 91, *see also* notes to ch.7
Horace, *Odes*: 114

ILS (*Inscriptiones Latinae Selectae*, ed. H. Dessau) : 52, 121
Isaeus, *Orations*: 45
Isidore, *Etymologies*: 34

Jerome, *Letters*: 14, 31, 32, 33, 127, 135, 176, 177, 179, 180
John Chrysostom, *Homilies*: 121, 125, 129, 130, 131
Juvenal, *Satires*: 127, 131, 134

Libanius, *Orations*: 133
Livy, *History of Rome*: 18, 90, 135, 154, 171
Lucretius, *de Rerum Natura*: 27, 28
Lysias, *On the Murder of Eratosthenes*: 10, 20, 23, 33, 42, 67

Macrobius, *Saturnalia*: 154, 176
Martial, *Epigrams*: 97, 156, 158, *see also* notes to ch.7
Menander, *Dyskolos*: 87
Musonius, *Discourses*: 29, 30

Nepos, *Lives*: 23
New Testament, *Acts of the Apostles*: 30, 31, 173, 174
New Testament, *Epistles of Paul*: 30, 31, 173, 174, 175
New Testament, *Gospel according to St Mark*: 30, 31
New Testament, *Gospel according to St Matthew*: 30, 121, 144

Ovid, *Fasti*: 167
Ovid, *Metamorphoses*: 103, 143

P.Brem. (Papyri in Bremen Staatsbibliotkek): 133
Paulus, *Ad Plautium*: 111
Paulus, *Ad Sabinum*: 111
Paulus, *Responsa*: 56
Pausanias, *Description of Greece*: 85, 86, 166
Pelagius, *Letter to Demetrias*: 122, 136
Petronius, *Satyricon*: 103, 114, 134, 151, 154, 156, 170, 171
Plato, *Euthydemus*: 165

Plato, *Laws*: 20, 172
Plato, *Symposium*: 134, 137, 153
Plautus, *Aulularia*: 168
Plautus, *Braggart Warrior*: 159
Plautus, *Mostellaria*: 24, 91
Plautus, *Poenulus*: 150
Pliny the Elder, *Natural Histories*: 90
Pliny the Younger, *Letters*: 27, 36, 136, *see also* notes to ch.7
Plutarch, *Advice to the Bride and Groom*: 122
Plutarch, *Alcibiades*: 86
Plutarch, *Caesar*: 163
Plutarch, *Convivial Questions*: 167
Plutarch, *Lycurgus*: 46, 47
Plutarch, *Numa*: 56

Salvian, *On the governance of God*: 33, 34
Semonides, *Iambics*: 121, 122
Sextus Empiricus: 49
Sidonius Apollinaris, *Letters*: 156, *see also* notes to ch.7
Sophocles, *Antigone*: 164
Sophocles, *Trachiniae*: 144
Soranus, *Gynaecology*: 131
Sozomen, *Ecclesiastic History*: 128, 129
Suetonius, *Augustus*: 18, 52, 91
Suetonius, *Divus Julius*: 163
Suetonius, *Nero*: 91
Suetonius, *Tiberius*: 54

Tacitus, *Annals*: 2, 54, 114, 144

Varro, *de Lingua Latina*: 86, 154
Virgil, *Aeneid*: 26, 95, 134
Virgil (Pseudo-Virgil), *Moretum*: 103
Vitruvius, *On Architecture*: 24, 25, 26, 27, 81, 155, 156, 158

Xenophon, *Constitution of the Lacedaemonians*: 45, 46, 47
Xenophon, *Oeconomicus*: 21, 22, 23, 24, 25, 30, 33, 35, 37, 40, 41, 44, 122, 124, 130, 162.

INDEX

Abraham 144
accommodation (*see also* hospitality)
    commercial and public stations 145–6
    guestrooms/*hospitalia* 156
adoption 40, 55, 56
adultery 29, 38, 54, 55, 125
Advice to the Bride and Groom 122
aedes/aedificare/aedificium 16
Aegisthus 19
Aelius Aristides 131
Aeneas 26
Aeschines 105
Aeschylus 18–19
Africa, Roman 12–13 (*see also* Egypt)
Agamemnon 18–19
agency, female 52
Alcibiades 86
Alexander the Great 87, 127
Alfenus Varus 108
America, furniture and 91
anchisteia 36
Andrianou, D. 84, 86, 87, 88
andrôn 4, 9–10, 41, 65–6, 67, 78, 153–4, 156 (*see also* dining areas)
andronitis 9, 20, 23
Annals 144–5
Antinous 143
Antiphon 164–5
antiquity, term 5–6
Antony 179

Apamea 156
Apicius 154
Apollo 162, 164, 165
Apollodorus 42–3
Apollonius II 174–5
Apuleius 103, 112–13, 117, 151
Aquila 174
archaeology
    Athens 62–9
    of the Bay of Naples 83, 92–3, 95
    Delos 72
    guestrooms/*hospitalia* 156
    hearths and 165–6
    houses combining residence and labour 104–7, 110–12, 117
    material evidence 3–4, 59–60
    Pompeii 93–101, 168–9
    Thorikos and Ano Voula 69–71
    use of spells and 139
Archias 91
architecture
    andrôn 4, 9–10, 41, 65–6, 67, 78, 153–4, 156
    atria. *See* atria
    porticos 24, 65, 77
Aristotle 20, 22–3, 25, 36, 41, 46, 162, 164
art (*see also* mosaics)
    Roman Empire 171
    sculptures 73, 75–6
artefacts 61

asceticism 31, 33, 137, 140
Athenaeus 87
Athene 17
Athens
   fifth and fourth centuries BCE houses 63–9
   the Agora 61–2, 63–9, 78, 86, 104
   the Areopagus 62, 64, 65, 74, 75, 78, 104, 105
   the Athenian Akropolis 61–2
   Attica 69–71, 86, 104
   courtyards 76–7
   Dionysia at 167
   Hecatea 165
   households in 36
   houses combining residence and labour 104–5, 117
   houses in the later Hellenistic/Roman periods 71–5
   legitimacy of children in 37, 38
   marriage 37
   the Parthenon frieze 86
   property ownership and 39, 40
   transformation of homes in the late Roman period 75–7
Atreus 19
atria
   architecture and purpose of 11–12, 75
   the impluvium 74–5
   lararia in 168–9, 170
   living and working units and 110, 111, 115
   Pompeii 77
   status and 78
Attica 69–71, 86, 104
Augustine 33, 125, 177, 179
Augustus 18, 28–9, 30, 31, 52, 53–4, 91, 123–4
authority
   formal display of 91
   furniture and 91
   parental 50
   religious 175–6
autonomy, of Greek heiress and 39–40

Bacchus 171
Balbus, House of 169
banquets
   ancient Greek 87, 152–4, 164
   hospitality and 158
   Roman 57, 154–6
Baucis 143
Bay of Naples, archaeology of 83, 92–3, 95
beautification 122–3
beds and couches 65, 76, 82, 87, 88, 91, 96–7, 154–5
Berry, Joanne 197 (*see also* Chapter 4)
Bible
   Acts of Paul 31
   Acts of the Apostles/Pauline epistles 173–4
   the Gospels 30, 121
   household codes 31
   New Testament 144
   Old Testament 141–2, 144
Bowes, Kim 177
Bray, Julia 7
Bronze Age 5, 61–2, 84, 164
Byzantium 6

Calatoria Themis 12
Calypso 16, 17, 18, 26
Capernaeum 175
carnal desire 33
Carthage 12–13, 14
casa 15–16
Cassandra 19
castration, voluntary 127 (*see also* eunuchs)
Catiline 108, 164
Cato 92, 169
celibacy 32
cena 154
Cenchreae 174
change; houses and religious change 171–5
charity 142
Charlemagne 5–6
chastity 139
child-bearing 124
childlessness 32
children
   child/infant mortality 56, 123 (*see also* mortality rates)
   childcare 132
   foundlings 56
   guardianship (*tutela*) over 51, 137
   infanticide 123, 124
   legitimacy of 29, 37, 38
   the right to kill a child 49

INDEX

in the Roman Empire 49
in the Roman household 56
slavery and 12, 56, 57–8, 124
Spartan 46, 47
Christianity
  accommodation and 146
  Christian imagery 140
  divorce and 121
  erotic pleasure and 123
  gender roles in homes and 140
  gendered divisions of labour and 133
  in the home 4–5, 176–7
  homes in early Christian thought 28–34
  homosexual relations and 126
  hospitality and 141–2, 144
  marriage and 31–3, 122, 140
  mourning practices and 137
  oikos and 30, 32
  public and private spaces and 139–40
  religious change and 173–5
Chrysostom, John 121, 125, 129
Cicero 25–6, 56, 90, 108, 114, 125–6, 144, 162–3, 164, 168, 173
Circe 17, 84
Ciron 164
citizenship 5, 29, 36, 38, 162
city and state 25
civic engagement 36
class (*see also* elites)
  status groups 27
  women's work and 41
Claudius 177
Clodius 25–6, 162
Clytemnestra 18–19
coci 103
colonialism, Greek 19–20
Columella 28
comedy, Roman 24
commercial accommodation 145–6
commissationes 154
common law (*ius gentium*) 29
common spaces, in Roman homes 26
community, gods of 4–5
confessio 178
confiscations, records of 86
consilium 49
conspicuous consumption 87
Constantine 5, 29, 32
convivium 48, 154, 155

Corinth 75, 174
couches and beds 65, 76, 82, 87, 88, 91, 96–7, 154–5
country estates 12–14, 136–7, 140 (*see also* farmsteads)
courtyards
  Athens 76–7
  courtyard houses 64–5, 67, 71, 74, 75
  Delos 72
  farmsteads in Attica 71
  Olynthos 65
craftsmanship and trade 10, 11, 104–5, 108–10, 111–12, 115, 116, 117
Creusa 26
cubicularii 103
cubiculum 110, 113, 115, 123, 135–6
cults
  cult of Bacchus 171
  cult of Mithras 178
  cult of Serapis 174–5
  domestic 44–5, 178
  religious 161–2
culture(s)
  ancient Mediterranean 143, 145
  cultural capital 77
  gender and cultural production within the home 133–7
  homes and 15–16
  houses and 75
  Islamic 6
  religion and 173
  Roman 167, 171
  slavery and 57
  visual culture 171
cupboards 95–6
Curio 125–6
Cynic, the 29–30

Daedalus 86
Damasus 177
Dark Ages 5, 85
deipnon 152
deities (*see also* names of individual deities)
  genius 12, 167, 168, 169
  gods of community 4–5
  gods of the house/city 164–7
  hearth deities 4–5, 10, 45, 139, 165–7
  home, gender and 137–40
  in homes 161, 167–71

hospitality and 143
household 26, 44–5
Jewish god Lydia 174
lares 12, 26, 28, 139, 167–8, 169, 170
penates 26, 28, 139, 167, 168
sculptures of 73
Delos
   courtyards 72
   housing of 71–4, 78
   living and working units in 106–7, 116, 117
   mosaics 10
   religion 174–5
   temple inventories 86
deme houses 70, 79
Demeas 151
demes 36, 162
Demetrias 122, 136
democracy, Greek 7
demos 19
Demosthenes 38, 41, 42, 87, 117
di penates. See penates
dining areas 74, 75, 77, 91 (*see also* andrôn)
dinner parties 75, 92, 130, 134, 155 (*see also* banquets)
Diomedes 148, 150
Dionysia at Athens 167
divorce 31, 38, 40, 51, 54–5, 121
domestic cults 44–5, 178
domestic service 2, 4
domestic sphere, morality and 5
domestic staff 27
domestic violence 33
domesticity 21, 52–3, 121
domina 2, 13, 14
dominus 13, 14, 16
domiseda 121
domos 16, 19
domus
   hospitality and 158
   living and working units in 110, 111, 112, 114–15
   the meaning of 1, 16, 34, 48, 120
   religion and 163, 177, *179*
   in Roman life and law 23–8
   the state and 3
dowries 38, 50–1, 54
drama, Roman comedy 24

education
   Classical 5
   of slaves 132
   Sparta 47
   women and 47, 134–5
Egypt 55–6
ekklesia 30, 32
Electra 19
Eleusis 86
elites
   adoption and 56
   hospitality and 142, 147, 158
   houses of in Athens 75–7, 78
   luxury goods and 90–1
   Roman 48–9, 53, 56
   women 41–2
emotion, homes and 25–6, 28
endogamy 37, 50
entertainment, of guests 156
Epictetus 29–30, 132
Epigrams 156, 158
epigraphic habit 36
epiklêros 39
Eratosthenes 20
erotic pleasure 122–3
Etymologies 34
Euboea 104
eunuchs 127
Euphiletos 20–1, 23
Eurycleia 18
Eurytos 144
Eustochium 135
Euthydemus 165
evil eye 138
exile 29, 54
exogamy 37, 50

Fabius Amandus, House of 96
fabrics 4
family(ies)
   concept of 4
   extended families 36, 49–50
   familia 4, 12, 16, 27, 35, 48
   family structure of Greek households 36–7
   Germanic families 7
   in the Greek and Roman worlds 35–6
   the Greek family at home 40–5

Greek family law and practice 36
identity and 36, 50
Islamic families 7
legislation supporting the 53–4
nuclear 35
power of the father 25
Roman Egypt 55–6
in the Roman Empire 29, 30–1
the Roman family and home 48–58
slaves and 12
the study of 6–7
farmsteads 70–1, 92 (*see also* country estates)
Fasti 167
fertility, divinization of 139
finances, household 42
Finley, Moses 18
First Millennium 6
Forma Vrbis 110
Fortuna Annonaria, Domus della in Ostia 163
fosterage 56
foundlings 56
Fowden, Garth 6
Francia 6
free citizens 120
freedmen 120
furnishings 3, 82, 83
furniture
    America and 91
    couches and beds 65, 76, 82, 87, 88, 91, 96–7, 154–5
    the evidence for Roman furniture 88–92
    of farmsteads 92
    in the Greek world 84–8
    information provided by 82
    seating 98
    storage furniture 95–6
    tables 97–8
    tracing the development of 83–4
    wooden chests 95–6
    wooden furniture 4, 83, 84, 92, 93, 94, 101

Gaius 49, 51–2
gastronomy 154
gender
    as an analytical category 119
    and cultural production within the home 133–7
gender studies 2–3
gendered division of labour in the home 127–33, 140
the Greek family and 41
homes and 1, 9, 23, 119–20, 124
homes, deities and 137–40
hospitality and 181n.2
inheritance and 120
male and female spheres 3, 9, 21–2
male lineage 120
public spaces and 133–4
rituals and 139
sexual conduct and 125–6
the study of 6
symposion and 153
textile production and 128–9
genius 12, 167, 168, 169
George, Michele 197 (*see also* Chapter 2)
Germanic families 7
The Gift 18
gift-exchange 18, 152, 156, 158
Glaukos 148, 150
Goddesses, Whores and Slaves 6
gods. *See* deities
Gortyn 39, 40
Greece
    Athens. *See* Athens
    banquets 87, 152–4, 164
    colonialism 19–20
    the family at home 40–5
    family law and practice 36
    family structure of Greek households 36–7
    furniture in the Greek world 84–8
    Greek democracy 7
    the Greek heiress 38–40
    the Greek home 7–10, 23
    Greek households 36–48
    Greek language 16
    Greek literature 5
    the Greek political system 36
    Greek tragedy 18
    Hellenistic era 71–5, 87, 106
    houses 59, 81
    houses combining residence and labour 104–7, 117
    houses in the Roman period 71–7

inheritance 38–40
Iron Age Greece 5, 61–2
marriage 37–8
oikos in Greek thought 16–23, 35, 36
slavery 48
Gregory of Nyssa 137, 140
guardianship (*tutela*), for women and
    children 51, 52, 137
guestrooms 156
guests (*see also* hospitality)
    entertainment of 78
    the receiving of 74
gunaikôn/gunaikônitis 66, 67
gynaeceum 4, 104
gynaeconitis 9, 20, 23

Halieis 65, 66, 166
Halos 106, *107*
Hannibal 144
Harper, Kyle 129
hearth deities
    Hestia 4–5, 10, 45, 139, 165–6
    Vesta 4–5, 139, 167
hearth rituals 139, 167
Hecatea 165
Hegeso, stele of 85
Helen 148
Heliogabalus 125
Hellenistic era 71–5, 87, 106
helots 46, 48
Herakles 144
Herculaneum
    craftsmanship and trade 104, 108,
        110, 111, 112
    furniture and furnishings 4, 83,
        84, 93
Hermes 138
Hesiod 22
Hestia 4–5, 10, 45, 139, 165–7
hestiân 147
hetairai 153
hierarchy, Roman banquets and 155–6
Hippodamus of Miletus 7–8
Homer 1, 15, 18, 84, 86, 141–2, 148, 164
Homeric Hymn to Aphrodite 165
Homeric Hymn to Hestia 165
home(s) (*see also* houses)
    ancient hospitality and 147–52
    Christianity and 4–5, 176–7

common spaces in Roman homes 26, 41
concept of 1–2
culture and 15–16
deities in 137–40, 161, 167–71
in early Christian thought 28–34
emotion and 25–6, 28
gender and 1, 9, 23, 119–20, 124
gender and cultural production within
    the home 133–7
gender, deities and 137–40
gendered division of labour in the
    127–33
the Greek home 7–10, 23
houses and 15, 16, 25, 27
the language of 15–16
the meaning of 15, 17–18
modern concept of 23–4, 26
non-fixed features 81 (*see also*
    furnishings; furniture)
pagan homes 4–5
physical environment of 7
as a place of intimacy 27
privacy in the Roman home 26–7
religion in the home 10
religious meaning of 162–4
as reproductive and erotic spaces
    120–7
and social conditions of workers
    112–18
the study of 2–3
transformation of homes in the late
    Roman period, Athens 75–7
values of the 20
women and 121, 124
work and the 2, 4, 10, 11, 24, 103–4
worshipping at home 167–71
homesickness 15, 16
homosexual relations 126–7
Horace 91, 114
hospes 146
hospitalia 156
hospitality
    ancient Mediterranean 142–7
    ancient Mediterranean – entering the
        house 147–52
    banquets and 158
    Christianity and 141–2, 144
    deities and 143
    divine 143, 144

the *domus* and 158
elites and 142, 147, 158
the entertainment of guests 78
explained 141
gender and 181n.2
Homeric/Old Testament 141–2
hospitium priuatum 145
hospitium publicum 145
importance attributed to 9
law and 146
moral obligation to provide 17
ordo hospitalitatis 152–8
privacy and 4
proxenia (public hospitality) 145
the receiving of guests 74
religion and 173
the Roman home and 26–7
as a sacred value 145, 146
social status and 158
social structuring and 147
strangers and 158
xenia 145, 156, 158
xenoi 146, 148, 152
hostis 146
households
in Athens 36
in Egypt 55–6
Greek households 36–48
household codes, Bible 31
household deities 26, 44–5
household finances 42
household management 22, 23
household rituals 45, 168, 169
identity and 44
as a religious community 175–80
slaves in the Roman household 12, 28, 48, 57–8
the state and 3
women as guardians of 41–2
houses (*see also domus*; home(s))
5th and 4th centuries bce Athens 63–9
ancient hospitality and 147–52
combining residence and labour in Athens 104–5, 117
combining residence and labour in Olynthos 105–6
courtyard houses 64–5, 67, 71, 74, 75
craft or commercial activities in 10, 11, 104

culture and 75
of Delos 71–4, 78
deme houses 70, 79
elite houses of Athens 75–7, 78
gods of 164–7
Greece 59, 81
home and 15, 16, 25, 27
house-churches 30
identity, owners, religion and 162, 171
Islamic 9
in the later Hellenistic/Roman periods, Athens 71–5
living and working units in Delos 106–7, 116, 117
mixed units 104, 106, 117–18
of Olynthos 7–8, 9–10, 14, 66, 68
public dimension of Roman houses 48
religion and 6, 12, 161
religious change and 171–5
in the Roman world 10–11, 81
semi-fixed features 81, 82, 83, 94, 101
social relations and 48
status and 75, 81
transformation of homes in the late Roman period, Athens 75–7
human sociability 29–30
hunting 13
hyperôia 106

identity(ies)
Athenian citizenship and 162
family 36, 50
household 44
houses, owners and religion and 162, 171
Ikmalios 84
Iliad 16, 148, 170
imagery, Christian 140
impluvia 74–5
industrialization 128
inequalities, of wealth 8
infant mortality 123 (*see also* mortality rates)
infanticide 123, 124
infidelity 33, 38
information
material evidence 3–4, 59–60
provided by furniture 82

inheritance
   gender and 120
   Greece 38–40
   Sparta 46
intellectual activity, women and 134–5
intellectual retreats 136–7
intimacy, the home as a place of 27
invitations 151
Iron Age Greece 5, 61–2
Isaeus 164
Ischomachus 21–2, 28, 124
Isidore, St. 34
Isis-Fortuna 178
Islamic caliphates 6
Islamic families 7
Islamic houses 9
Itinerary of Egeria 175

Janus 167
Jason 18, 148
Jerome 32–3, 127, 135, 176, 177, 179–80
Jerusalem 173
Jesus Christ 175
Julius Caesar 90, 163
Julius Dominus, mosaic of 12–14
Jupiter 143, 144
justice, *polis* 20
Juvenal 127, 131, 134

kai su mosaics 138–9
Karanis 83
Kathedra 45
Kerr, Robert 26
klêros 46
koinonia 22, 29

labour, gendered division of in the home 127–33, 140 (*see also* work)
land ownership, Sparta 46 (*see also* property)
language, of home 15–16
lanifica 18, 129
lararia 5, 108, 110, 115, 168–9, 170, 171, *179*
lares 12, 26, 28, 139, 167–8, 169, 170
Latin language 16
Laws 172

law(s)
   Augustan social legislation 28–9, 31–2, 53–4, 55, 123–4
   common law (*ius gentium*) 29
   domus in Roman life and law 23–8
   Greek family law and practice 36
   the Greek heiress and 39–40
   hospitality and 146
   inheritance 120
   law of Moses 31
   legal frameworks 3
   legal right of patria potestas 49
   legislation supporting the family 53–4
   Lex Iulia de adulteriis coercendis 54
   Lex Iulia de maritandis ordinibus 53
   Lex Papia Poppaea 53
   of male guardianship 51–2
   pacta dotalia 50
   of the *polis* 20–1
   Roman 25, 28–9
   Roman marriage and 50, 51
   slaves and 57
   sumptuary laws 87
Le Guennec, Marie-Adeline 197 (*see also* Chapter 7)
legitimacy, of children in Athens 37, 38
Lesbos 135
Libanius 133
liberti 48
Life of Macrina 137
Life of Thecla 31
lifecycle rituals 139
liminary rites 148
literacy 5
literary activity 135, 136
literature 3, 4, 5
Livia 18
Livy 90, 171
longue durée 107, 117–18
Lot 144
Lucius 151
Lucretia 18
Lucretius 27–8
luxury goods 87, 90–1
Lycurgus 45, 47
Lydia 174
Lysias 20, 23, 42

Macarius 177

Macedonia, royal tombs 87
Machado, Carlos 197 (*see also* Chapter 8)
Macrina 137, 140
Macrobius 176
magical practice 139, 140
Maiuri, A. 111, 118
male infidelity 125
male lineage 120
manufacturing, in the home 103–4 (*see also* work)
manus 51
marble working 105
Marc Antony 125–6
Marcella 179–80
Marcus Aurelius 132
marriage (*see also* divorce)
    adultery 29, 38, 54, 55, 125
    brother–sister marriage 55
    Christianity and 32–3, 122, 140
    cum manu (with *manus*) marriages 51
    dowries 38, 50–1, 54
    Greek 37–8
    infidelity 33, 38
    Mediterranean 37
    oikos and 29
    paternalism and 37–8
    Roman Egypt 55
    Roman Empire 29, 31–3, 50–3
    sine manu (without *manus*) marriages 51, 52
    slave marriages 57, 124
    Sparta 47
Martial 156, 158
materfamilias 49, 50, 52
matrona 23
Mauss, Marcel 18
Medea 18, 148
Melania 178
Menander 87, 88–9
Menelaus 148
mensa 154–5
Mercury 143
Metamorphoses 103, 112, 117, 143, 151
Milo 151
Minerva 168
Mithras 178
mixed units 104, 106, 117–18
mobility, hospitality and 145
Mols, Stephan 84, 92, 96, 101

Mommsen, Theodor 146
monastic asceticism 31 (*see also* asceticism)
Monnica 33, 137
monopodia 97, 98
moral obligation, hospitality as 17
morality, domestic sphere and 5
mortality rates 55, 56, 123
mosaics
    Carthage 14
    Delos 10
    House of the Greek Mosaic 67
    House of the Parakeet Mosaic 65, 66, 67
    kai su mosaics 138–9
    mosaic 'of Julius Dominus' 12–14
    mosaic of Venus 172
    Olynthos 8, 9, 10
    in Roman houses 155, 158, 171
mourning verse 137
Musonius Rufus 29, 30
Mycenaean settlements 5
myth 18

nation states 5
Nausicaa 17
Neolithic period 84
Nepos, Cornelius 23
Nero 91, 145
networks, hospitality 145
Nevett, Lisa 6, 198 (*see also* Chapter 3)
New Testament 144
Nichoria 63
Nissin, Laura 93, 97
non-fixed features 81 (*see also* furnishings; furniture)
nostalgia 15, 16
nostos 15, 25, 28
nurses 131–2

Octavian 90
Odysseus 15, 16–18, 21, 28, 84, 128, 143, 144, 164
Odyssey 1, 15, 16–18, 26, 84, 103, 142, 143, 144, 148, 164, 170
oeci 155
Oedipus 18
oiketai 29
oikia 23, 24, 29, 36
oikodomeo 16

oikonomia/oikonomoi 16, 21
oikos
   Christianity and 30, 32
   the Greek heiress and 38–40
   in Greek thought 16–23, 35, 36
   hospitality and 158
   marriage and 29
   the meaning of 1, 16, 120
   oikos Theou 30
   the *polis* and 3, 8, 10, 23, 36
   the state and 3
Old Testament 141–2, 144
Olynthos
   allotments in the country 13
   the *andrôn* feature 66
   courtyard-portico area 65
   hearths and 166
   houses combining residence and labour 105–6, 117
   houses in 7–8, 9–10, 14, 66, 68
   mosaics 8, 9, 10
ordo hospitalitatis 152–8
Orestes 19, 21
Ostia 109, *163*
otium 136
Ovid 143, 167

Pagan homes 4–5
Pagan worship 178
papyri 55
parental authority 50
Parker, Robert 166
Parthenon frieze, Athens 86
Pasqui, A. 96
paterfamilias 16, 28, 49–50, 168, 169, 178
paternalism
   Augustan social legislation and 54
   marriage and 37–8
   Roman Empire 49, 51
patria potestas 25, 49–50, 51
patriarchy 25, 31
Patricius 33
patroiokos/patrouchos 39
patronage 11
Paul, St. 30–1, 173–4
Pauline epistles 173
Paulus 111
pedagogues, slave 132–3
Pedanius Secundus 2

Peisistratos 148
Pelagius 122, 136
penates 26, 28, 139, 167, 168
Penelope 15, 17, 18, 21, 22, 84, 128, 143
Perdikkas of Macedon 7
pergula 108
Pericles 37
perioikoi 46, 48
peristyles 77
persecution
   of the cult of Bacchus 171
   religious 177
Peter, St. 173, 175
Petronius 103, 151–2, 154, 170, 171
Petronius Stephanus 12
Phaeacia 17
phallic imagery 138
Philemon 143, 174
Philip II of Macedon 7, 105
Philippi 174
Philoneos 165
philoxenia 142
Phoebe 174
pietas 50
Piraeus 105
Plato 20, 137, 165, 172
Plautus 24, 91–2, 150, 159, 168
Pliny the Younger 136
Plutarch 45, 122, 167
polis
   emergence of the 5
   laws of the 20–1
   oikos and 3, 8, 10, 23, 36
   the religious life of 167
politics, the Greek political system 36
Polyeuktos 42
Pomeroy, Sarah 6
Pompeii
   atria 77
   commercial activities within the houses 4
   craftsmanship and trade 104, 108–10, 111–12, 115, 116, 117
   domestic religion and 168–9
   furniture and furnishings 82, 83, 88–9, 95–6
Porphyrio 91
porticos 24, 65, 77
postliminary rites 148

poverty 114
power
    of the father of the family 25 (*see also* paterfamilias; paternalism)
    social 57, 58
Praetextatus 176
preliminary rites 148
Priapus 138
Priene 106
Priscilla 174
privacy
    hospitality and 4
    in the Roman home 26–7
private/public spheres 1, 23, 26
Procopius 126
Projecta casket 122–3
property, women and 39, 40, 51, 52 (*see also* land ownership)
proxenia (public hospitality) 145 (*see also* hospitality)
Ptolemaic dynasty 55
Ptolemy II Philadelphus 87
public and private spaces, Christianity and 139
public dimension, of Roman houses 48
public spaces, gender and 133–4
public sphere, gaining influence in the 152
public stations 145–6
Pylos 84

Quintus 144

Rawson, Beryl 6
reception, practice of 142–3
recommendation letters 151
religion (*see also* deities)
    Christianity. *See* Christianity
    culture and 173
    Delos 174–5
    domestic 10, 137–40, 168–9
    the *domus* and 163, 177, 179
    gods of the house/city 164–7
    hospitality and 173
    house-churches 30
    households as a religious community 175–80
    houses and 6, 12, 161
    houses and religious change 171–5
    Pagan homes 4–5
    Pagan worship 178
    religious authority 175–6
    religious cults 161–2
    religious life of slaves 169
    religious life of the *polis* 167
    religious meaning of homes 162–4
    religious orthodoxy 176–7
    religious persecution 177
    worshipping at home 167–71
res publica, *oikos/domus* and 3
rituals
    hearth 139, 167
    household 45, 168, 169
    lifecycle 139
Robinson, D.M. 7
Roman Empire
    art 171
    banquets 57, 154–6
    children in the 49, 56
    country estates 14
    culture of 167, 171
    dining habits in 154
    divorce 54–5
    domus in Roman life and law 23–8
    East Roman Empire 6
    Egypt 55–6
    the evidence for Roman furniture 88–92
    families 29, 30–1, 48–58
    homes in early Christian thought 28–34
    houses in the 10–11, 81
    influence of Greece on 23, 25
    law 25, 28–9
    living and working units in 107–12
    marriage 29, 31–3, 50–3
    paterfamilias 49–50, 52
    paternalism 49, 51
    Roman Africa 12–13
    the Roman family and home 48–58
    slaves in the Roman household 12, 28, 48, 57–8
    women and 12, 23, 49, 154
Romance languages 15, 16
Rome 176, 177–80
Romulus 26

Saller, Richard 49
salutatio 48, 99

Salvian of Marseilles 33–4
Samos 85
Sanctuary of Hera on Samos 85
Sappho 135
Saturn 176
Schmitt-Pantel, P. 152
sculptures 73, 75–6
seating 98 (*see also* furniture)
seclusion and segregation, of women 121–2
semi-fixed features 81, 82, 83, 94, 101
    (*see also* furniture)
Seneca 56
Serapis 174–5
servants 103
sex
    male sexual aggression 139
    sexual conduct 5, 125–6
    sexual fidelity of women 120–1, 122, 124
    sexual relations 4
    and slave women 124, 140
    social status and 126
Sextilius Rufus 112
Sextus Empiricus 49
shrines, *confessio* 178 (*see also lararia*)
Sidonius Apollinaris 156
Simon, House of 105
Sippe 7
slavery
    abusive mistresses 130–1
    children and 12, 56, 57–8, 124
    cubicularii 103
    culture and 57
    domestic service and 2
    education of slaves 132
    eunuchs 127
    familia 4
    Greece 48
    male labour 132–3
    religious life of slaves 169
    Roman freedmen 120
    sex and slave women 124, 140
    sexual conduct and 5
    slave marriages 57, 124
    slave pedagogues 132–3
    slaves in the Roman household 12, 28, 48, 57–8
    weaving and 129
    work performed by female slaves 131

sociability, human 29–30
social conditions, of workers 112–18
social control 64, 72
social hierarchies 173, 174, 176
social honour 122
social power 57, 58
social practices 11
social relations, houses and 48
social status
    banquets and 152, 155
    hospitality and 158
    houses, owners and religion and 171
    sex and 126
social structuring, hospitality and 147
socio-politics, banquets and 152
Socrates 165
Soranus 131
Sozomen 128–9
spaces, common spaces in Roman homes 26, 41
Sparta 39, 40, 45–8, 135
spells, use of 139
spinning 104, 129
spiritual eroticism 123
Spurinna 136
standards of living, rising 72–3, 78
state(s)
    city and 25
    households and the 3
    nation states 10
status
    houses and 75, 81
    seating and 99
    slaves and 57
status groups 27, 50
stibadium (*sigma*) 155
strangers
    hospitality and 158
    love/fear of the 142, 147
strongboxes 95
supellex 90, 92
surveillance 64, 79, 81
symbola 148–50, 151
symbolic reminders 148–50
symposium 9, 65–6, 82, 134, 137, 152–3
synagogues 173, 174
syssition 46–7

tabernae 108–12, 114
tables 97–8
tablinum 11, 12
Tacitus 114, 144–5
Telemachus 17, 148
temple inventories 86
Terence 24
Tertullian 127
tesserae 148–50, 151
textile production 128–9 (*see also* spinning; weaving)
Theopropides 24–5
theoxenia 143–4
Thompson, Dorothy Burr 62
Thorikos 69–71
Thyestes 19
Tiberius 54
towers, deme houses 70
town, country and 12–14
trade and craftsmanship 10, 11, 104–5, 108–10, 111–12, 115, 116, 117
Tran, Nicolas 198 (*see also* Chapter 5)
triclinia 97, 98, 115, 116, 154–5, 170
Tullia 56
tutela 51–2

urbs and *res publica* 25

Valens 177
Valentinian I 177
values
    Augustan social legislation and 53–4
    of the home 20
    hospitality and 145, 146
    of Roman marriages 52
Van Gennep, A. 142, 147–8
Varro 88
Venus 170, *172*
Veranius Hypsaeus 115
vernae 57, 58
Verucchio 88
Vesta 4–5, 139, 167
villas 13
Vindolanda 83
violence
    Augustan social legislation and 54
    domestic 33
    male sexual aggression 139
    right to kill a wife or child 49

visual culture 171
Volubilis 109

Walker, Susan 8–9
Wallace-Hadrill, Andrew 110, 198 (*see also* Chapter 1; Introduction)
wealth
    country estates and 14
    display of 87
    inequalities of 8
weaving 10, 18, 52, 104, 106, 128, 129
Wilkinson, Kate 198 (*see also* Chapter 6)
women
    child-bearing 124
    childcare and 132
    dinner parties and 134
    domestic labour 4
    domestic violence and 33
    education and 47, 134–5
    elite 41–2
    female agency 52
    female homosexual activity 127
    feminine labour 4, 128
    feminine virtue 18, 128, 129
    Greek and Roman 23
    the Greek heiress 38–40
    as guardians of the household 41–2
    guardianship (*tutela*) over 51, 52, 137
    the home and 121, 124
    homemaking responsibilities of 22
    intellectual activity and 134–5
    patriarchy and 31
    property and 39, 40, 51, 52
    the right to kill a wife 49
    Roman dining habits and 154
    in the Roman family 49
    Roman houses and 12
    seclusion and segregation of 121–2
    sex and slave women 124, 140
    sexual fidelity of 120–1, 122, 124
    social life of 28
    Sparta 46
    spinning, weaving and 52–3
    the study of 6
    the virtuous wife 18
    work and class 41
    work performed by female slaves 131

wooden chests 95–6
wooden furniture 4, 83, 84, 92, 93, 94, 101
wool-working 129–30
work
    craftsmanship and trade 10, 11, 104–5, 108–10, 111–12, 115, 116, 117
    domestic service 2, 4, 27
    gendered division of labour in the home 127–33, 140
    Greek houses combining residence and labour 67, 104–7
    the home and 2, 4, 10, 11, 24, 103–4
    home and social conditions of workers 112–18
    intellectual labour of slaves 133
    living and working units in Delos 106–7, 116, 117
    living and working units in *domus* 110, 111, 112, 114–15
    living and working units in the Roman world 27, 107–12
    manufacturing in the home 103–4
    marble working 105
    servants 103
    women, class and 41
    work/life balance 24

xenia 145, 156, 158
xenoi 146, 148, 152
xenophobia 142, 143
Xenophon 21, 22, 23, 37, 40–1, 45, 122, 124, 130, 162

Zarmakoupi, M. 116
Zeus 17, 44, 138, 144, 162, 164, 165